Spire Studies in Architectural History
Volume 1

Episodes in the Gothic Revival

six church architects

edited by

Christopher Webster

Spire Books Ltd

PO Box 2336, Reading RG4 5WJ
www.spirebooks.com

Spire Books Ltd
PO Box 2336, Reading RG4 5WJ
www.spirebooks.com

CIP data: a catalogue record for this book is available from the British Library.

Designed by John Elliott

Printed by Information Press Ltd, Eynsham, Oxford.

ISBN 978-1-904965-34-3

Endpapers
Front: Holy Trinity, Ossett, West Yorkshire, an existing chapel to which Thomas Taylor added the two storey block on the right of the image (1820-6). It contained accommodation for 300 Sunday scholars at services.
Rear: St John the Baptist, Prosser Plain, Buckland, Tasmania, R.C. Carpenter (1846-48), the Ecclesiological model which was exported to the Empire.

Contents

Thomas Rickman, St John, Oulton,
West Yorkshire, 1827–9, lithograph
c.1830, a view from the north-west.

Introduction

Christopher Webster

In seeking evidence for the 'battle of the styles' in late-Georgian architecture, one could hardly do better than read nearly adjacent articles in the September 1834 edition of J.C. Loudon's short-lived *Architectural Magazine*. Of Anthony Salvin's recent *Catterick Church, in the County of York*,[1] the anonymous reviewer noted 'Our ancient church architecture is again in the ascendant, proudly triumphing over all the abominations of the dark age of English design ... which commenced with the [Reformation].'[2] Turn over the page and there is a 'Notice', taken from the *Foreign Quarterly Review*, of Leo von Klenze's *Collection of Architectural Designs*,[3] which quotes its author: 'Grecian architecture can and must be the architecture of the world, and that of all periods; nor can any climate, any material, and difference in manners, prove an obstacle to its universal adoption.' Commendable balance, and typical of Loudon's editorship. However, for the Gothic camp, events that unfolded just two years later, in 1836, must have seemed propitious in the struggle to see their favoured style move from the periphery to the mainstream of English architecture. On 31 January Charles Barry was announced as the winner of the competition organised to select a design for the Houses of Parliament; the new edifice – 'the largest construction project the country had ever witnessed' and a building that would stand comparison with 'the splendid monuments of St Petersburg and Paris'[4] – really was to be Gothic. In August, A.W.N. Pugin published *Contrasts*. Its author's aggressively dogmatic prose could have been predicted to generate opposition – and it certainly did – but it also reflected widespread concern about the state of England in the late-Georgian period; Pugin was by no means alone in believing that when modern society was compared with that of the Middle Ages, it was found wanting.[5]

An interesting link between these two important events in the Gothic Revival story is that they were largely driven by those outside the architectural profession, rather than those within it. In 1836, Pugin was, at best, a would-be architect, and anyway the principal support for his cause came from those concerned about social reform; within the profession, he generated much ridicule, especially among the old guard. It was precisely this sector of the profession that had reacted with a mixture of disbelief and anger when it was announced that entries for the Palace of Westminster competition had to be either Gothic or Elizabethan. Despite their best endeavours to open the competition to Classical designs – the style in which the profession's luminaries believed they had the best chance of impressing the judges – the parliamentary committee established to oversee rebuilding refused to budge, determined that the new building should be an overt reference to Britain's ancient royal and democratic traditions.

By the early 1840s, the pendulum was undoubtedly swinging in the Gothic direction. Many of the Classicists who dominated the late-Georgian profession had either died or retired, and the rising generation was more willing to embrace Gothic, although Classicism's reign was far from over. The formation of the Cambridge Camden Society in 1839 and the appearance of its journal, *The Ecclesiologist,* two years later – along with a host of regional architectural societies that came in its wake – virtually guaranteed new churches would be Gothic. And a stream of publications on the theme of medieval architecture ensured that all strata of society, from affluent[6] to poor,[7] could enjoy the hugely popular past time of exploring the monuments of England's pre-Reformation past.

Among the early commentators on the stylistic shift was James Fergusson, whose 1862 *History of the Modern Styles of Architecture*[8] includes a chapter on 'The Gothic Revival'.

However, Fergusson was no enthusiast for revivals of any style and nineteenth-century Gothic, even with the most studiously copied battlements, pointed arches and vaulted corridors, was 'neither defensible [in a military sense], nor monastic, nor Medieval ... [this] is the fatal feature of the whole system' of modern revivals.[9] Nevertheless, he felt moved to acknowledge that 'there were certain obvious advantages to be gained by the introduction of Gothic Architecture in church-building ... The first of these was, that when applied to a modern church every part could be arranged as originally designed, and every detail used for the purpose for which it was originally intended.'[10] At the present time 'Gothic has obtained entire possession of the Church ... Generally it may be said that Gothic is the style of the clergy, the Classical that of the laity.'[11]

In *A History of the Gothic Revival*, Charles Eastlake, publishing only ten years later, displayed none of Fergusson's ambivalence. The revival 'represents' – his narrative was, of course, written in the present tense – 'one of the most interesting and remarkable phases in the history of art'.[12] And by the 1860s, the revival 'had so far prospered as to survive popular prejudice, to be recognised and approved by a considerable section of the artistic public, and to monopolise the services of many accomplished architects. The Classic school was by no means extinct, but it was in a decided minority, and chiefly represented by [the older] members of the profession.'[13] In short, Eastlake could claim stylistic victory for the revival. And in this assessment, he was careful to include secular buildings alongside ecclesiastical examples to demonstrate the style's universal validity in a modern context.

George Gilbert Scott had already sought to do this. His *Remarks on Secular and Domestic Architecture, Present and Future* of 1857 set out to extend the 'success … of the great movement by which Pointed architecture has been revived for ecclesiastical purposes' to produce 'a corresponding effect upon our secular buildings'.[14] He also wished to counter the argument that the style, 'though eminently suited to churches … is not fitted for other classes of building' by demonstrating that far from being 'an antiquarian movement' as was often claimed, it was, in fact 'pre-eminently free, comprehensive, and practical; ready to adapt itself to every change in the habits of society, to embrace every new material or system of construction, and to adopt implicitly and naturally, and with hearty good will, every invention or improvement, whether artistic, constructional or directed to the increase of comfort and convenience'.[15] Perhaps more than any other architect, he led by example and demonstrated that the style was capable of very effective use for banks, hotels monuments, hospitals and government buildings. E. W. Godwin produced town halls, Deane and Woodward a museum, Alfred Waterhouse an Oxford college, William White a row of modest shops, and countless architects designed houses of every conceivable size. In short, there seemed no building type that defied Gothic expression.

Yet there remained lingering doubts about historicism as a viable approach to the issue of style. In his Introduction, Fergusson notes, 'The highest praise that can be bestowed on a modern building is, that its details are so perfectly copied from some other style as to produce a perfect counterfeit, such as would deceive any one … [but] our Parliament Houses are not medieval, notwithstanding the beauty or correctness of the details; nor do any of our best modern churches attain to a greater truthfulness or originality of design … The consequence is, we shall never look upon them with the same satisfaction as we do those of the True Styles [Fergusson's term for pre-Reformation architecture] … nor can we feel sure that the construction we see is a necessary part of the design, and not put there because something like it was placed in a similar situation for some other purpose in some other age … it degrades architecture from its high position of a quasi-natural production to that of a mere imitative art.'[16]

Fergusson's readers would indeed have had no difficulty in identifying those things worthy of 'imitation' in 1862, but for earlier generations, the study of Gothic was still very much in its infancy. For John Carter (Chapter 1) and Thomas Rickman (Chapter 2) establishing the canons of Gothic authenticity had barely started. Carter, 'unique in his attainments in Antient English Architecture',[17] sought to 'provide information and instruction to the rising generation of Antiquaries and Architectural Professors'.[18] According to Terry Friedman, 'The core of his polemical activity lay in his advocacy of the supremacy of medieval ecclesiastical architecture in the modern age anchored in a quest for an undiluted Gothic authenticity both in restoring old, especially cathedral fabrics and in designing new parish churches and chapels.' Rickman too is better known for his publications than for his buildings, 'The most important English writer on architecture between Wren and Pugin' as Michael Port points out, and, in George Gilbert Scott's summary: '[I]n this country chiefly through the minute observations of a Quaker student – the visions of the strange past rose before a newly awakened world.'[19] 'No one' writes Port, 'had the personal knowledge of English churches that Rickman garnered, and no one of his contemporaries the analytic skill to "discriminate" them to the same degree.'

Thomas Taylor (Chapter 3) has never been afforded the status of Carter or Rickman, but his is a career of considerable interest. His projected books came to nought so it is via his buildings that his contribution to the Gothic Revival must be judged. He was probably the very first nineteenth-century architect to establish a career as a church designer; interestingly, his acquaintance with 'Gothic authenticity' came from his earlier work as a topographical painter, specialising in medieval remains. Linking Carter, Rickman and Taylor is this salutary fact: their interest in Gothic and their pioneering ability to exploit the style effectively did not arise from a conventional architectural education or career. For Carter and Rickman, their understanding of the style was a development from their antiquarian interests; for Taylor, it came from his successful vocation as an artist.

A generation later, the career of R.C. Carpenter (Chapter 4) was perfectly timed to capitalise on the early triumphs of the Ecclesiologists. Crucially, they sought a different sort of Gothic authenticity, one that would allow celebration of an Anglican liturgy that was much closer to pre-Reformation Roman Catholicism than anything that Rickman's or Taylor's patrons would either have dreamed of or dared to specify. A substantial chancel was essential, but so too steeply pitched roofs, altars raised on steps, uniform, east-facing benches and a revival of the arts of church decoration. In both his country churches, impeccably modelled on medieval examples, and in his 'town' churches, where he − like Pugin − identified the Austin Friars' church in London as a perfect model for a big, gallery-less modern edifice, he was a designer of central importance in establishing the models for lesser mortals to follow. It is a mark of his influence that he, along with Scott, was responsible for a set of prototypes that, for a decade or more, an army of architects adopted to satisfy the growing demand for Higher expressions of Anglicanism.

The beginnings of G.E. Street's ecclesiastical practice (Chapter 5) is almost concurrent with Carpenter's, yet already there were signs that the English 'authenticity' of the latter's work was too limiting. By the 1850s Street was enthusiastically studying continental alternatives as a means of enriching his own stylistic repertoire, and publishing his findings to act both as guides for travellers and inspiration for his fellow architects. Neil Jackson refers rightly to Street's biggest project, the Royal Courts of Justice (1874-82) in the Strand as 'clearly the swan-song of the Gothic Revival', yet while this was true for secular commissions, the style was so well-established for ecclesiastical work that its currency was far from over, as J.T. Micklethwaite's career shows (Chapter 6).

Micklethwaite − important for his writings, his new churches as well as his sensitive conservation projects − was one of a number of gifted late-Gothic Revivalists who, after the various mid-Victorian experiments with polychromy, continental Gothic and 'muscularity', returned to an Englishness of great delicacy and refinement. His carefully designed fittings were always of the highest quality, and of his St Paul, Wimbledon Park (1888-96), Basil Clarke opined 'the late Victorian suburban church at its best'.[20]

Among Fergusson's conclusions in his rant about revivals in general and the Gothic phase in particular was this: 'It required, therefore, neither ability nor thought on the part of the architect to attain appropriateness … The public had become sufficiently instructed through the labours of Rickman and others' to demand correct Gothic. 'Every library furnished the requisite materials, every village church was a model; neither thought nor ingenuity was required.'[21] He makes it seem so mindless − even banal − yet as the chapters in this book demonstrate, the quest for Gothic authenticity was hard won and once achieved, served merely as a stepping board from which a succession of exceptional architects could produce buildings of outstanding quality well into the twentieth century; the best of them are, in Professor Curl's assessment, 'sublime'.[22]

Notes

1. Published by John Weale in 1834.

2. J.C. Loudon (ed.), *Architectural Magazine*, 1, 1834, 273.

3. For July 1834, p. 108, quoted in ibid., 275.

4. H. de Haan and I. Haagsma, *Architects in Competition*, Thames and Hudson, 1988, 32.

5. P. Stanton, 'The Sources of Pugin's Contrasts' in J. Summerson (ed.), *Concerning Architecture*, Penguin, 1968, 120-39, esp. 132.

6. Many examples could be quoted, including those published by John Britton between 1801 and the mid-1840s, Charles Wild's *An Illustration … of the Cathedral Church of Lincoln*, published by the author, 1819, or the Cambridge Camden Society's *Churches of Cambridgeshire*, Stevenson *et al.*, 1845.

7. Weekly papers aimed at the 'diffusion of knowledge' among the lower classes, for instance the *Penny Magazine* (1832-45) or *Saturday Magazine* (1832-43), sold at one penny per edition, regularly carried illustrated reviews of cathedrals and major churches through the 1830s and beyond.

8. J. Fergusson, *History of the Modern Styles of Architecture*, John Murray, 1862. For Fergusson, see Summerson [note 5], 140-52.

9. Fergusson [note 8], 313.

10. Ibid., 319.

11. Ibid., 329.

12. C.L. Eastlake, *A History of the Gothic Revival*, Longmans, Green, 1872, 1.

13. Ibid., 333.

14. G.G. Scott, *Remarks on Secular and Domestic Architecture, Present and Future*, John Murray, 1857, vii.

15. Ibid., viii.

16. Fergusson [note 8], 2-3.

17. 'B' [J. C. Buckler], 'Memoir of the Late Mr. John Carter, F.S.A.', *Gentleman's Magazine*, 87, 1817, 365-6.

18. *Gentleman's Magazine*, 73, 1803, 106.

19. Sir G.G. Scott, *Personal and Professional Recollections*, ed. Gavin Stamp, Paul Watkins, 1995, 390.

20. B.F.L. Clarke, *Parish Churches of London*, Batsford, 1966, 277.

21. Fergusson [note 8], 319-22

22. J.S. Curl, *Victorian Churches*, Batsford, 1995, 111.

1

John Carter (1748–1817) and the late Georgian struggle for Gothic authenticity

Terry Friedman

Within a month of his death at the age of 69 on 8 September 1817 John Carter was memorialised as 'An Artist of superior eminence, and unique in his attainments in Antient English Architecture'; 'his knowledge and experience were great'; 'As an Antiquarian Draftsman his abilities were truly estimable; – he was extremely faithful in his delineation, – delicate and elaborate in his drawings'; 'the unadorned and absolute facsimiles of the objects pourtrayed [sic] … His death, certainly, may be considered as a national loss.'[1] The core of his polemical activity lay in his advocacy of the supremacy of medieval ecclesiastical architecture in the modern age, anchored in a quest for an undiluted Gothic authenticity both in restoring old, especially cathedral fabrics, and in the design of new parish churches and chapels.[2]

Carter was born in London in 1748 and at the age of 26 began earning his 'first money' as a draughtsman supplying illustrations of his own designs for Francis Newberry's *Builder's Magazine*, of which more shortly.[3] In 1784 he was appointed draughtsman to the Society of Antiquaries of London, producing a groundbreaking, exquisitely illustrated series of publications devoted to major medieval ecclesiastical buildings which, in his own words, were intended 'not alone to please the eye by the beauties of the whole display, but to give information and instruction to the rising generation of Antiquaries and Architectural Professors'.[4] His extensive excursions around the country produced the six-volume *Views of Ancient Buildings in England*

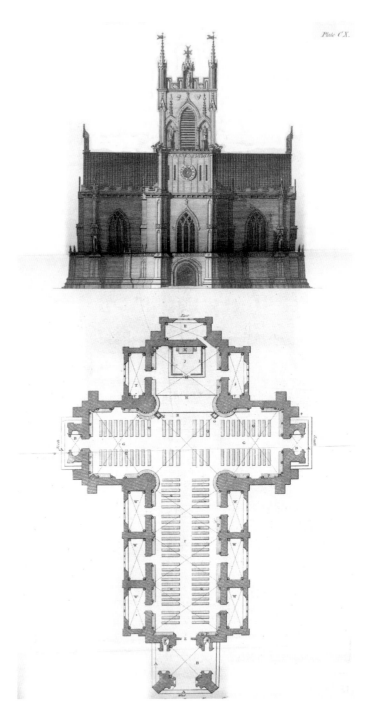

Plate CX.

1.1: John Carter, 'Design for a Church …View taken at the West End' and 'Plan', 1 January 1777, engraving by I. Royce in the *Builder's Magazine*, 1779, pl. cx.

(1786-93) and two-volume *The Ancient Architecture of England* (1795-1814), both substantially illustrated. In addition, large numbers of sketches and finished drawings survive.[5] Indeed, no other English architect had previously explored the potentials of true Gothic so diligently, except for James Essex, who died in 1784, the very year Carter rose to prominence.[6]

The subject of this chapter is Carter's activities as a *practising* designer of Gothic churches, which though hampered by a paucity of executed examples have, nonetheless, unfairly received almost no close scrutiny from architectural historians. In particular, this chapter concentrates on two buildings: St Nicholas, Moreton, Dorset (1777), hitherto unassociated with the architect but harbouring convincing circumstantial evidence and reflecting his ideas published in the *Builder's Magazine*; and St Peter's Roman Catholic chapel, Winchester (1792), his masterpiece and often cited as an icon in modern architectural literature, but rarely discussed in detail. In addition, James Donaldson's Woburn or Tavistock Chapel, London (1802, demolished 1900) is examined, an unusually interesting building of dubious artistic virtue subsequently unaccountably excluded from the history of the Gothic Revival, yet at the very heart of the issues concerned in the present chapter.

The *Builder's Magazine*

The *Builder's Magazine: or Monthly Companion … Consisting of Designs in Architecture* was published in instalments between 1774 and 1778 (with the first collected edition appearing in 1779). According to the title page, the aim was to cater to 'Architects, Carpenters, Masons, Bricklayers, &c. as well as for Every Gentleman who would wish to be a competent Judge of the elegant and necessary Art of Building' offered 'In Every Stile and Taste, from the most magnificent and superb Structures, down to the most simple and unadorned.' These included 'Designs for … Churches … and other Public Buildings … in the Greek, Roman and Gothic Taste.' Only fourteen designs in the *Magazine* fall within a Gothic remit.[7] The majority of these look back to Batty Langley's *Gothic Architecture, Improved* (1747), and they hardly prepare one for the remarkable 'Design for a Church' dated between 1 January and 1 July 1777, uniquely represented by seven plates, accompanied by a fuller explanatory text than found elsewhere in the publication, suggesting Carter held it in special reverence. Compared to his other Gothic schemes, it alone is both free of frippery and self-evidently serious, more closely resembling an authentic medieval church in its heyday and more geared for potential actual construction, as the technical plate devoted to internal roof timberwork suggests.[8] Perhaps here is a visual demonstration of the

1.2: John Carter, 'Design for a Church…West Door', 1 July 1777, in the *Builder's Magazine*, 1779, pl. cxxx.

'Complete System of Architecture … so disposed, as to render the Surveyor, Carpenter, Mason, &c. equally capable to erect a Cathedral' advertised on the title page. While J. Mordaunt Crook's seminal *John Carter and the Mind of the Gothic Revival* (1995) summarily dismissed the scheme as 'really little better than the sort of thing [Carter] criticized so fiercely'[9] in the work of others, this is certainly not entirely true.

Looking closely, it is a proposal for a cruciform structure which, if built, would have measured overall 190 feet west to east, with the nave and chancel both rising to 48 feet. Carter obligingly takes the reader on a methodical tour of the building, signposted in a fully keyed ground plan (**1.1**).[10] Ascending the west steps and through the porch with its 'grand

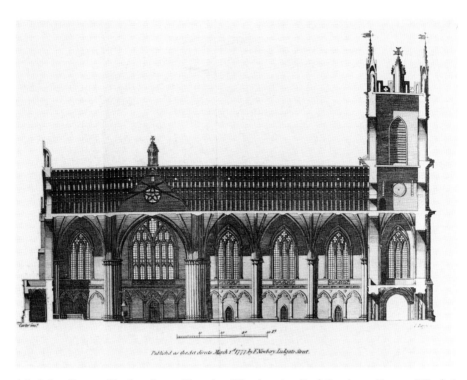

1.3: John Carter, 'Design for a Church…The longitudinal Section…East to West', 1 March 1777, in the *Builder's Magazine*, 1779, pl. cxvi.

1.4: John Carter, 'Design for a Church', longitudinal section north to south, 1 April 1777, in the *Builder's Magazine,* 1779, pl. cxix.

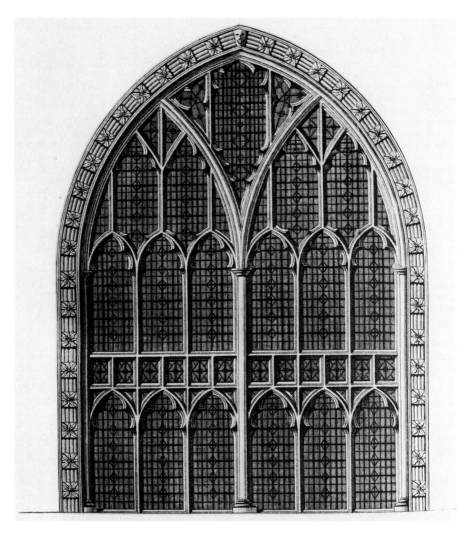

1.5: John Carter, 'Design for a Church … The outside of the great north window', 1 June 1777, in the *Builder's Magazine,* 1779, pl. cxxvi.

door' (**1.2**), then descending one step into the body of the church (**1.3**) and looking towards the chancel and transepts, the body is filled with 'Seats for the common people Q.' Then 'having come to the center of the building … to the left is … the pulpit and reading-desk M' and 'to the right … the font O', both attached to a 'cluster of columns'. 'We now ascend the three steps leading to the altar [K with] LL Seats for the Ministers … the railing round it, I', to its right 'the door leading to the sacristy R', a place for storing 'the utensils, the ornaments of the church, ministers vestments, &c.', flanked by 'a vestry-room S', and a 'Room for the reception of the ministers, &c T.' Above the altar was 'the east window' (**1.5**).[11]

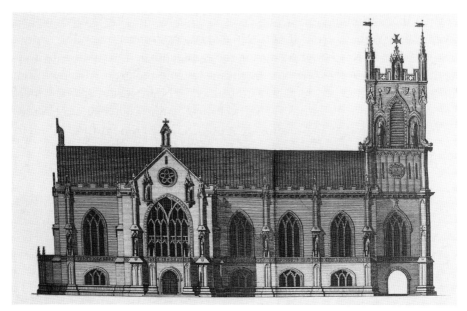

1.6: John Carter, 'Design for a Church … Elevation of the North Front…from East to West', 1 February 1777, in the *Builder's Magazine*, 1779, pl. cxiii.

Throughout the building Carter introduced authentic Gothic details which would have been recognisable to knowledgeable antiquaries of the day, and to those few architects with medieval interests. The most distinctive feature of the west tower (**1.1, 1.6**) is the Somerset-inspired turret composed of corner pinnacles of alternating crenellation and merlons, but given more emphatic canopied niches in the centres of each side containing (unidentified) statues in place of conventional pinnacles.[12] The repeated blank quatrefoils framing the west door (**1.2**) recall the early thirteenth century reveals of the upper windows of Lichfield Cathedral choir.[13] The self-contained, single-storey chapels 'over burying places of honourable families' flanking the three bays of the body (**1.1** marked W, and **1.6**) derive from the Perpendicular King's College Chapel, Cambridge, 'justly term'd one of the finest buildings in Europe … after the Gothick manner', which Horace Walpole reported in the fortuitous year of 1777 as having had its 'beauty … now … restored, penetrated me with the visionary longing to be a monk in it'.[14] Carter's immoderately massive compound crossing piers were almost certainly inspired by those in Exeter Cathedral (1270s-1340s) which he had recently drawn (**1.7**).[15] But what is the function of this superfluous anomaly in the 1777 church scheme where they support only an insignificant superstructure, since above the cross-vault is only a roof cavity crowned by a diminutive flèche (**1.3, 1.4**). Perhaps this arrangement was intended to suggest the continuing growth inherent in large medieval structures, such as Westminster Abbey, begun about 1050 and largely completed by 1534 when work ceased, although revived during the eighteenth century when the west end and north transept were finally finished, while the great crossing tower, despite many attempts, remained unrealised.[16] Nonetheless, Carter's piers impressively frame the entrance to the chancel, acting as dramatic backdrops to the attached pulpit and reading desk positioned on the north-east, and to the font with a suspended cover on the south-east (**1.1, 1.3, 1.4**, marked M, N, O), a post-Reformation innovation following the removal of the chancel

1.7: John Carter, 'View of the north cross aisle of Exeter Cathedral, (taken 1777)', pen and ink and wash. (*British Library Board, Add. MS. 29925, f. 8.*)

screen and the bringing of the sermon and baptism into the arena of the congregation.

The seating arrangement, with stone benches provided for 'the gentry' integrated in blind arcading along the perimeter, and serried rows of benches for 'the common people' filling the body and arms (**1.1**, marked P and Q) represented a rethinking of both pre- and post-Reformation practices, where in the former regime congregants were rarely provided such comforts except as concessions to the elderly and infirm. Neither side galleries nor box pews, so usual at the time, clutter the interior, so anticipating Victorian improvements in churches.[17] Even more prophetic was Carter's introduction of subtly ascending steps in the worshippers' progress from west to east, culminating in a raised and railed enclosure surrounding the altar and reredos (**1.1** marked H-K, **1.3**, **1.4**) – a remarkable anticipation of the Ecclesiologists' call some 60 years later for greater Catholic feeling in church design.[18]

Carter's ecclesiastical Gothic credo, encapsulated in the 1777 church, appears at the conclusion of the *Builder's Magazine*:

> The student is to observe, that as all churches should be built in the Gothic taste, as being more suitable to such structures than the Grecian taste, so likewise every part appertaining to it must be in the same style … For true it is, nothing can be more absurd than mixing one taste with the other, as is too commonly the case, for instance, the towers of Westminster abbey, what a medley of Grecian and Gothic architecture is there! The choir of the same place is *decorated* with a screen of Grecian columns, &c. to the altar, while every other object round is Gothic! … the choir of Canterbury cathedral is Grecian, and numberless other places in England, can produce instances as ridiculous as these. I think no true considerate admirer of Grecian architecture can with confidence maintain that such *medley work* shews real taste, it can only shew a love of novelty, which will always reflect a disgrace on the intruder of Grecian architecture on Gothic remains. If any of these venerable piles need repair, or any alterations, let it be designed in the exact manner of the original work, and seek not, by introducing some new whim or fancy, to cast a *mark of scorn* on what indeed should be our pride to imitate and preserve in its original purity and grandeur. Some architects of late years have invented an extraordinary taste for Gothic buildings, as the seats of justice in Westminster-hall --- the arches that compose the same are *purely modern*, and I may say, with the rest of the ornaments, need no other conviction of their deformity and extravagance than to be compared with the old Gothic --- this is one of the noblest rooms in the world rendered odious, when before it was so truly beautiful and magnificent. I must confess myself a zealous admirer of Gothic architecture --- affirming with confidence, nothing can be more in character, and better adapted to

1.8: John Carter, attributed, west front, St Nicholas, Moreton, Dorset, 1776. (*Author, 1996.*)

a place of worship, than that awful style of building, and that Grecian and Roman architecture should be confined to mansions and other structures of ease and pleasure.[19]

It is impossible within the scope of this chapter to speculate on any possible one-to-one relationships between the 1777 church and particular medieval models, except in the cases of Westminster Abbey and Exeter Cathedral, as we have seen. According to Carter's obituarist, he lauded the former as 'the architectural wonder of [the] Kingdom' and 'from his own mouth … all his leisure time [as a young man] was employed in examining and drawing … all its parts, under every point of view' and that here the authorities 'introduced him into the world of Antiquities'.[20] This is important because not only was the Abbey then regarded as an unrivalled repository of the most authentic specimens of ancient Gothic forms and ornament, but also the focus of the Georgian controversy surrounding the schizoid mixture of Gothic and Classical in the same building – what Horace Walpole aptly called 'the bastard breed' but Carter more graciously, as we have seen, '*medley work*'.[21] Carter very likely read Stephen Wren's *Parentalia* (1750), containing the 1713 memorandum by his grandfather, Sir Christopher, Surveyor to the Fabric, on an enlightened policy for the restoration and completion of the building: in this he notes that for 'new Additions I have prepared perfect Draughts ... such as I conceive may agree with the original Scheme of the old Architect, without any modern Mixtures to shew my own Invention' which are 'still in the *Gothick* Form, and of a Style with the rest of the Structure, which I would strictly adhere to [since] to deviate from the old Form, would be to run into a disagreeable Mixture, which no Person of a good Taste could relish'.

Certainly the 1777 church can best be understood as a conflation of distinctive historical features to create an archetypal pattern for the future, yet, as well, it played a seminal role in late eighteenth-century church design. Take the example of St Nicholas, Moreton, Dorset, dated 1776 on the entrance door corbel, a distinguished but inadequately documented building hitherto unattached to an identifiable architect but, in the present writer's opinion, a strong contender as Carter's creation; or at the very least representing an early expression of Carterian forms and decoration.[22]

The plan is unusual: a three-bay nave with integral semicircular chancel (**1.8**) and a central, square, three-storey tower attached to its south side flanked by single-storey pew blocks accommodating family and servants respectively (**1.9**).[23] The bold, simple geometric forms and individual details – ogee-arched door, trefoil tracery windows, pierced stone louvres of the tower's bell-stage and rosetted quatrefoil parapets all round – are closely akin to the 1777 church.

The Roman Catholic chapel, Winchester

The opportunity that propelled Carter into the penultimate realm of Gothic authenticity was his 1791-2 commission to design a new, free-standing Catholic chapel in Winchester, one of the first built since the Reformation, in an atmosphere of uncommon religious tolerance following the Second Relief Act, which allowed the erection of recusant places of worship, provided they excluded steeples and bells.[24]

Carter's client (and 'great friend') was the Revd Dr John Milner (1752-1826), the future vicar apostolic of the Western District of England, who was appointed priest of the Winchester Mission in 1779 and took responsibility for the general concept of the building.[25] They employed experienced tradesmen: the principal carpenter, joiner and carver, John Lingard, received £433 9s. 5d. and probably acted as clerk of the works; among others

1.9: John Carter, attributed, south elevation, St Nicholas, Moreton, 1776. (*Author, 1996.*)

mentioned in the wage sheet and accounts is William Cave, a member of a local Catholic family of painters, who was paid a total of £97 16s. 10d. for undertaking 'a good Altar Piece and five Pictures and all the Ornamental Painting'; the total cost of construction was £917 1s. 1d.[26] No preparatory drawings have been traced and tragically only the empty shell of the chapel survives (**1.10**), though fortunately Milner published invaluable engraved views of the exterior and interior in 1809 (**1.11**), accompanied by a lengthy and detailed description; together with later images these help recreate for modern readers something of the glamorous appearance of Carter's building in its heyday.[27]

Milner began his published peregrination at the arched entrance to the compound, 'an exceedingly good specimen of the Saxon style ... a genuine antique' reinstated from the demolished church of 1174 attached to nearby St Margaret's Hospital, a rare instance of Georgian preservationist activity as well as an authentic affirmation of the new chapel's medieval ancestry.[28] The entrance elevation, measuring 75 feet long by 35 feet high to the summit of its pinnacles (replaced in 1888 by simple crenellation), a 'light Gothic building, coated with stucco, resembling free-stone; with mullioned windows, shelving buttresses, a parapet with open quatrefoils and crocketed pinnacles, terminating in gilt crosses',[29] displays a row of five identical three-light Perpendicular windows, each measuring 12 feet by 4 feet 6 inches, a pattern closely resembling St Augustine, Skirlaugh, Yorkshire (*c.*1401–5), renowned as a perfect, homogeneous piece of late medieval architecture.[30] The use of quatrefoil bands were much favoured in the *Builder's Magazine* as well as at Moreton (**1.1, 1.6, 1.8, 1.9**). The corbels of the chapel's window canopies feature heads of bishops, kings and queens 'with their respective emblems' inspired by statues in the screen at the west front of Exeter

1.10: John Carter, exterior, St Peter's Roman Catholic Chapel, Winchester. (*Author, 2000.*)

Cathedral, which Carter sketched in 1792.[31] The 'ground' glass 'admits the light but prevents any object from being seen through it'. The entrance porch was originally 'surmounted with a niche, containing a small statue of St Peter, holding his keys', while below the royal arms accompanied a Latin inscription translated as 'Erected in the 33d year of the reign of George III, king of Great Britain, and Ireland, &c. Happy, Temperate, the Assertion of Innocence, the Father of his Country'. These were clearly intended as affirmations of Roman Catholic loyalty to the Crown.[32]

Inside, opposite the entrance, was a staircase leading to a loft-like gallery containing an organ – once the property of Handel, subsequently enclosed in 'a case of Gothic work' – supported on a double row of 'light pointed arches and slender columns, faced with Gothic railings' (**1.12**). The gallery offered 'an advantageous view' of the glories of the chapel body, accurately recorded in the Cave-Pass engraving (**1.11**).[33]

Running through Milner's description and undoubtedly his personal contribution to the decorative programme, though too complex to detail here, was elaborate Old and New Testament iconography which had by then all but vanished from post-Reformation Anglican churches. On the long unfenestrated wall and mirroring the ogee and cusped arch windows were Cave's *chiaro oscuro* paintings on canvas, *The Salutation of the Blessed Virgin*, copied from the Winchester College Chapel altarpiece by François

1.11: John Carter, 'Inside View of the Altar End', 'Outside View of St. Peter's Chapel, Winton' (Winchester) and 'Norman Doorway Leading to the Chapel, from St. Peter's Street'. (*J. Milner*, The History Civil and Ecclesiastical, & Survey of the Antiquities, of Winchester, *vol. 2, 1809, Supplement, 2nd ed., engraving by J. Passe after James Cave.*)

1.12: John Carter, interior towards the organ gallery, St Peter's Chapel, Winchester. (*Pre-1926 photograph, Hampshire Record Office.*)

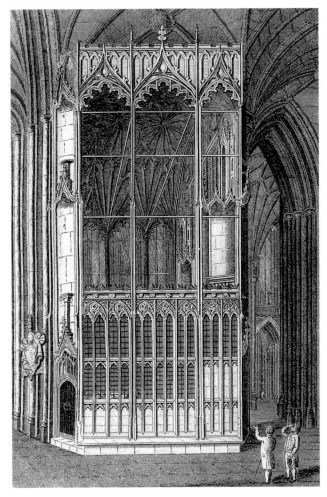

1.13: 'South View of the Outside of William Wykeham's Chantry, in Winchester Cathedral'. (*J. Milner, The History Civil and Ecclesiastical, & Survey of the Antiquities, of Winchester, vol. 2, 1809, Supplement, 2nd ed., engraving by J. Passe after James Cave.*)

Lemoine, although here the background represented 'part of the present chapel'; *The Last Supper* after Hans Holbein; *Christ Giving the Keys to St Peter* after Poussin, updated with views of St Peter's Chapel and St Peter's, Rome; *The Death of Ananias* based on Raphael's cartoon but 'placed at the altar of the present chapel' and *Christ Casting the Moneylenders from the Temple*, located under the gallery, with the background showing the 'lower end of this chapel'. In other words it was a visual expression of the continuity of the Catholic faith through its nearly 1,800-year history, in the manner of medieval ecclesiastical storytelling. The ogee and cusped tracery patterning of the walls probably derive from William of Wykeham's Chantry in the nearby cathedral (**1.13**), which Milner reckoned 'the most perfect specimens extant of the time when they were performed … The ornaments … rich, without being crowded; the carvings … delicate, without being finical'.[34]

Moreover, of crucial importance was Carter's close association with Horace Walpole's Strawberry Hill, which he recorded in a series of beautiful watercolour views between 1788 and 1790 showing some of its internal walls patterned overall with trefoil and quatrefoil low relief plasterwork.[35] Separating each narrative panel and corresponding window bay were 'tall [engaged] columns with plain capitals and bases … painted of a straw colour' set against 'French grey' walls, supporting a rib vault with central bosses at the intersections 'painted and gilt with various sacred emblems' of Christ.[36] The body was separated from the two-bay sanctuary by a delicate railing of trefoil arches, mirroring that extending across the gallery.

The fittings and furnishings, 'all in the same style, and copied from originals of ancient date',[37] included a pair of 'gorgeous lamp pedestals … borrowed from the city cross' (**1.14**).[38] The priest's chair (visible on the far left

1.14: The Butter Cross, Winchester, fifteenth century. (*Author, 1996.*)

29

1.15: Tomb of Aymer de Valance, Earl of Pembroke, Westminster Abbey.

in **1.11**) 'imitated' the thirteenth century Coronation Chair in Westminster Abbey made for Edward I, a poignant resurrection of an inimitable furniture model from the nation's pre-Reformation past.[39] The altar, a 'Gothic table … supported by arches in the same style … painted white with gilt mouldings', featured 'instead of an antependium' a panel depicting the *Lamentation of Christ* 'copied from a celebrated picture by Dominichino, in the possession of Lord Arundell' of Wardour Castle (a leading Catholic aristocrat), here 'painted in chiaro oscuro, to represent carving'. Atop the table was a 'tabernacle … peculiarly rich and elaborate; being a model of the west end

of York Minster, but with such variations as [its] nature and use … require';
that is, the door was carved with 'the emblems of Christ's Passion', with the
paired towers instead of windows containing 'canopied niches [having] gilt
emblematical statues [of] Faith, Hope, the Love of God, and the Love of our
Neighbour'. The choice of York as model, which Carter later hallowed for
being built during Edward III's reign, when 'the English nation seems to
have arrived at the meridian of its glory', and which he especially admired
because it had escaped James Wyatt's deadly hand of 'improvement' – Carter's
antiquarian and ecclesiological circles famously condemned the architect as
the 'Destroyer' of this style.[40] Both he and Milner believed implicitly that
the future of English church design of whatever Christian denomination lay
exclusively in a return to pre-Reformation Catholic 'Pointed' forms, and it
was this, among other things, that made the Winchester Chapel seminal to
the early development of late Georgian Gothic.[41]

Above the table was a cinquefoil-arched reredos, 10 feet 6 inches by 8
feet 6 inches, with pinnacles terminating in pomegranates (suitably symbolic
of resurrection) and crowned by a lily (denoting purity), again painted white
with gilt mouldings and other ornaments, measuring 16 feet by 12 feet.
This was based on the fourteenth-century tomb of Aymer de Valence, Earl
of Pembroke in Westminster Abbey (**1.15**), but with its quatrefoil-framed
equestrian relief replaced by a 'transparent painting upon glass of a Dove;
which, by means of light that is let in upon it from behind, produces a
surprising and pleasing effect'. A stylistically disparate yet nonetheless
dramatic note was struck by Cave's copy of Raphael's *Transfiguration*, 'the
first picture, in point of merit, extant'.[42]

It is worth mentioning here that Carter's 1792-3 octagonal chancel
addition to St Mary and All Saints, Debden, Essex (**1.16**), constructed of
wood and plaster vaulting, while 'a parody of Gothic structure' (as it certainly
would still have been at this date), by 1797 came to house the monument
to R.M.T. Chiswell, lord of the manor (**1.17**): it was an altogether more
convincing adaptation than was the Winchester reredos of Aymer de Valence's
tomb.[43] The heraldic-panelled tomb chest is familiar from numerous medieval
examples in the Abbey, while the quatrefoil band framing Chiswell's epitaph
derives from Lichfield Cathedral choir's clerestory windows via Carter's
door design (**1.2**). Precociously detailed and crisply carved, the monument
represented one further step in his quest for Gothic authenticity.

Returning to the Winchester Catholic chapel, flanking the reredos
were doors 'rich with Gothic carvings'; topped by a frieze and cornice,
the former 'charged with carved and gilt foliage and flowers', in turn over
these were ranges of 'closed Gothic arches, carved and gilt', in the centre of

1.16: John Carter, design for the chancel addition to St Mary and All Saints, Debden, Essex, longitudinal section north to south, with burial vault, 1792-3, pen and ink and wash. (*Trustees of Sir John Soane's Museum, London, 47/10/16.*)

each 'relieved canopies' containing figures of St Peter and St Paul 'painted in light and shade, to imitate sculpture'. The crowning register, within the vault area, was filled with 'a closed embattlement, carved and gilt, containing alternate niches and quatrefoils'. On close inspection this is the pattern of the 1777 church parapet (**1.1, 1.6**), now decorated with angels 'in the act of adoration towards the altar' and 'some emblems of the blessed sacrament ... interrupted by two large niches with figures of St Birinus and St Swithin. Milner's message was clear: with the establishment of this chapel he was hopeful of reclaiming the town, indeed the whole of the British nation, in the name of pre-Reformation Christianity.

The door to the left of the reredos led to a secondary, private entrance (shown in the 1809 external view) and via a flight of stairs to a 'private gallery ... of inverted Gothic arches, with gilt mouldings; being a species of antique rail-work, which is open, for the benefit of persons who attend the divine service ... A grey silk curtain hangs behind the railings, and conceals such persons from the sight of the congregation'.[44] They would primarily have included over-cautious fellow members but undoubtedly also curious non-Catholic interlopers, such as James Dugdale, author of the encyclopaedic *New British Traveller, or Modern Panorama of England and Wales* (1819), who correctly recognised that the chapel's 'general idea was to give a modern imitation of the English, or pointed style, with its corresponding decorations in the middle ages'.[45] The ensemble was altogether a remarkable achievement.

1.17: John Carter, monument to R.M.T. Chiswell, St Mary and All Saints, Debden, 1797.

Since Carter designed few religious buildings after Winchester and Debden, what evidence is there that this ideal was expressed in his subsequent polemical writings? Although he published 212 closely argued, often esoteric essays in the *Gentleman's Magazine* between 1798 and 1817 under the provocative title 'Pursuits of Architectural Innovation' – a text today hardly more than dipped into even by the most zealous antiquarians and architectural historians – much of what he chose to publish dealt with improvements to medieval cathedrals and large parish churches rather than with new Gothic ecclesiastical undertakings by other architects, let alone ones in which he was somehow involved. In this regard we are in luck.

The Woburn or Tavistock Chapel

In 1801 James Donaldson (*c.*1756-1843), now an almost totally forgotten figure except for being the father of Thomas Leverton Donaldson, founder of the RIBA, realised his only recorded religious scheme, for Woburn or

Tavistock Chapel in Tavistock Place, Russell Square (demolished 1900) (**1.18**).[46] Its unusual front elevation consisted of a tripartite stepped centrepiece with buttresses framing each section, recalling medieval Austin Friars' church (the Dutch Church), London,[47] though only in its general composition since Donaldson had emasculated his scheme in the interests of metropolitan proprietary chapel typology,[48] while at the same time expanding the front elevation latterly. Thus, the main block was flanked by a pair of square, crenellated pavilions, themselves also each framed by a pair of lower entrance links (the innermost communicating with internal galleries), altogether forming a picturesque sweep of seven connected units appropriate to a terrace-house development. The chapel immediately attracted critical attention germane to the present study.

In May 1802 the *Gentleman's Magazine* published a brief letter from 'PANCRAS' (an unidentified pseudonym), accompanied by a view similar to **1.18**, describing 'The New Gothic Chapel' as built of brick, 'stuccoed in a very masterly manner' giving 'the appearance of a dark stone building. The windows, battlements, and minute ornaments, are all chaste imitations, and extremely well executed.'[49]

In the following month appeared another anonymous but more

⚓IDEAOGRAPHICAL VIEW of the NEW-CHAPEL, TAVISTOCK-PLACE, RUSSELL SQUARE. ⚓

1.18: James Donaldson, 'An Ideaographical View of the New Chapel, Tavistock-Place, Russell Square', London, 1802, etching. (*Trustees of The British Library, London, King's Maps, xxvii, 29 (3).*)

significant letter, dated 8 June, signed 'I.M.' It praised Carter profusely by name – as a person 'so much better qualified than I to expose the bad taste of modern architectural reformers and innovators' and 'more conversant with the disposition and beauties of our antient national structures'; furthermore 'Architectural Antiquities are more indebted than to those of any other man living, not only for acquiring just notions in these matters, but also for the preservation of some of the most precious monuments of ancient art and magnificence.'[50] The author may have been, as a subsequent correspondent claimed, a 'colleague of Mr. Carter' or perhaps, as the present writer suspects, Carter himself in disguise.[51] Here Donaldson's veniality is explicitly spelt out: where are 'windows, *of the same period* ['the genuine works of our ancestors, in the pointed order ... called *Gothic*'] ... to be seen, some of them forming a highly pointed, others a flat arch [with Tudor hood-moulds], and others no arch at all ... where plain mullions are to be found, crossing each other in the Chinese form, without the least tracery, or even the characteristically trefoil head?'; 'where uniform piers, without breaks or embellishments of any kind, buttresses up a façade, being capped with large square abacuses, and finished with hatched billets [a Romanesque ornament of regularly placed short blocks], by way of crocket pinnacles?'; 'flat battlements, without coping or mouldings'; 'the new idea of representing the emblem of Christianity by a traverse hole on the tympan, instead of exalting it to the summit of the pediment'; 'the double row of diminutive niches, occupying the place where we look for the bold columns and arches of the grand portico'; 'the disproportion in a chapel that is designed to be in the antient style, of making its breadth ... nearly equal to its height'. All here were 'burlesque imitations' of the true Pointed Style. Carter's worst nightmare.

Later in June 'AN ARCHITECT' (assuredly Carter) ridiculed 'PANCRAS' as either 'one totally unacquainted with the moods of Architecture he presumes to illustrate' or 'means his communication as an insult to the cause of Antiquity', adding to the earlier list the errors of a central arched recess replacing a doorway and of positioning the principal front at the south rather than the west end (an understandable expedient imposed by existing town planning) and placing the communion table at the north rather than the east, which Carter condemned as 'interior innovations, peculiar to modern church arrangements' setting 'the ancient disposure of such principal decorations at defiance'. But because he recognised the chapel as 'indeed ... one of the first pretended revivals in the town of our Antient Architecture ... the public ... should ... be properly apprised of its real error [otherwise] they might be induced to conceive it a model to guide their taste in any future erection of the like nature'.[52]

'PANCRAS' promptly counter-attacked by insisting he was a 'friend to ancient English architecture' and that Tavistock Chapel 'as a symptom of the returning religious art of building ... must at least be allowed equal to many of our oldest country churches'. He preferred its 'better and handsomer design' to a ballroom, a chapel or a Quaker meeting-house and questioned why the 'Grecian [that is, Classical] style' of the early eighteenth-century Queen Anne churches by Archer, Gibbs, Hawksmoor and James had found official favour. In explanation of his use of the phrase 'chaste imitations' of Gothic he cited sources for the thirteenth-century tracery windows over the entrances in St Nicholas, Sutton, Surrey (rebuilt 1862-4), St Helen, Bishopsgate, London 'besides fifty others in the country' and endorsed Westminster Abbey and 'other equally rich English cathedrals' as 'models ... for it is undoubted that they afford every grand sublime effect that the art of man can attain in Architecture'. Yet, he also believed that 'others have a right to prefer Grecian' and personally recommended 'the pleasing descriptions of such authors as Mrs Radcliffe' (author of *The Mysteries of Udolpho*, 1797) by which 'a taste is imbibed for the awful and venerable style of our ancestors'.[53] Such a picturesque approach exposes the confusion over stylistic appropriateness debated during the hiatus between the golden age of Georgian Gothic culminating in the 1790s, and the launch of the 1818 Church Building Commission along with its subsequent progress under Pugin and the Ecclesiologists.

This prompted a fuller critique in the August 1802 issue of the *Gentleman's Magazine*, for the first time signed 'J.C. – Surveyor (by inclination) of the various Styles of the Ancient Architecture of England' and undertaken in a resolute, Churchillian refutation. Deplored was the liturgically unnatural reorientation of the internal plan running north to south, rather than the long-standing west to east axis, preconditioned by having to integrate an ecclesiastical building into a rigid estate development. There was no historical precedent for repositioning twin entrances in the outer bays flanking 'arched recesses and small compartments projecting from the main wall': 'In our antient architecture the door of entrance was in the centre'. While the doors were of pointed form, over them were 'horizontal labels, applicable only to the square-headed doors and windows of the Tudor aera'. The upper windows of 'equilateral pointed form' were divided by mullions of 'so *petit* dimensions ... they must be nearly invisible (this runs with your modern eldarado sash-frames) ... without tracery or any antient finish whatever'.[54] Pilasters at the outer angles of Donaldson's front ('in our antient architecture no such figures, buttresses occupying these parts') supported on plinths and pedestals 'a sort of pinnacles notched at their angles, to supply the place of

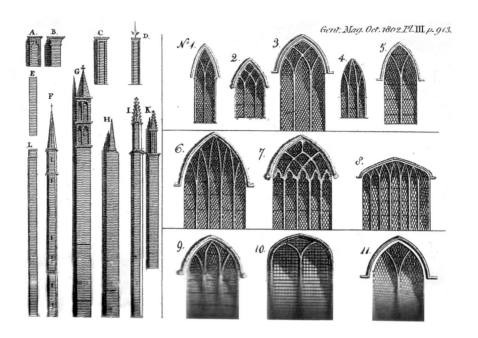

Gent. Mag. Oct. 1802 Pl. III. p. 913.

1.19: J.P. Malcolm, Woburn or Tavistock Chapel, London, 'slight sketches ... of windows and abutments ... where originals might be produced of which the windows. &c. in the new chapel were chaste imitations': nos 3, 11 'in the new chapel', no. 1 Exeter Cathedral west front, no. 5 Sutton, Surrey, no. 2 Carshalton, Surrey, no. 4, Duffield, Derbyshire, nos 6, 8, 9 St Helen, Bishopsgate, London, no. 7 Bentley, Derbyshire, no. 10 St Dunstan, Fleet Street, London; A. E. Durham Cathedral, B. St Catharine's Chapel, Abbotsbury, Dorset, G, D. St George's Chapel, Windsor, F. Norwich Cathedral, G. Gloucester Cathedral, H. Hereford Cathedral, I. K. Salisbury Cathedral, L. Selby Abbey. (Gentleman's Magazine, October 1802, p. 913, pl. III.)

crotchets' (detailed in a vignette in **1.19**); their 'enormous cornices' as well as the central gable 'are purely modern'.

Of the interior Carter painted a desperately grim picture, assuring readers 'there is no cause visible to make us believe the builder was any way so inclined' towards religious tendencies. The 'clustered columns without bases' (of 'Grecian architecture, not ... our antient styles'), 'enormously large' capitals, 'prodigious columns – crowning ... arches ... without ribs or mouldings of any kind', 'Much of the work ... of the common house sort' though 'some ... leans towards our antient modes' yet 'cut out in a manner which does not convince us that a zealous attachment to "chaste imitation" was once thought of', and so forth.[55]

Next to enter the fray was J.P. Malcolm, author of *Londinium Redivivum* (1802-7), who 'PANCRAS' described as a 'Gothic Enthusiast' and who identified and illustrated (in crude generalised vignettes) a considerable number of specific medieval models employed in Tavistock Chapel (**1.19**).[56] Carter wrote again on 3 November 1802 (from Winchester) attacking Malcolm for drawing proofs in favour of Tavistock's 'chaste imitations … from a few mean and trifling antient churches in and about London, and from prints', the latter particularly futile exercises which 'can be of but little service to guide the construction of a new building', being 'so small a scale, and their forms so incorrect, that they appear more the production of memory than faithful delineations from the originals'. He thought it 'impossible to give a true representation of any part of such works, in a building about to be set up, without an exact plan, elevation, the mouldings, and ornaments, &c … made on the spot from the model fixed on to be religiously adhered to'. Stressing the vital importance of relying on accurate, detailed source material, which was one of the chief beauties of Winchester, he cited his own exquisite renderings for Durham and Gloucester cathedrals drawn 'on the largest scales possible' for the Society of Antiquaries' 1801 and 1809 publications, respectively. Carter then proceeded to demolish Malcolm's purported models. The 'plain intersecting mullions' of the windows (**1.19**, nos 7–8) were 'erroneous' since they were either 'irrelevant … modern whimsies' or detailed 'to save the expence of reparation … to give more light' or 'appear … more consonant to the ideas of modern architectural men'. As to specific ancient buildings, St Dunstan, Fleet Street's fenestration (no. 10) had undergone 'many *alterations* and *beautifying* … in our time', while the 'small window' on Exeter's west front (no. 1) 'does not bear the original finishings: the late Architect of that church [probably William Blackburn, died 1790, appointed Surveyor in that year], with whom I was well acquainted, did more than once satisfy me in this respect'.[57] Carter presumed that Malcolm had neither visited nor surveyed the cited cathedrals at Ely and Gloucester.

Here is a perfect demonstration of the virtues of knowledgeable first-hand observation coupled with careful historical research so keenly promoted by Carter, who now signed the article 'J.C. Surveyor (by inclination) of the various Styles of the antient Architecture of England, not from "Prints," but from the real Remains of antient Buildings among us' and closing his argument by maintaining 'the consistency of all my observations … made on the best of motives, the defence and honour of our antient Architecture, and for the instruction of young students in that line of professional employ'.[58] However, he was not to enjoy the last word on this fraught issue promoted by the *Gentleman's Magazine*.

Yet another anonymous contributor to the December 1802 issue censured Carter's 'unprovoked attack upon Tavistock chapel', which the former claimed 'displayed considerable knowledge of that science [of Gothic architecture], in which he has distinguished himself both as an Antiquary and an Architect'. That Carter should 'endeavour to impose ... the *errors of education* and *early habits* ... upon the world ... is one melancholy proof, among many, how completely a man may become the slave of superstition, and the dupe of his own sophistry'. Milner's *The History ... of Winchester* was held up as 'a deplorable instance ... which exhibits great learning and taste in antiquity, and that style of architecture ... termed *ecclesiastical*' yet 'contrived to weave a continued sneer upon the Reformed Faith, and a libel upon the religious establishments of his country', setting 'all the mummeries, follies and blasphemies of Popery ... against the simple, rational, sublime institutions of Protestantism'. By inference the reader was surely prompted to recall St Peter's Chapel. Our cryptic correspondent then turned his spleen on Carter's attack on Tavistock Chapel as an 'invidious censor', 'the jealousy of a little mind, which can discern nothing but faults in the works of a *rival artist*' and suggested that the chapel 'was not intended as a complete specimen of Gothic architecture. It has other and better claims to approbation. It was intended as an useful auxiliary to the mother church [medieval St Pancras];[59] and, when it is fairly contrasted with that, it will not be thought to disgrace its origin. What-ever may be its imperfections, it must surely be preferred, in point of beauty and effect, to its much-neglected parent.' Moreover, its capacity to accommodate 1,500 persons excluded from the latter 'through want of room ... would have more weight with every friend to the Church of England, than the strictest conformity to the purest models of antient architecture, could not be doubted'.[60]

The liturgical and stylistic polarities between the all too conspicuous refinements of Winchester and the self-evident ineptitudes of London, separated by only ten years; between the misinterpreted virtues expressed in the above closing December letter and the prophetic verdict of a July 1802 letter from 'I.I.' that the latter was 'a sufficient proof of the incapacity of our present architects to restore the *genuine* Gothic', epitomises the dilemma English ecclesiastical architecture found itself embroiled during these pivotal decades.[61] In retrospect, Tavistock Chapel seems the sad conclusion of backward, outdated late-Georgian indecisiveness, while St Peter's and even the 1777 church emerge as pioneering icons of Gothic exclusiveness and authenticity as well as expressions of a true National ecclesiastical style. Carter had advocated these essential qualities as early as the *Builder's Magazine*:

The Gothic architecture has, for these few years past, fallen greatly under the censure of the immoderate admirers of Grecian architecture, yet if we candidly consider, we shall find both styles have their separate beauties and use. The Grecian taste certainly best suits those publick buildings; such as palaces, courts of justice, exchanges, hospitals, music-rooms, banqueting-rooms, mansions, &c. but for religious structures, Gothic, undoubtedly, ought to be preferred: the difference is easily to be decided: by spending a few hours in St. Paul's [Cathedral] and Peter's [Abbey], Westminster, we may easily and seriously tell which has the greatest effect on the mind; which pile of building conveys the more devout ideas; which fills the senses with the greatest attention of the heaven above us; which leads us more to contemplate on the life to come? – If I may take the liberty to judge, it is St. Peter's; St. Paul's never can impart those sensations; it has the contrary effect. We behold that wondrous object with a familiar eye: we consider that as raised to pass the hours in business, pleasure, and delight; no pious thought possess the mind, as while we are gazing on the vaulted roof of St. Peter. Therefore condemn not Gothic entirely, but as occasion serves, and the subject requires, give preference to it. This little digression is meant to take partial impressions from the minds of the students which they may likely have imbibed, that Gothic architecture is a depraved taste, and ought never, on any account, to be introduced; and to remind them and others, that Gothic architecture has been ages back the taste of Englishmen, and not entirely be led away by Grecian architecture alone, because it is the invention of foreigners.[62]

There is another very important aspect to this debate. To where could an architect turn to satisfy the growing army of worshippers who demanded a Gothic design around 1820? In R.D. Chantrell's oft-quoted words 'Although generally well grounded in Greek and Roman architecture [the architect] found himself called upon to construct works utterly at variance with Greek and Roman principals.'[63] The many pattern books of Peter Nicholson, the most widely read of the post-Waterloo authors, contained only designs for classical churches; W.F. Pocock's *Designs for Churches and Chapels* (first edition 1819) included much useful information, but was weak on Gothic.[64] Conveniently, Carter's *Builder's Magazine* was reprinted under the editorship of an obscure 'Architect & Builder' named Andrew George Cook and entitled the *New Builder's Magazine and Complete Architectural Library … Consisting of Designs in … Architecture*, using the original plates: the new editions were published in 1819, 1820 and 1823; significantly, there were also undated ones that are likely to have appeared several years earlier.[65] In all of them Carter's 1777 church was faithfully reproduced – it even carried Carter's name, although the date was removed in order to disguise its true age. It was the most accessible example of a recent Gothic church design illustrated in

and summarily categorised by … Rickman who not only made sense of the confusion of styles in his explanatory volume but by clear and simple diagrams provided a wealth of parts which would be useful in composition, accompanied by advice as to what should or should not be copied.'[5] 'Few sciences can boast of so good an elementary treatise.'[6]

Born in Maidenhead, Berkshire, in 1776, Thomas Rickman, eldest son of an apothecary, came of a family 'entrenched in the solid core of the Quaker middle class',[7] believing in scrupulous behaviour in daily life. He began medical studies, but in 1803 took up accounting, both crafts calling for exactitude and suited to the Quaker ethos. Noted from childhood for an exact observation, he applied this skill to ecclesiastical buildings.

Rescued from bankruptcy by his elder brother John, in November 1807, he moved from London to Liverpool, eventually in 1810 joining an insurance broker's, at a respectable salary of £150 a year.[8] His generous employer promoted his career and his interest in architecture.[9] A visit to Porden's Gothic rebuilding of Eaton Hall stimulated Rickman's architectural development, particularly the use of cast-iron window tracery,[10] and he began seriously to sketch churches.[11] His lack of training he laboured to correct by copying from Britton's *Architectural Antiquities* and similar works,[12] and took advice from friends.[13]

As well as traversing the country to examine churches and cathedrals, Rickman helped organise literary societies in Liverpool, a means of social advancement.[14] He lectured on architecture to his Philosophical Society on 27 September 1811, when 70 attended.[15] Further lectures formed the first draft of his *Attempt*, setting out a schema of a rise to a 'finest epoch' followed by decline.[16] A fellow member, a printer, James Smith, invited him to contribute articles on architecture to his part-work, *Panorama of Science and Art*.[17] Further lectures in March–May 1812 served to establish Rickman's architectural credentials.

Conscious that existing publications did not guide 'the practical Architect to those Principles which a careful examination of our best Ecclesiastical Edifices has convinced me are as clearly marked as those of the Orders of Greece & Rome', and aware of mounting demand for church extension, Rickman published his papers in book form in July 1817 as *An Attempt to Discriminate the Styles of English Architecture* (**2.2**). It opens with an illustrated treatise on Antique (Grecian and Roman) architecture, describes the English styles (also with plates of compositions or details) and concludes with a list of 452 buildings, of which Rickman himself had examined at least 135.[18] He stated his aims, at once theoretical and practical, quite clearly in his Preface:

2.2: Rickman, frontispiece to first and second editions of *An Attempt,* an assemblage of features in a church of un–English height. This was moved to plate XVII in the third edition but was dropped from subsequent editions, probably as too unrealistic.

To furnish, at a price which shall not present an obstacle to extensive circulation, such a view of the principles of Architecture, more particularly that of the British Isles, as may not only be placed with advantage in the hands of the rising generation, but also afford the guardians of our ecclesiastical edifices such clear discriminative remarks on the buildings now existing, as may enable them to judge with considerable accuracy of the restorations necessary to be made in those venerable edifices that are under their peculiar care; and also, by leading them to the study of such as still remain in a perfect state, to render them more capable of deciding on the various designs for churches in imitation of the English styles, which may be presented to their choice.[19]

Outstanding in clarity and conciseness, at half a guinea the first edition of 500 copies sold rapidly and at profit[20] – it was indeed well timed, just before the wave of church extension broke on England's shores. And, unlike previous works of a similar character, grounded in the literary tradition of the eighteenth-century Gothic Revival, the *Attempt's* account of churches was based extensively on personal observation – increasingly so in subsequent editions.

Although not the first endeavour to systematise the development of Gothic architecture in England, Rickman's *Attempt* was the first to give 'substance and meaning' to the progression of styles 'by assigning to each its proper characteristics',[21] and assigning dates to them; 'a complete taxonomy of medieval style, a method for studying, dating, and conceptualizing antiquity which was one of the cornerstones of ecclesiology'.[22] Noting that 'the clear distinctions are now almost entirely confined to churches' because of the alteration and destruction of secular buildings,[23] Rickman first analyses and defines the parts and features of a church. Uncertain whether any Saxon architecture survived,[24] he commences his 'discrimination' with the Norman style, prevalent to the end of Henry II's reign, and proceeds to the Early English (to the death of Edward I), Decorated English (to Edward III's death) and finally Perpendicular English. This exact terminology is interesting, for although he had not then travelled overseas, Rickman discerned from prints and friends' reports, that English buildings possessed a character different from continental churches, whether or not English architects were foremost in Gothic styles.[25] 'This remark shows at once that there is more to Rickman than just nomenclature.'[26]

The terms 'Early English' and 'Decorated' had been employed by previous architectural writers,[27] but Rickman's descriptions are, as Pevsner pointed out, 'more precise than any before'.[28] He is also the first to use 'Perpendicular' as a stylistic designation, though, as Dr Baily has noted, Wren in *Parentalia* had commented that the Romans 'laid all their Mouldings horizontally … the Gothick Way on the contrary carried all their Mouldings perpendicular',[29] a remark echoed by Humphry Repton in 1797.[30]

Rickman was not content merely to distinguish stylistic phases: he also set out his aesthetic judgements, which became prevalent. In his introductory remarks he refers to 'the simple, yet beautiful Early English style'; commenting that

> Not much has been done in either restoring or imitating this style; it is certainly not easy to do either well, but it deserves attention, as in many places it would be peculiarly appropriate, and perhaps is better fitted than any for small country churches. It may be worked almost entirely plain, yet if ornament is used, it should be well executed.[31]

The 'Decorated English style', he observes 'may be considered as the perfection of the English mode'.[32] Although Pevsner refers to Rickman's 'partiality for Perpendicular', it is quite clear from the *Attempt,* from his 'Letters' in *Archaeologia*, and from his correspondence with Edward Blore (1787-1879) that Rickman thought the Decorated style, 'this most valuable style', was the height of English Gothic,[33] setting the criterion for the Ecclesiologists.

What the *Attempt* did lack was large-scale drawings of specific details, such as Auguste Pugin and E.J. Willson were to supply in *Examples of Gothic Architecture* (1828-30), and which architects could use to reproduce correct detail; the plates Rickman drew, compositions of his own (as the antiquarian publisher John Britton complained),[34] were not more than a guide. He recognised this deficiency, remarking in his Preface on the need for a 'more detailed view of English architecture' and calling for a large number of plates, an expensive undertaking. He wrote to Blore in November 1818, 'Thy proposal of making an enlarged Edition of my Book with real examples is what I have all along contemplated as to be done at some future period.'[35]

Although in January 1819 Rickman was beginning 'to think more seriously of a larger extension', the increasing flow of new architectural work proved too much, and it was set aside.[36] Instead, Rickman simply described another 345 buildings from further tours, for an extended edition, again of 500 copies, in 1819. Drawings in the British Library probably relate to the abandoned project, having the highly finished character of material designed for publication.[37] An interleaved copy of the second edition of *An Attempt* found by Megan Aldrich in the Avery Architectural Library, New York, apparently Rickman's working copy, has tracings from contemporary illustrated architectural books.[38] It is clear that Rickman always had hopes

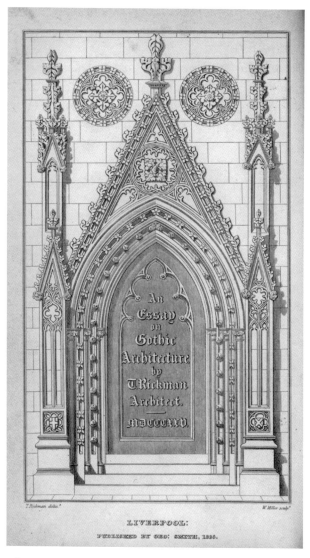

2.3: Rickman, Frontispiece to third edition of his *Attempt*, 1825, engraved by his brother-in-law; similar to the west porch of some of his churches.

of publishing a much more fully illustrated edition, including drawings of actual buildings and details, such as he amassed in folders now in the Bodleian Library.[39] Nonetheless, his work is one of huge significance and established the basis on which the vast superstructure of Victorian Gothic Revival architecture was built.

By the end of 1822 even the second edition of the *Attempt* was almost exhausted.[40] Rickman set about the lengthy task of writing county essays,[41] as well as drawing a new frontispiece (**2.3**) for the hugely enlarged third edition of 1,500 copies[42] which appeared in 1825. Investigatory tours (especially in December 1823-March 1824 through Lincolnshire and

Yorkshire to Scotland) and advice from Blore and other friends yielded nearly 2,000 more English buildings (including all the cathedrals), as well as over 300 Scottish and Irish.

The fourth edition, of 1835, augmented with fruits of tours in 1825, 1826, 1830 and 1831, mentioned 3,844 buildings, of which Rickman had personally examined 1,689,[43] arranged on a new basis: significant churches were described at length, and the others grouped according to their styles, so that more information could be included in less space. The etching of a drawing of a ruined chapel at Evesham by Rickman's late partner, Henry Hutchinson (1800-31), provided an impressive frontispiece (**2.4**). Two plates, one of Grecian, the other of Roman or Italian orders, replaced three of Classical architecture less useful to the layman; and Rickman replaced his earlier etchings of English architecture with revised and extended lithographs from his drawings, a much larger proportion taken from named sources. Thus for plate VIII in the third edition, 'a Perpendicular tower with a lantern' and 'a Decorated tower and spire', he substituted plate VI, with the same

2.4: Etching by J. Le Keux from a drawing by Henry Hutchinson of a ruined Perpendicular chapel at Evesham, Frontispiece to 4th edition (1835) of Rickman's *Attempt*, striking a much more Romantic note than hitherto.

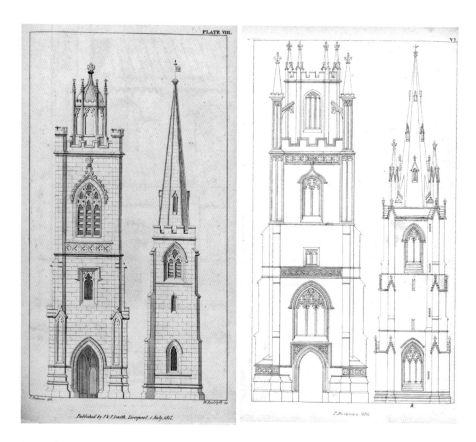

2.5: Left, plate VIII from the first edition (1817) of *An Attempt*, showing a Perpendicular tower and a Decorated tower with spire, compositions by Rickman, *c.*1812. Right, plate VI from fourth edition of *An Attempt* (1835), showing steeples of Lowick (Perpendicular) and Heckington (Decorated) – real examples for architects to copy.

designations, but with Lowick's tower and Heckington's steeple replacing his own compositions (**2.5**). Plate X introduces ten fonts (a particular interest of Rickman's) from named churches; and five Decorated windows in plate VIII are set between reduced versions of his Early English and Decorated compositions, plates XI and XII of the third edition; steps therefore to that hoped-for book of genuine examples. Notes on French architecture based on tours in northern France made in 1830 with Hutchinson, and in 1832 with William Whewell (1794-1866),[44] author of *Architectural Notes on German Churches* (1830), together with an appendix on Saxon architecture, he added from his papers contributed to the Society of Antiquaries,[45] to which he had been admitted in 1830.

After his death, rights in the *Attempt* were sold to Parker's of Oxford, who

2.6: St Michael, Toxteth, Liverpool (1812–13), looking east: Rickman's first church, for iron-master John Cragg, with nave and aisles.

produced further editions in 1848, 1862 and 1881. Rickman's systematisation has stood the test of time and seen off its competitors.

The architect

Like Welby Pugin, Thomas Rickman is more important for his writing than for his buildings. Nevertheless his architectural practice too is important in the evolution of nineteenth-century architecture.[46] That he was self-taught does not detract from its importance, for architectural training in an architect's office was often little more than a matter of copying drawings. Robert Dennis Chantrell (1793–1872), as a pupil of John Soane, spent much of his time copying drawings or preparing accounts.[47] Rickman already had an accountant's skills at his fingertips. Though less skilled in draughtsmanship, he was constantly sketching old buildings.[48] He harvested drawings from the rich crop of contemporary antiquarian books, such as Britton's *Antiquities*, 'and put together the details in the form of designs'.[49] In October 1811 a chance encounter with Edward Blore – celebrated for his exquisite and exact draughtsmanship – in the churchyard at Doncaster led to an important friendship, Blore's 'occasional instructions … in manipulation' completely altering Rickman's 'style of architectural drawing'.[50]

This may perhaps be observed in the difference between the first

churches were allocated. Rickman pursued commissions in Lancashire, Yorkshire and the Midlands, and even in London.[84] For all these, designs had to be drawn, success was uncertain,[85] and he was never able to break into the metropolitan ring.[86] But by June 1820 Rickman had won four commissions.

St George's, Birmingham (demolished in 1960), Rickman's first Commissioners' church, established a pattern: in his favoured Decorated, with west tower, 'well designed, especially in its upper part', flanked by porches; walls of brick with ashlar facing, 'stouter indeed than those in some of Pugin's churches'; and an east end marked with flying buttresses. Internally, the five 'nave arches have a bolder span, and the aisle windows are splayed more deeply than was usual in contemporary work';[87] a lofty, slightly pitched ceiling was panelled with ribs and bosses (**2.7**). Galleries, behind the nave arcade, were low-hung, and the deeply rebated, large, three-light clerestory windows, of the same iron tracery as the aisle windows, continued with blind panelling below, a feature that was to re-appear in many Rickman churches. St George's cost £12,752, for 1,900 sittings.

More commissions were secured by Rickman's ability to work within his estimates,[88] and to work effectively with local clergy and their committees. Success at Barnsley led to a double commission at Preston:[89] St Peter was Decorated (like Barnsley and with the same windows), St Paul, severe Early English in order to reduce the cost; but their preparation was closely integrated in the drawing office.[90] Rickman again sought variety in building three churches in Blackburn parish; one in Early English, another in Decorated and the third in Perpendicular.[91]

Rickman was a man of extraordinary energy: 'he could, without material inconvenience, pass two nights of three in travelling'.[92] In his workbooks, a series which he began on Friday, 27 October 1821, when he was aged 45, he states the time spent on the various daily activities, calculated in hours and half-hours. In the first two weeks recorded, his average working day was 11½ hours long, the shortest being 7½ hours.[93] It was not only his ability to 'think Gothic', but also this indomitable energy that enabled him to build up a practice that from 1822 through 1833 returned him an average £1,239 a year.[94]

He wrote from Birmingham to his friend Blore in August 1822, explaining that he was now chiefly resident there, 'as I find it the most convenient center' for attending to commissions. He added, [95]

> my opportunities of exhibiting our various Styles of English Architecture are encreasing ... I have also begun the rebuilding of Hampton Lucy Church near Stratford on Avon where I hope to have no Galleries & only a few Seats & to exhibit a very rich Specimen of Decorated Work. ...

As to Grecian work I have a Chapel at Gloucester [96] – a Gents House in the City & a considerable house[97] for Geo Dowdeswell Esqr late Chief Judge of the Supreme Court at Calcutta in a most beautiful spot between Gloucester & Ledbury. These with various Works both public & private in & about this Town & Liverpool give us full employ.

The competence of Rickman's practice, to which his partner Henry Hutchinson made an important contribution, attractive designs, reliable estimates, and well-supervised construction by reliable tradesmen, ensured a steady flow of new church commissions from private patrons, or for repairs or enlargements, as well as from the Commissioners. There was a steady demand, too, for funerary monuments.[98] The practice was also active in secular work: Rickman was surveyor to the Birmingham General Hospital, a constant responsibility; the Edward VI Free School persistently mulling ideas for rebuilding on a new site; there were town and country houses for industrialists and nabobs;[99] a bank wanted a handsome Classical building;[100] the Canal Company new offices; a foundry a new warehouse; gaols at Worcester and Derby; news rooms at Preston and Carlisle;[101] an agent's house for Lord Dudley; farm works on country estates; Worcester Infirmary's new wing; alterations to the bishop's palace at Chester; rebuilt country parsonages; and the national competitions that might make a reputation, like that for completing King's College Cambridge in 1824: all demanding carefully considered but speculative designs. While the economy flourished, the pressures mounted, until deflated by slump late in 1825; banks failed (including Rickman's), and commissions dwindled for a year or two before picking up again.

Obviously such a load of work required the services of a staff. Rickman told Edward Blore in August 1822 that he now had four apprentices and three clerks.[102] He followed the somewhat old-fashioned mode of indenturing apprentices till they were 21, charging a premium which by 1830 was 300 guineas,[103] and there was a steady flow of them. Hutchinson, like Rickman himself, experienced bouts of ill-health, and died, probably of consumption, on 22 November 1831. Rickman declined to have another partner, relying heavily on his brother until his mental instability became uncontrollable.[104] Fortunately a former pupil, Jonathan Bell, just returned from Italy, was able to take charge of the office in January 1833.[105] But his own increasingly poor health eventually drove Rickman to secure as partner from the start of 1835 Richard Charles Hussey (1802-87), who had intermittently assisted him earlier,[106] and by the spring of 1838 he had to transfer the whole business into Hussey's hands.[107] He emerges from his diary as a strict but pleasant employer.[108]

The question obviously arises, who did what? Was Rickman's practice (to take extremes) more like George Gilbert Scott's or George Edmund Street's? A generation later, Scott had a huge, highly organised office capable of working up Scott's rapid expressive sketches:[109] 'details and everything else were always ready to the minute'.[110] Mr Street, who 'as a rule … drew all details with his own hand in pencil', on the other hand, 'was always behind'; there were constant delays, clerks of works 'waiting for details'.[111] Without such comments from staff it is of course difficult to ascertain exactly who did what, but Rickman's workbooks and diaries throw light on how the office functioned. Each commission received a number, and Rickman entered the time, in half-hour units, that he spent on each daily.

While still living in Liverpool, Rickman sent Hutchinson the drawings of St Martin's, Birmingham (a fruitless rebuilding project) 'for him to make the finished Drawings from'. In Liverpool, Edwin and assistants had 'proceeded with the Drawings [for Warrington church] tolerably well … I examined the Drawings at home and settled some of the Arrangements'. Similarly, 'began Hesketh's castle & done so much of the outline that Henry can I doubt not go on with it'.[112] From such entries one would assume that Rickman, like Scott, made preliminary sketches that his staff worked up for him to check; 'examinations & instructions' are frequent entries, a half-hour for each commission. Preparation of specification and estimates, a lengthy job, preceded signing and despatching designs.

But often he took a major hand in the drawings himself: for his important Ombersley commission, an expensive church financed by the Marchioness of Headfort: 'I have today got on with the Ombersley Drawings tho not so fast as I could wish but I hope by working hard to get thro this Week.'[113] On the Sunday following he did not go to Quaker Meeting, in order to concentrate on Ombersley, and on the Tuesday noted 'With great exertion & leaving our Dinner till 6 o'clock we have got done & sent off the Ombersley drawings consisting of twenty sheets made out the Specifications & everything necessary this Job has been one of the closest application I ever had … Edwin has been in this job of most essential service.'[114] Here he was clearly making finished drawings, not mere sketches. However, while an elevation of the front for Derby Prison occupied him for seven hours on 10 and 11 December, it was a week later, after his staff had presumably drawn out the fair copies, that he spent 9½ hours on report, estimate and specification.[115]

This suggests that for some of the works (where perhaps his interest or peculiar skill was involved, as with Ombersley) Rickman would himself engage in the entire process; for others, like the gaol, he would spend a considerable time drafting, but leave the final execution to the office staff before checking and signing the drawings. He collaborated closely with Edwin and Hutchinson: he noted that Edwin, probably a better draughtsman than Thomas, had done the most elaborate elevations in the competition for completing King's College Cambridge, 'so far as to be ready I hope after Henry [Hutchinson] has done what he is now about'; and the next day 'I have proceeded today with the Court Elevation of the fellows Lodgings'.[116] In 1829, the year of the Cambridge University Library competition, considered below, his son recalled: ' Perkins [an assistant], and Lewis of London, were employed over his perspectives, on which he spent much time with his own hands.'[117] He worked at the same table as Hutchinson,[118] and close co-operation on many projects seems likely. In his diary, 4 February 1830, working on a mansion at Rottingdean for T.B. Lennard, M.P., he notes 'H[enry] H[utchinson] made perspectives', and after prolonged daily labours on this project notes on 13 February, 'With H H and at E[dwin] S R[ickman's] writing signing and entering and packing Designs.' Then, sadly, the client might jib at the cost or want alterations: we find 'Reduced' or even 'New design' against a workbook entry.

For the monument at Hampton Lucy that Rickman designed for his deceased partner, the inscription he drafted read: 'concerned with Thomas Rickman in design and erection of Rose Castle, St John's College Cambridge, Society of Arts Birmingham, Churches: St David Glasgow, three in Blackburn, three in Birmingham, Oulton, one in the parish of St P[hilip] in Bristol and various others including the church of Hampton Lucy'.[119] As it is sometimes implied that Hutchinson should be given the credit for the best Rickman churches, this list is important, and may be compared with the evidence of the workbooks and diaries.

Whenever he was en route to inspect sites or works Rickman seized the opportunity to inspect as many churches as he could. He would travel by stagecoach all night, allowing him to walk or ride to churches in daylight. Setting off at the end of December 1823, he made an extensive three-month study tour through Lincolnshire northwards through Yorkshire, Durham and Northumberland to Edinburgh, and on to Stirling and Perth, returning through St Andrews to Edinburgh, and thence via Dunfermline to Dumfries and Carlisle and so home to Birmingham in late March 1824 to plunge into writing up accounts, examining the works at Hampton Lucy church and going to Eatington House to discuss alterations with its owner, Mr Shirley.

This tour is of considerable significance. In the first place, the length of his absence is noteworthy. Clearly, his practice, with its offices at Birmingham and Liverpool, was running efficiently, his partner and assistants competent enough to conduct the considerable amount of business on hand without his presence for a period of some three months.

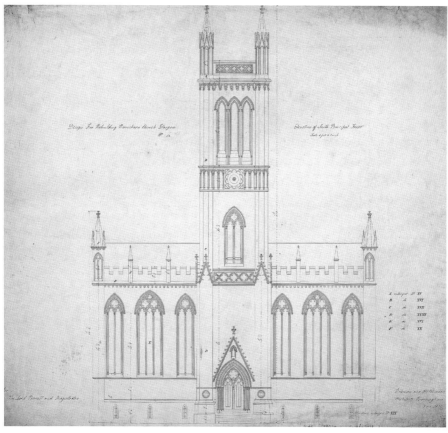

2.8: St David, Ingram Street, Glasgow – 'The Ramshorn Church' (1824-6), with its innovative tower. (*RCAHMS (RIAS Collection) Licensor* www.rcahms.gov.uk)

Moreover the purpose of the tour was to provide Rickman with material for both his design library (so to speak) and the greatly extended third edition of his *Attempt*: his labours exceeding those of Pevsner. In a single day, 12 January 1824, for instance, he examined nine churches,[120] mostly on foot; followed by Lincoln Cathedral and four Lincoln churches the next day. At Brigstock he was 'obliged to break into the Church because the Clerk was gone out'.[121] He devoted exceptional attention to Heckington church, Lincolnshire, a paradigm of his favourite Decorated style, on 7 January 1824, when he spent '2 hours making remarks only and then walked back by moonlight to Sleaford'; and again on 10 January, going there 'soon after nine & worked till past three taking sketches & measurements … so that I can draw the best part of the Church'[122] – a 'perfectly pure decorated Church all of one Character … West Tower & Spire very lofty & plain but of excellent composition', on which he made no less than twelve pages of drawings.[123]

'One of the most perfect models in the kingdom ... every part of the design and execution is of the very best character' he remarked in the *Attempt*.[124] This work was the more urgent as already twelve months before, Rickman had been warned that the second edition stock was 'reduced to a very few copies'.[125]

The tour also enabled Rickman to widen his acquaintanceship, and make contacts with potential for new commissions. In Edinburgh, staying with his brother John, he met the city's leading architects, Burn and Playfair.[126] Visiting Glasgow, Rickman saw James Cleland (1770-1840),[127] Glasgow's superintendent of public works, who 'took me to the Cathedral & the Ramshorn Ch[urch] which is to be rebuilt & he wishes me to make a Design & is to speak to the Provost & the magistrates tomorrow ab[ou]t it'. As good as his word, the following day Cleland told Rickman that 'the Magistrates had ordered us to make the designs & desired me to come to his office tomorrow Morning for the data'. He duly 'gave me the plans to work from & also two books on Glasgow'.[128]

St David's, Ingram Street, Glasgow, or the Ramshorn Church,[129] is unique in Rickman's corpus; its principal, southern front may look on paper a pre-archaeological, symmetrical Gothic Revival design, but in the street it has a bold presence (**2.8**). It is a Scottish church, not English, designed on a traditional T-plan,[130] probably at the behest of James Cleland, to whom the high basement is ascribed.[131] 'The detail is scholarly and the capable management of the T-plan indicates a close study of native practice.'[132] Dr Macaulay notes its 'considerable range of [Early English] detail, hitherto unexplored by other architects'; the 'bold and striking' composition 'strikes a new note in church design ... best summarised by the soaring lines of the tower with its open parapet and airy pinnacles'.[133]

Although he was to acknowledge his partner's involvement, this was a building to which Rickman devoted a great deal of time: on receiving plans from Cleland, he had immediately 'set to work', and after 'three Hours hard work' was able to send Hutchinson 'the Data & instructions'. Returning to Edinburgh within the fortnight, 'I found the Glasgow Drawings come', so Henry had worked up Rickman's sketches.[134] A month later in Birmingham, Rickman examined more finished drawings and sent off a batch of queries to Cleland, whose reply provoked a new arrangement of the plan and elevation (5, 6 April 1824). From 19-28 April Rickman was devoting six or eight hours a day to the church, particularly to the tower details, which alone took him more than 24 hours. Long days were spent on the drawings and specification from 3-8 May, and at the end of the month to cope with alterations 'ordered' by Cleland.[135] Cleland may have plotted the traditional Scottish T-plan,[136]

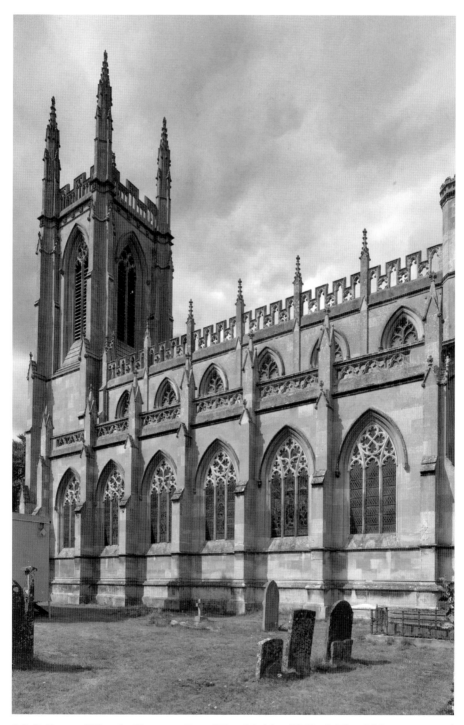

2.9: St Peter ad Vincula, Hampton Lucy, Warwickshire (1822-6). The richly ornamented Decorated tower, nave and aisle from the south-east. (*Geoff Brandwood*.)

2.10: Hampton Lucy, looking north-west. The rebating of the clerestory windows furnishes a decorative feature in the wall-space between window and arcade arch. (*Geoff Brandwood*.).

but Rickman devoted 108 hours in April-May 1824 in designing the body of the church, longer than he spent on any other contemporary work; to which one must add a further 24 hours designing the vital Presbyterian pulpit in June. Cleland's 'crypt' (really a ground-floor feature) makes the church stand tall, its bold tower – 'the first of such boldness among Scottish Gothic Revival buildings'[137] – rising high above the centre of its seven-bay front.[138] Galleries on three sides were supported on slender cast-iron columns, and the plaster ceiling is ribbed to represent quadripartite vaulting.

Thus we have here a church with input from Cleland and Hutchinson, but that appears, from the time he spent on the design, to be essentially Rickman's work. The introduction of Geometrical (iron) tracery into the windows is a significant detail:[139] for all his admiration for Early English, Decorated was to Rickman the pinnacle of Gothic.

Four other private commissions for churches, erected outside the Commissioners' bounty, are regarded as the peak of Rickman's achievement: 'Hampton Lucy, Ombersley, Oulton and Stretton-on-Dunsmore show what he could do if funds permitted.'[140] Not all, however, were as lavishly funded as this suggests. In three, Hutchinson was involved; but Stretton was largely designed after his death.

St Peter ad Vincula, Hampton Lucy, was indeed expensive (**2.9**). It was designed to seat 400, in contrast to Rickman's Commissioners' churches, where for a similar expenditure he had to seat 2,000. A trust established in 1778 for repairing the church had by 1822 accumulated to over £9,000, and the pluralist rector, John Lucy, decided to build a new church altogether, meeting any deficiency from his own pocket.[141] The situation struck Rickman as 'most beautiful'; staying there overnight, he lost no time in arranging both his 'Ideas about the Building which seem to meet those of J. Lucy.'[142] He gave Hutchinson his ideas, and the latter began a plan; together, they 'settled most of the work for Hampton Lucy'. Then, presumably, to the office. But on 25-7 March Rickman spent 15 hours on the west elevation, and on the following two days nine hours on a section, 'which looks very rich'. As he records nothing about other elevations, the rest may have been detailed by Hutchinson.

On 2 April, 'The Hampton Lucy drawings are done so that I go there tomorrow', when 'We all looked over the Drawings ... all seemed much pleased with the Design.' The work went well; Rickman settled about the carving with the contractors on 27 July after they all had attended the ceremonial laying of the first stone. Further drawings were despatched in January 1823, and inspecting the work a few days later, Rickman found 'the carving very well done & a great quantity worked'.[143] In August sketches for the tower and windows, and details of mouldings, required 27 hours work over a week. Rickman on 25 March 1824 thought the church 'looks very well particularly the Parapet and Battlement'; they settled with Lucy 'to finish the Body & leave the Tower', presumably because Lucy needed additional funds. The east window was in by July, when Rickman spent six days on designing the font and screens for the baptistery and the altar. Towards 1824's end Lucy evidently decided to go ahead on the tower: Rickman spent merely half-an-hour examining and signing drawings for the tower at the new year, presumably the working-up of his drawings made in August 1823; and in December 1825 Lucy chose the pattern for belfry windows.[144] The church was consecrated in November 1826.[145] The final cost is said to have been £23,000,[146] comparable with the most expensive of the Commissioners' churches, all, except for stone-vaulted Chelsea, Classical in style.

The result is undoubtedly one of the century's best churches. Pevsner calls it the firm's '*magnum opus*'.[147] Smooth ashlar facing in warm Postlip and Chipping Campden limestone, a tiny chancel (now distorted by Scott's apse) and perhaps in so lavish a structure the absence of transepts may betray its date, as does the iron window tracery, but Rickman's encyclopaedic knowledge of medieval churches gave his wealthy patron a truly Gothic church, that few of his contemporaries could approach. There are, of course, not many medieval parish churches with aisles with pierced parapet and nave embattled, the buttresses gabled and pinnacled: the precedent might be St Mary's, Beverley, or Terrington St Clement, Norfolk (both known to Rickman), but the effect is rather of a great church such as St George's, Windsor, or Bath Abbey. It is, as Pevsner states, 'Dec throughout',[148] with a 114-foot, three-storeyed, richly angle-buttressed tower, with tall two-light belfry windows on each face, crowned by a pierced battlement and four tall corner pinnacles with gablets and crocketting as in a fifteenth-century Gloucester or Somerset church; clerestoried, with crowning pierced battlements, and a pierced parapet to the aisles of a type singled out in the *Attempt* as particularly beautiful: 'a waved line, the space of which is trefoiled'.[149]

The aisleless one-bay chancel is distinguished by a window much taller than the five large three-light aisle windows; it is surmounted externally by a crocketted gable, similar to that over the west door, rising into the battlement. The clerestory windows are uniform, quite widely spaced, divided internally by springing shafts of the quadripartite plaster vault; deeply rebated, the recess carried down almost to the crown of the arcade arch, its lower part filled with two-light cinquefoiled, gabled and crocketted panelling, as in St Mary's Beverley, a characteristic Rickman feature. The slender columns of

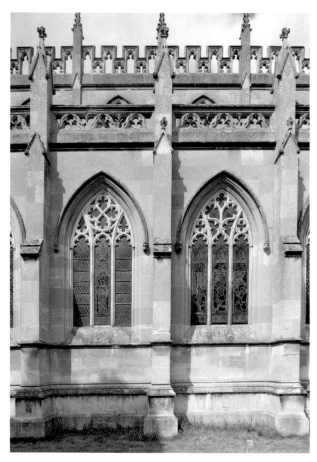

2.11: Hampton Lucy, south aisle, two bays showing variations in iron window tracery. (*Geoff Brandwood*.)

the five-bay nave arcade have attached shafts with small variously-carved capitals. Like the nave, the aisles have plaster rib-vaulting (**2.10**). The east window contained stained glass by Newbolds of Birmingham.[150]

Hampton Lucy is not an imitation of any one church, but particular features resemble those in various churches: the aisles' traceried parapets recall Wrington, Somerset, the tower Heckington, Lincolnshire, a church Rickman considered 'one of the most perfect models in the kingdom'.[151] The complex curvilinear tracery of the aisle windows, of two patterns, recalling Grantham's varieties, but executed in cast iron from Rickman's moulds (**2.11**), were his contribution to the infinite variety of reticulated window tracery, furnished from his exceptional familiarity with medieval models.[152]

Another outstanding parish church was St Andrew, at Ombersley, Worcestershire, ancestral seat of the Sandys family, represented by the Marchioness of Downshire. Again, a trust fund existed for rebuilding

2.12: St Andrew, Ombersley, Worcestershire (1825-8), from the south-east. The first working drawings date from 1821. (*Geoff Brandwood.*)

the church. As early as February 1821 Rickman was instructed to make working drawings,[153] but not until June 1825 was building agreed on,[154] matters arranged with the trustees,[155] and tenders settled.[156] The church was completed in June 1828 and consecrated on 22 June 1829.[157] Although built after Hampton Lucy, Ombersley was evidently designed first. The listing description comments: 'Decorated style imposed on essentially Georgian plan.' But 'nave and aisles' is not 'essentially Georgian': St Andrew is a highly-articulated church such as the Ecclesiologists loved, though the roofs may be too low and a ten-foot chancel too short for them. The design is simpler than Hampton Lucy: tower, nave, chancel and transepts are embattled, but in plain mode, and the aisles have a plain parapet; the nave is only four bays, though the east end is more complex with transepts (employed as vestries) and the additional bay to the chancel. Aisle window tracery is identical with Hampton Lucy. Most conspicuous difference is Ombersley's tall recessed spire, enriched with lucarnes and flying buttresses *à la* Louth

(**2.12**). According to Pevsner, the cost was about £18,000, of which the trustees appear to have contributed £7,000, and Lady Downshire the rest.[158]

Internally, slender piers with cast-iron cores support wide arches, their inner shafts with moulded capitals similar to Hampton Lucy, but the vaulting shafts rise from corbels above the continuous hood mould, instead of rising from the base. Wooden gallery-fronts are recessed behind the arches in Rickman's characteristic manner, the access from lobbies either side of the tower – adequate funds meant that Rickman did not have to use the tower for staircases as in his economic Commissioners' mode. A string some way above the arch crown demarcates the clerestory level; the blind panelling below the clerestory windows is much simpler than at Hampton

2.13: Ombersley, nave and north aisle; the gallery front is set behind the columns of the nave arcade, a Rickman characteristic. (*Geoff Brandwood*.)

Lucy, resembling rather his first church for the Commissioners, St George, Birmingham.[159] The ceiling has quadripartite plaster vaulting with carved bosses (**2.13**).

His third privately financed church was St John's, Oulton, in the parish of Rothwell, West Yorkshire. The local magnate, John Blayds, a Leeds banker, decided to provide a church for the township, and his son wrote to Rickman for designs. Rickman promptly went to Leeds on 10 January 1827, tested the site, and sketched plan (**2.14**) and elevations on 13 January. Blayds *père* approved, accepting the architect's rough estimate of £7,500. Rickman then spent some 24 hours over the next four days working on his designs, and on 27 January noted that Hutchinson had finished all the drawings, which 'looked very well'; after some further 20 hours work on the stained glass, the drawings were sent to Blayds on 2 February, approved, with small alterations, on 14 February, and the final approval given on a site visit 'arranging alterations' on 6 March, Rickman drawing up the new design, 13–31 March, nearly 60 hours work.[160] As work progressed, Rickman designed a pulpit in November 1828, modified by Blayds. The church was consecrated on 22 December 1829.[161]

If one assumes, as all the evidence suggests, that the general character of these churches was devised by Rickman, one has to admire the fertility of his invention, and his breaking away from convention, as in the treatment of the clerestory at Hampton Lucy and the introduction of an apsidal east end to a real chancel here at Oulton (**2.15**). Worsley sees the design as 'a distinct change from the Georgian tradition':[162] like Ombersley, its parts were clearly articulated – west tower and spire standing forward of the six-bay nave,

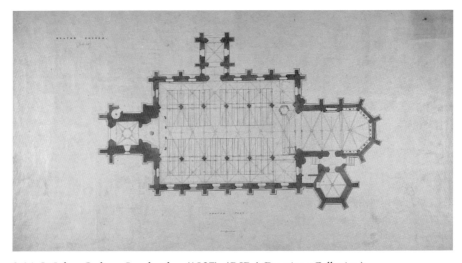

2.14: St John, Oulton, Leeds, plan (1827). (*RIBA Drawings Collection.*)

2.15: Oulton, interior looking east. The substantial chancel and arcaded apse are remarkable. (*Ruth Baumberg.*)

three-bay chancel, north porch, and unique hexagonal vestry at the south east (**2.16**). The differences, however, are marked: the position of the tower, the lack of transepts, but provision of a north porch and distinct vestry, the apse, and of course the style: Early English at Oulton, a style Rickman had used successfully for the Commissioners, at Chorley, Lancashire (1822-5), and contemporaneously with Oulton at St Mary, Mellor, Lancashire, also aisled and plaster-vaulted, which cost £5,496.[163] But Blayds got a quality bargain, even at the reported £15,000.[164]

Oulton is one of several of the partnership's buildings for which they published the specification.[165] Best Barnsley stone was prescribed for the exterior, best Oulton for the internal piers and arches; pulpit, font and other details of best Bramham Moor 'equal in quality to what is used in the reparations of York Minster'. External stonework was to be fine tooled, the

2.16: Oulton (1827-9), from the south. The high degree of articulation and the choice of Early English are remarkable features for this date, and the hexagonal vestry, inspired by the vicinity of York Minster's chapter house, is unique. (*Ruth Baumberg.*)

internal to be rubbed. Stones were to be set in putty 'mixed with a little fine washed sand', and the joints pointed. External joints were to be 'filled with oil mastic or other cement, so as to make them perfectly weather proof'. Building was to be carried up at a roughly uniform level throughout, backing and ashlar carried up together and bonded together every third course with cast-iron dovetailed cramps. The ashlar courses were to diminish regularly from 18 inches at the bottom to 12 inches high under the cornice, the roof slates similarly graded in size. Ceilings of nave and aisles were to be groined, with composite timber angle ribs (**2.16**), all groinings having enriched plaster bosses with ventilation openings behind, and plaster window shafts to have an iron core (but the Early English windows of course required no iron tracery). A wrought-iron chain bond was to be let in and leaded round the spire (recessed, with flying buttresses to the pinnacles, in the Louth style) between the lower and upper windows.

Stretton-on-Dunsmore, between Hampton Lucy and Coventry (where Rickman was also busily engaged on several commissions for church and charities) was his fourth privately financed financed church, again from a previous vicar's bequest of £4,000, invested in 3 per cent Bank of England stock. Commissioned in mid–1831, All Saints (**2.17**) may be most purely Rickman, Hutchinson being in the late stages of his fatal illness. It proved troublesome; a special Act of Parliament was thought necessary appointing diocesan and archdeacon trustees; the sum available long uncertain because of legal fees and fluctuations in Bank stock.[166] Having viewed the site with the vicar, and found a good clay foundation at four feet, Rickman made a new design, sketches for the circular clerestory windows alone taking him five hours. Another new plan was sketched at the end of November 1831, after Hutchinson's death, and approved on site 'generally' by the ecclesiastics, with specific reservations, on 30 December.[167] Two months later: 'At last the B[isho]p and Archdeacon have settled to sanction Stretton church as now drawn with their Alterations';[168] but only on 9 May 1832 was Rickman told to begin forthwith, though the sum available was not finally ascertained till late September: only £4,000; so further drawings were necessary.[169] His draft letter to the archdeacon explains how he proposed resolving the problem:

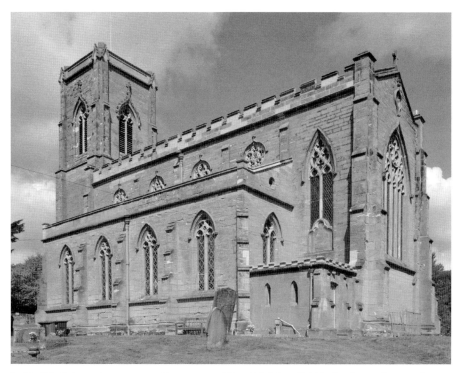

2.17: All Saints, Stretton-on-Dunsmore, Warwickshire (1831-7), from the south-east. Lack of funds imposed relative simplicity, but Rickman achieved a distinctly articulated church. (*Geoff Brandwood.*)

2.18: Stretton-on-Dunsmore, looking east. Rickman rescued the niches flanking the altar from proposed economies. The remarkable embattled stone reading-desk and pulpit, left and right of the chancel, have no precedent. (*Geoff Brandwood*.)

having carefully examined the drawings T[homas] R[ickman] is able to say that he will be able to make the required reduction of cost without affecting the Size or Stability of the Church but not without in TR's view materially taking from its interior Beauty tho' it will still be a handsome Church.

The Altar piece is now taken to be of Stone with two side Niches & Seats. This must all be taken away & very plain panels substituted in Plaster for the Commandments.
The two windows on the sides of the Chancel must be entirely taken away & the plain wall remain instead. The canopies of the Buttresses of the Tower now having rich Crockets & Finials must be made quite plain.

These reductions with a few others not easily described but making small reductions in cost will bring the work within the sum afforded if stock [the legacy] is sold at 90 or upwards.

To do this many of the present drawings will be required to be done once again the Specification altered & other considerable additional trouble.

I can now say that if the stock is sold at 90 yielding … [£]3874.19[s], 4[d.] leaving this sum net applicable to the building. Then he will engage to provide persons who shall build the Church according to the present design (with the above reductions) together with the warm air Stove & the Fence of some good & sufficient Kind round the new part of the Church yard & repair the old part thereof.[170]

Protracted discussions followed and in the event not all the proposed reductions were implemented: the built church retains a single window on either side of the chancel, as well as the stone niches in the corners either side of the altar (**2.18**). The contract price was £3,800, additions before

2.19: St Matthew, Kingshill, Bristol (1833–5), from the south-west: a galleried, Perpendicular church in local stone, with a Bristol spirelet over the tower stair-turret. (*Author.*)

consecration amounted to £715, and with commission and fees, the total cost was £5,348, covered by subscriptions, a rate, and various means obtained by the vicar, as well as the 'drawback' of customs and excise duties.[171] When the first stone was laid on 9 June 1835 a village fête was held. Rickman then decided on Bath stone for the piers of the nave arcade and for the west gallery front. Though unwell in early 1836, Rickman was at Stretton on 30 August to see Vicar Powell set the top stone of the south-west pinnacle of the tower.[172] All Saints was consecrated on 16 May 1837.

Rickman here was working to a tight budget, comparable with his contemporaneous economical (£5,533) Commissioners' church at Loughborough, Emmanuel, though that had to hold twice as many. Even so, Stretton-on-Dunsmore is a notable achievement. It has a family resemblance to Hampton Lucy: pared down, tower buttresses unornamented, aisle buttresses terminating below the solid parapet, the nave plainly battlemented, and lacking a structurally differentiated chancel (save for its larger side windows). The east window and the proposed painted figures Rickman discussed with his new partner, Hussey; the tracery is a five-light variation of one of the three-light Hampton Lucy aisle windows. The nave has quadripartite vaulting with moulded ribs and carved bosses, slender attached shafts with moulded capitals on foliated corbels.[173] Pevsner acknowledges 'the details

2.20: St Mary, Lower Hardres, Kent (1831-2), elevation drawing. The simplicity of an Early English village church, an innovation at this time. (*RIBAD*.)

[of the church] are remarkably accurate … Late Perp piers of well-informed section and the curious but quite convincing motif of blank Perp panels below the clerestory oculi' – that handling of the space between arch crown and clerestory window that is a Rickman hallmark. But Pevsner rejects the ashlar walling as too smooth for the archaeologically-minded succeeding generation; though it is of a more medieval character than Hampton Lucy's truly smooth-cut stones.[174]

Space does not permit of similar examination of Rickman's other churches, but some of his later, less expensive ones, call for notice. Rickman had long been active in the Bristol area, had built the Commissioners' turreted Holy Trinity in 1829,[175] and three years later was invited to design a church, St Matthew, for the respectable suburb of Kingsdown. First designs proved too expensive, but in May 1833 he decided on a 'cler[estory] ch[urch]' with 'good random walls', in June arranged new plan and elevations; and in August was able to record 'Bristol Church comfortably settled. Higgs & Goodwin are to have it & considerably under the estimate.'[176] The church was about two years a-building. Rickman gave his characteristic clerestoried form a Perpendicular character: galleries on three sides behind four-centred arches called for the large transomed windows much used in the Commissioners' churches, the panelled ceiling is flat, and there is no attempt to mark out a chancel – the east window is flanked by turrets with quatrefoil tops that are in fact chimneys. But one of the tower's angle buttresses serves as a stair-turret, terminating in a Bristol spirelet, and the random Pennant rubble walling suggests a church of a decade later (**2.19**).[177]

While some of Rickman's later churches have the open-span interiors, galleries and external lack of articulation that the expression 'Commissioners' church' may summon up, many are of what in the light of nineteenth-century developments one may call a more 'advanced' (i.e., archaeologically accurate) character. Emmanuel church, Loughborough (1835-7), for the Church Building Commissioners, was another nave-and-aisles church, similar to Oulton (but with flat roofs), with tall west tower, and it did have a chancel – since lengthened – and a characteristic rebated clerestory. Pevsner comments: 'No longer the paperiness of the Commissioners' churches of c.1820.'[178] Another late Commissioners' church, of 1837-9, St Stephen, Sneinton, Nottingham (much enlarged in 1912), in Early English, with apse, transepts and crossing tower,[179] was hailed by T.C. Hine as 'the first example of the revival of pure Gothic architecture' in Nottinghamshire.[180] On the imprecise evidence of the workbooks, Rickman's assistants J. Frith and R.C. Hussey may both have contributed here.[181]

The most interesting of these later designs, however, is that for Lower

Hardres, Kent (**2.20**). Rickman's Birmingham friend, Revd J.H. Spry, became a canon of Canterbury in 1828, and brought Rickman into several projects concerning the cathedral ultimately executed by others, such as rebuilding the crumbling north-west tower. These visits to Canterbury produced a commission to rebuild the church of Lower Hardres, a nearby village. For this, Rickman produced an entirely appropriate, but at that period unique design, 'conceived' in John Newman's words, 'as a humble village church, an imaginative leap before Pugin's example made such attention to appropriateness commonplace'.[182] Designed in early 1831, when Hutchinson was succumbing to his fatal illness, the likelihood is that the 'imaginative leap' was entirely Rickman's. He sketched a new plan in June, spending some 34 hours on design and specification.[183] Styled in economical Early English, with nave and chancel, faced in flint with ashlar dressings, the church has an asymmetrical tower over a south-west porch, rising to an octagonal stage as a base for a broach spire, altogether a remarkable feature for its date.

The evidence available indicates that Rickman was the initiating mind in his practice, and that his was the hand and mind that created this considerable corpus of churches of a character distinct from both Regency Georgian[184] and the common picture of the Commissioners' churches.

Rickman as a secular architect

Although, as an architect Rickman's prime significance is in the realms of

2.21: Matfen Hall, Northumberland (1832-5), in 'Elizabethan' for a rich industrialist landowner: entrance front. Rickman modified the windows over the porch to meet his client's views. (*Geoff Brandwood*.)

church architecture, he had a considerable practice in residential and public building. He sometimes acted as surveyor, laying out streets in Birmingham, on, for instance, the Colmore estate, New Hall Hill.[185] Occasionally he was asked for house designs in both Gothic and Classical, the client then choosing between them. His numerous town houses have been largely lost to sight,[186] together with much work of additions and rebuilding for the nobility and gentry.

Country houses

Rickman's most important domestic works, however, survive: those at Rose Castle, for the Bishop of Carlisle, and at Matfen, Northumberland, a new mansion for the landed industrial magnate Sir Edmund Blackett, Bt.

The Hon. Hugh Percy, translated from Rochester to Carlisle in September 1827, found his partly medieval seat, Rose Castle, inadequate for wife and nine children.[187] To overhaul the whole estate he called in Rickman, who found the castle 'beautifully situated on the N[orth] edge of the valley of Caldew with some good portions remaining but mostly poor modern work'. Required improvements included additional bedrooms over the schoolroom and butler (who was to have a strong closet and a cellar for wine in use); a w.c. on each floor; four coach houses and ten stalls for horses; and works on farm buildings.[188] Though Carlisle was a poor bishopric, Percy also held the rich prebend of Finsbury[189] in St Paul's Cathedral, London.

Rickman transformed the castle into a more convenient episcopal residence, throwing out two oriels in the state dining room and the state drawing room above it,[190] removing a tower to improve the entrance, building the Percy Tower on the west front and rebuilding staircases – he visited Moreton Old Hall (15 December 1829) in order to find a suitable model, 'but only saw a Newell one', being denied admittance to the family part. He also designed bookcases and other furniture, and obtained lamps for the staircase.[191] But the bishop became seriously concerned about the cost. Hutchinson had been intimately involved in this work, and after his death Rickman found his estimate, 'upon which he appears to have assured the B[isho]p something ab[ou]t 12,000£ sadly deficient both in matters to be done and the cost of those which he did take account of to finish'. Much chagrin followed, the bishop claimed he had been deceived, though not by Rickman, and only in July 1833 did Percy indicate he would pay up.[192]

Yet more expensive, at some £40,000, came Matfen Hall, near Newcastle, for recently-married Sir Edward Blackett, 6th baronet, mines and colliery owner, who inherited Matfen Old Hall from a grandmother. Rickman designed a modern 'Old English' mansion incorporating the old, but

2.22: Matfen Hall, Great Hall (1833), supposed to be a survival from a much older house. Galleried on two sides, the great stair rising opposite; the hammerbeam roof is unrivalled at this date. (*Geoff Brandwood*.)

Blackett wanted modifications such as adding a third storey to the south front, lowering the floors nearer the lawn, and scrapping fireproof ceilings to give more height and light to rooms, that the architect successfully resisted (**2.21**).[193] On site in September 1832 discussion was intense: 'We have had a Stage up to examine as from the Windows the Lawn &c'; but the next day, 'At length I hope I have settled the Plan & with a little alteration the Elevation – having made out the East side'; and a day later: 'I have settled the Elevation with Sir E and Lady B & I hope now to their satisfaction.'This foreshadows problems to come, the Blacketts having frequent changes of mind. Finding suitable stone was another problem involving discussion and search.[194] Meanwhile, the ground was excavated for foundations.

Back in Birmingham, Rickman worked on the interior arrangement and 'settled the Staircase'. He discussed with Haden,[195] the engineer, whether hot water or warm air heating was to be preferred, and found him 'quite of my Mind that … Warm Air [would be] much better', tanks taking a long time to heat and the hot water long to get down to the rooms. On 30 October he 'put the Chimneys to the Elevations'. Returning to Matfen he found his host 'very kind & fr[ien]dly but he talks of various alterations', and bringing friends into the discussions.[196] Through the clerk of works, Blackett then made further imprecise demands, driving Rickman to seek clarification in a letter that shows his scrupulous care in providing for the domestic convenience of his clients:[197] 'this will make his spoiling the Front his own Act if he does it'. Blackett replied that he did not now want any alterations.[198] So in December, Rickman spent some 25 hours work on the hall and ceiling.[199] He despatched two designs, one 'accordant with the Entrance front'; the other 'on the supposition that a building of earlier date had existed the Hall of which … had been retained & a house of later character built round it. This circumstance is very common & affords a means of giving an elegant variety to the Work'.[200] Blackett fell for this Early English hall crowned with a magnificent hammerbeam roof (**2.22**) recalling Westminster Hall, unprecedented in this era.[201]

Alas, by September Sir Edward was all of a pother: 'he wants many things altered but can not tell exactly how'. So it continued. After discussion, Rickman 'made a plan for joining the two Houses so as to save the old front up[;] some alterations … will I believe settle that'. But Blackett was 'so very capricious that he says things quite contrary to what he has said before'.[202] In June 1833 Rickman made minor alterations to the entrance tower design that Blackett had altered previously.[203] There was much examining of accounts before his next visit, 4-6 September, when the hall and patterns for the staircase railing were considered. In November 1833

2.23: Cambridge, St John's College, New Court (1826-9), cloister arcade closing quadrangle: could the central block, enclosing a great spiral stair, have been inspired by Chambord? (*Author.*)

Rickman calculated expenditure at over £11,000. On 3-4 March 1834 he made a memorandum of what had been agreed with Sir Edward: no niche, string or east window in hall, 'old house arrangements – left alone … Dining Room & Library & Vestibule & Hall *new* Doors & Architraves … Dining Room new panel Dado 3 ft. Drawing Room old work Dado 3 ft.'[204] On what appears to have been his last visit there, he discussed the roof and what work was to be done in the winter.[205]

Blackett suddenly dismissed Rickman in February 1835, on the grounds of his bad health, claiming that 'having chiefly planned and superintended my building myself I had no difficulty in taking the responsibility upon myself'.[206] There is little doubt, however, that apart from the choice of style and some minor details Matfen is Rickman's work, and its magnificent Great Hall is wholly his imaginative design.

Public buildings

Public buildings in this period were commonly put out to a competition for designs. Rickman, aiming high, regularly competed, but with little success. In March 1822, for instance, he and his staff vainly devoted much time to the King's College, Cambridge, competition for completing its quadrangle. Similarly for a new foundation, King's College, London,[207] in 1828, and the Law Institute in Chancery Lane, and then the proposed restoration of Magdalen College Chapel, Oxford,[208] their labours brought

2.24: Rickman and Hussey Gothic entry in competition for Cambridge University Library (1834): Rickman again displaying his hankering for a magnificent feature. (*RIBAD.*)

no gain. Neither did Rickman's personal consultations in 1831 with I.K. Brunel about designs for Clifton Suspension Bridge.[209]

More of a cliffhanger was the limited competition for Cambridge University Library and lecture rooms in July 1829, between C.R. Cockerell, William Wilkins, Decimus Burton and Rickman.[210] Rickman and Hutchinson produced both Grecian and Gothic designs.[211] The competition committee chose Cockerell's, but opposition in the Senate resulted in a second competition in June 1830, that Rickman and Hutchinson's design won, but it was laid aside, apparently for financial reasons, until November 1835, when the competitors were invited to send in amended designs: the result was an overwhelming vote for Cockerell.[212] Thus from none of these projects did the firm gain any work.

However, another limited competition brought a major collegiate commission: St John's College, Cambridge, needed more accommodation, and in 1825 applied to Wilkins, Arthur Browne (c.1757-1840),[213] and Rickman for designs in the style of its Jacobean Second Court, but on the further side of the river.[214] It was Dr J.W. Whittaker (c.1790-1854), vicar of Blackburn, Lancashire, a fellow of St John's, who recommended Rickman to his colleagues.[215] Invited only on 31 March, by a fortnight later Rickman had been to Cambridge and laboured to the point of settling 'nearly all the difficulties of the work'; it took about a week more to 'arrange all the Cambridge work except the Bridge', but that too was arranged the next day.[216] However, it was in mid-July that he began the first fair drawing, and not till 8 March 1826 that the college determined to employ the partnership.

Ever seeking to improve, Rickman revised his designs in June: 'the new fronts look much better than before'; but in November he redrew them, including 'a new lantern'. The college resolved on 6 January 1827 to 'adopt in general the elevations for the new buildings now before us'.[217] The famous bridge over the Cam, linking the new court to the old buildings, had been planned by Rickman in iron, but because stone was found to be cheaper than originally calculated, stone was settled on and Hutchinson made 'a beautiful design'.[218] There followed a decision to execute the new buildings in Ancaster stone instead of brick, and in May 1829 to construct the roof of the new cloister in clunch instead of wood and plaster. This very extensive work, Rickman's largest undertaking, cost nearly £78,000,[219] and was the largest collegiate work of the time. A somewhat cheerless, four-storey E-plan building, its court is closed, as at King's, by an open cloister with a central pedimented gateway (**2.23**) – as Pevsner observes, mixing 'a Classical motif with his Gothic'.[220] The projecting centre of the main range has angle turrets, so it resembles the college gatehouse; and internally its elegant circular stair is crowned with a glazed lantern perhaps inspired by Ely. Professor Deborah Howard has suggested the Château de Chambord as the source: its general layout with central staircase tower does resemble the plan of New Court, but given the partners' ignorance of French architecture at this date, the resemblance would appear to be fortuitous.[221]

But the open competition announced in July 1834 for a museum to house the collections bequeathed to the university by Viscount Fitzwilliam with £100,000 proved another Cambridge disappointment. Rickman, one of 27 competitors, sent in three designs.[222] Hutchinson had died in November 1831, his brother Edwin was under restraint for manic depression, and Rickman himself was in poor health,[223] so that it was not until December that he really got to work on the museum. Jonathan Anderson Bell (c.1808-65), recently returned from Rome, was in charge of the office and, on the evidence of the workbook, assisting with the museum designs,[224] perhaps contributing to the grandeur that characterises them. All three are represented in the RIBA Drawings Collection:[225] 'A', Corinthian with a portico open to a court; 'B' in Decorated Gothic, with a very high, attenuated tower, spiral Grand Staircase and hammerbeam-roofed hall (**2.24**); 'C' in Doric with an amazing central rotunda (surely based on Bell's recollections of the Roman Pantheon). Magnificent and imaginative as they are, it is not surprising that they attracted few senatorial votes.[226] The sensational Gothic version has been called 'as romantic and picturesque as anything since Fonthill … The exploitation of an open timber roof to such effect was probably unprecedented in the revival' (though already used by Rickman at Matfen). The same critic comments that the Doric rotunda 'without a surmounting dome, or at least a conical roof,' is unprecedented in either ancient or Renaissance architecture.[227]

Rickman's victory in the Sir Walter Scott memorial competition was set aside by Scottish politicking, but it was impossible for him to resist the challenge when in June 1835 a national competition for Houses of Parliament in the Gothic or Elizabethan styles was announced to replace those burned down in October 1834. Competitors had difficulty in getting detailed instructions, but from mid- September to early November the firm was principally occupied with this greatest of competitions. On several days in mid-November he was with Bell and Hussey or Bell alone, 'writing on & mounting Drawings', looking over plans, issuing instructions, until the 28th, in order to meet the deadline of 1 December.[228]

Competitors had to provide three perspectives from specified viewpoints, as well as plans, elevations and sections, and Rickman's are in RIBA Drawings Collection.[229] A diffuse and poorly organised design, it is clear why this was not one of the four entries selected by the judges. Subject to frequent attacks of ill-health and with much other work in hand, it is not surprising if Rickman's powers of composition began to fail. The Houses of Parliament was an extremely complex building and many of the competitors failed to observe the instructions accurately. Nor does planning a complex building seem to have been Rickman's strongest point, so far as one can judge from the Fitzwilliam and University Library competition entries.

Conclusion

Rickman's health had begun seriously to deteriorate in the spring of 1834; he had a series of 'apoplectic seizures' over the next three years; he gave up keeping a workbook at the end of 1837 and a few months later gave up the business to R.C. Hussey and, to meet debts, retired to a smaller house. Constant ill-health attended his final years. He died of cancer of the liver, 4 January 1841.

While it is not possible entirely to disentangle his own work from the contributions of his colleagues, Rickman appears a bold and innovative architect who composed effectively and picturesquely, had a keen aesthetic perception, designed dramatic and unusual interiors, and reintroduced the character of medieval church design into our ecclesiastical architecture. But in contrast to fellow-Goths James Wyatt and Francis Goodwin, he worked carefully and methodically, devoting great care to the more tedious aspects of an architect's work, recording, composing specifications, compiling tenders and checking accounts, elements that we may perhaps ascribe to his Quaker upbringing. In the closing decades of the Georgian era he was a towering figure in English architecture.

Acknowledgements

I am most grateful to the Mark Fitch Fund for a generous grant towards my research on Rickman buildings, and to Queen Mary, University of London for their generous support of my expenses regarding illustrations.

I am grateful for help to Dr John Baily, Charles Hind and his staff at the RIBA Drawings Collection, Professor Deborah Howard, Adrian James (Society of Antiquaries), Thomas Kennet (Canterbury Cathedral Archives), Malcolm Underwood (St John's College, Cambridge), Professor David Webster, and the staffs at the Society of Friends' Library, British Library, Lambeth Palace Library and the Church of England Records Centre. Geoff Brandwood has been most generous in taking excellent photographs for me, and David Cronin, Ruth Baumberg have been very helpful with illustrations. I owe a deep debt to Patrick Lefevre who has devoted much time to supplying computer arts that I have yet to master. Most of the Rickman churches that I have visited were open, and I am grateful to the incumbents and parochial authorities for their help and care of the churches in their charge.

Rickman's MS diary is in the RIBA Drawings Collection.
The following abbreviations are used below:

BoE	*Buildings of England*
BL	British Library
f.	folio
LPL	Lambeth Palace Library
RIBA	Royal Institute of British Architects
RIBAD	RIBA Archives & Drawings Collection at Victoria and Albert Museum, London

Notes

1. N. Pevsner, 'Rickman and the Commissioners', in *Some Architectural Writers of the Nineteenth Century,* Oxford U.P., 1972, 28.
2. *RIBA Journal*, 1875, 219, quoted in J. Baily, 'Thomas Rickman Architect and Quaker. The Early Years to 1818', unpublished Ph.D. thesis, University of Leeds, 1977, 348, an essential aid to which I am most indebted to understanding Rickman, and I am most grateful to Dr Baily for permission to quote from it. Sharpe had visited Rickman in 1836.
3. G.G. Scott, *Personal and Professional Recollections*, ed. Gavin Stamp, Paul Watkins, 1995, 390.
4. C.L. Eastlake, *A History of the Gothic Revival in England,* Longmans, 1872, 124-5. After the 1819 edition Rickman changed the title slightly to *An Attempt to Discriminate the Styles of Architecture in England …* Here the work is referred to simply as the *(An) Attempt* or *Attempt to Discriminate the Styles.*
5. J. Macaulay, *The Gothic Revival 1745-1845,* Blackie, 1975, 262.
6. Anonymous review, 'Manuals of Gothic Architecture', *Archaeological Journal*, 3, 1846, 380.
7. Baily [note 2], 52.
8. Ibid., 76-87, 116; Rickman, Diary, 4 Jan. 1810. Rickman's MS diary is in RIBAD. As a Quaker, Rickman dated his diary entries, e.g., '1 [day of week] . 3 (or 3mo.) [month]. 1 [day of month]. [18]21'. For clarity, however, I date them according to the more normal usage, and omit the day of the week.
9. T.M. Rickman, *Notes, on the life … of Thomas Rickman, F.S.A., architect,* Pitman, 1901, 16. They 'employed him in his leisure time, and probably on some occasions in office hours, to prepare plans for them for private and public buildings in which they were interested'.

10. Baily [note 2], 108-9.

11. The earliest surviving drawing is that of Ormskirk church, Lancs, dated 8 Feb. 1809, BL, Add. MS 37803, f. 39.

12. BL, Add. MS 37803, ff. 60, 63, 65; 57 (Malmesbury), 58 (Salisbury), 95 (Kirkstall), 96 (Attleborough).

13. Rickman, Diary, 7 May 1811. 'the occasional instructions received … from Mr Blore completely altered his style of architectural drawing', T.M. Rickman, *Notes* [note 9], 16.

14. D. Wilson, 'The cultural identity of Liverpool', *Transactions of the Lancashire and Cheshire Archaeological Society*, 147, 1997, 47-8.

15. Rickman, Diary, cited by Baily [note 2], 136, who points out that T.M. Rickman has the date wrong.

16. Baily [note 2], 136-40, using the minutes of the Literary and Philosophical Society, Picton Reference Library, Liverpool.

17. James Smith, *The panorama of science and art, embracing the sciences … the arts … the methods of working in wood and metal … and a miscellaneous selection of … processes and experiments*, Liverpool, 1815-17.

18. T.M. Rickman, *Notes* [note 9], 69. The remainder were from notes by Blore and other friends, and published illustrations, chiefly by Britton, Lysons and Storer.

19. T. Rickman, *Attempt,* 1817 and later edns, pp. iii-iv. Subsequent quotations come from the 3rd edition, 1825.

20. Diary, 17 Jan. 1818, stock was down to 180 copies.

21. Blomfield, *Journal of the Architectural, Archaeological and Historic Society for … Chester*, 2, 1861, 276.

22. C. Miele, 'Re-Presenting the Church Militant: the Camden Society, Church Restoration, and the Gothic Sign', in C. Webster and J. Elliott (eds), *'A Church as it should be'. The Cambridge Camden Society and its Influence*, Shaun Tyas, 2000.

23. *Attempt* [note 19], 39.

24. Though he accurately discerned that the lower stages of the tower of St Peter, Barton-on-Humber, were probably 'real Saxon', along with that of St Thomas, Clapham, Beds. *Attempt* [note 19], 45-6.

25. *Attempt* [note 19], 37.

26. Pevsner [note 1], 29.

27. Baily [note 2], 313, identifies Milner (1805) as using 'Early English' and J. Britton in *Malmesbury Abbey*, 1807, 'Decorated'.

28. Pevsner [note 1], 30.

29. S. Wren, *Parentalia,* 1740, 307.

30. H. Repton, *Sketches and Hints in Landscape Gardening,* 1794.

31. *Attempt* [note 19], 5, 70.

32. Ibid., 5, 87-8.

33. Pevsner [note 1], 34; T. Rickman, 'Four Letters on the Ecclesiastical Architecture of France', *Archaeologia*, 25, 1834, 173; correspondence with Blore, BL, Add. Ms 52587. Pevsner's confusion derives from Rickman's statement , 'I consider Gothic architecture in England at this time, about the end of Edward the Third's reign, to have reached its best power' (*Archaeologia*, 25, 1834, 173), but Rickman's citing Heckington and the naves of Exeter and York as exemplars make it clear that he

was thinking of Decorated, not Perpendicular. He refers several times to particular similarities between Dec. and Perp. (e.g. *Attempt* [note 19], 88-9, 94); but his identification of panelling as 'the grand source of ornament' (ibid., 98) identifying the Perp. would appear to meet with Nicola Coldstream's approval, *The Decorated Style: Architecture and Ornament, 1240-1360,* British Museum Press, 1994, 58-9. In an autograph letter to J. Britton, he writes of 'the Decorated Style that best of all Styles full of difficulties of construction' (D.J. Holmes Autographs online catalogue, item 19690).

34. *The Architectural Antiquities of Great Britain,* 5, 1827, 94, cited by M. Aldrich, 'Gothic Architecture Illustrated: The Drawings of Thomas Rickman in New York' in *The Antiquaries Journal,* 65:2, 1985, 427.

35. BL Add. MS 52587, f. 23, 14 Jan. 1818.

36. Ibid, Rickman to Blore, ff. 29 (14 Jan. 1819), 32 (20 Dec. 1819).

37. BL, Add 37803; Baily [note 2], 411-14, suggests ff. 74-80; (but ff. 73-98 are all very carefully drawn). But Baily has identified some in this made-up volume taken from Britton (e.g. ff. 57, 58, Malmesbury Abbey and Salisbury Cathedral), that are dated 1810 and 1811, and these may have been prepared for Rickman's Liverpool lectures.

38. Aldrich [note 34].

39. Bodleian Library, MS Dep. b.140.

40. Rickman, Diary, 18 Nov. 1822.

41. As early as 23 Nov. 1822 Rickman was working 'hard at my Essay tonight & have now nearly finished my Extracts from my Books on to my Papers' (Diary). On 14 Jan. 1823 he finished his account of Ely Cathedral, and he continued laboriously (e.g., spending 18½ hours on Devon and 23 on Dorset, 11-13 and 15-17 Nov., BL, Add. MS 37794) until his three-month tour in Dec. 1823-Mar. 1824 The intensity was ratcheted up by Sep. 1824: Winchester Cathedral and parts of Hampshire (Diary, 1 Sep.); 'finished Hampshire & part of Hereford so that I hope to send these two Counties if not more to G Smith [Liverpool publisher]at the End of the Week'; Kent and Lancashire (2, 17-18, Sep.); a great part of Lincolnshire prepared for writing, and then written up (2; 17-18; 25, 28-30 Sep.). In Nov. he was still hard at it, Northants on 17-19, Oxfordshire 24-5 Nov.

42. The number of copies in each edition is taken from a letter in Rickman's brother Edwin's handwriting in Dr Baily's possession, [note 2], 318.

43. T.M. Rickman, [note 9], 75.

44. Fellow and later Master of Trinity College, Cambridge, author of *Architectural Notes on German Churches,* 1830, subsequently (1836) extended to cover his French tour with Rickman.

45. Published in *Archaeologia,* 25, 1834, 159, 'Four Letters on the Ecclesiastical Architecture of France'; and 26, 1836, 26, 'Further Observations on the Ecclesiastical Architecture of France and England'.

46. H.-R. Hitchcock, *Early Victorian Architecture in Britain,* Yale U.P., 1954, 13: 'Thomas Rickman … had preceded Pugin in several ways as a serious reformer of Georgian neo-Gothic.'

47. C. Webster, *R.D. Chantrell (1793-1872),* Spire Books, 2010, 59.

48. T.M. Rickman, [note 9], 6.

49. Ibid., 16.

50. Ibid., 16. Recording supper with Blore, 2 Jul. 1812, Rickman noted 'he [Blore] did part of a drawing as a pattern & such Drawing I have never seen he gave me a few Simple Instructions by which I hope that I shall be able to manage more decent work', Diary, cited Baily [note 2], 120. Rickman spent some time then and later in practising shading mouldings according to Blore's advice (Diary, 2, 3 Jul.; 2, 21 Aug. 1812). The workbook sketches made on tour are mostly of window tracery or fonts.

51. BL, Add MS 37803.

52. Ibid., ff. 38, 66.

53. T.M. Rickman [note 9], 15-16; Rickman, Diary, 31 Jul. 1813; BL, Add MS 52587, f. 7, 16 Sep. 1817.

54. Baily [note 2], 121. Cp. BL, Add. MS 37803, ff. 89-94.

55. BL, Add. MS 52587, ff. 3-4, 7 Sep. 1814.

56. T.M. Rickman [note 9], 14.

57. C. Hartwell and N. Pevsner, *BoE: Lancashire: North*, Yale U.P., 2009, 599. 'Scarisbrick still continues to engage much of my work a new Staircase has been built & a new antiroom there will give us much Scope for roofing which we intend to make good groinings & the old Drawing Room has been restored', Rickman to Blore, 7 Sep. 1814, BL, Add MS 52587, ff. 3-4.

58. Described in his patent, no. 3716 of 1813.

59. Baily [note 2], chap. 6. See 'Flat-pack Christianity – the "cast iron church"' in *Church Building*, no. 110, Mar./Apr. 2008, 26-9.

60. Ibid., 165-6.

61. Quoted by A. Saint, *Architect and Engineer*, Yale U.P., 2007, 74; St George's, Everton, is there illustrated, internal and external views, 73.

62. Baily [note 2], 179.

63. Plan and elevation in RIBA Drawings Collection, reproduced in M.H. Port, *Six Hundred New Churches*, Spire Books, 2006, 47.

64. Baily [note 2], 253-8; T.M. Rickman [note 9], 12. Rickman's designs are *RIBA Drawings Collection Catalogue, O-R*, Gregg, 1974, 140 [13].

65. RIBA [note 64], 141 [25].

66. T.M. Rickman [note 9], 20. Designs for that for R.P. Buddicom in Everton church survive in RIBA [note 64], 140-1 [11] and [26].

67. T.M. Rickman [note 9], 20-1.

68. Baily [note 2], 335-6; T.M. Rickman [note 9], 20-1; Rickman, Diary, 19 Dec. 1817.

69. See Port [note 63].

70. Rickman, Diary, 22, 31 Jan., 19 Feb., 8 Jun. 1818.

71. Ibid., 7, 11, 14, 22 Mar. 1818.

72. Church Commissioners' file 21744, pt 1, Bishop Law to Lord Liverpool, 7 Aug. 1818. (Church of England Records Centre.)

73. Rickman, Diary, 2, 3, 21, 27 Jul.; 4, 6 Aug. 1818.

74. Port [note 63], 61-7, 110.

75. National Archives, Office of Works, letterbook 6/183, no. 18.

76. Rickman, Diary, 2, 12, 22 Sep. 1818.

77. Ibid., 29 Sep. 1818.

78. National Archives [note 75], WORK 6/183, no. 25, 5 Dec. 1818.
79. Rickman, Diary, 7, 13 Nov., 7-9, 14 Dec. 1818; 11 Jan., 19, 29 Apr. 1819. See Port [note 63], 166, and M.H. Port, 'Francis Goodwin (1784-1835)', *Architectural History*, 1, 1958, 61-3.
80. Rickman, Diary, 14 Dec. 1818, 15 May 1819.
81. Ibid., 8, 22, 25 Jun., 2, 20, 27, 30 Jul. 1819.
82. National Archives [note 75], WORK 1/9, 468.
83. T.M. Rickman [note 9], 22-4.
84. As may be followed in his diary.
85. At Chorley (Lancs) the local committee had, after Rickman's designs were rejected several times, desired the Crown Architects to 'point out a proper person and give him directions', but the Architects had no such remit, so the committee persevered with Rickman, who produced an entirely new design in Early English. See Rickman, Diary, 7, 28 Feb., 5, 31 Mar. 1820; National Archives [note 75], 1/9, 99, 272; 1/11, 26 Nov. 1821, 7 Feb. 1822.
86. See Port [note 63], chapter 8. Recovered from a period of illness, in Sep. 1836 (when the Bishop of London was launching a new church-building campaign) he made a further vain attempt, writing to both the bishop and his friend Canon Spry, BL, Add. MS 37802, ff. 235v-38v.
87. Eastlake [note 4], 123-4.
88. Rickman, Diary, 28 Mar. 1820, 8 Mar. 1822.
89. Ibid., 4 Dec. 1819; CC [note 72], file 17887, pt 1; Church Building Commission, building committee minute book 4, 315. The Church Building Commission papers are at the Church of England Records Centre.
90. CC file 17887, pt 1, CBC [note 89], building committee minute books 4, 359-60; 6, 93, 120-2, 151.
91. CC file 15217, pt 1; see Port [note 63], 94, 155-7 for illustrations of these churches.
92. T.M. Rickman [note 9], 57, quoting Rickman's partner R.C. Hussey.
93. BL, Add. MS 37793, 27 Oct.-10 Nov. 1821.
94. BL, Add. MS 37802, f. 71. 1832 and 1833 had seen a sharp decline.
95. BL, Add MS 52587, ff. 33-4, T. Rickman, 19 Colmore Row, Birmingham, 8mo (Aug.) 20 1822.
96. Christ Church, Brunswick Square. Occasionally obliged to use Grecian, Rickman disapproved of it for ecclesiastical work: St Pancras new church, London, 'confirms my Ideas of the unfitness of Greek for an English Church', Diary, 21 May 1823.
97. Contracts totalled £6,935 [to nearest £] (including mason, £754, chimney pieces £290, brickwork £1,307, carpenter & joiner £2,750, plasterer £809, plumber £44, slater £168, painter & glazier £258). BL, Add MS 37793, f. 26
98. Cp RIBA [note 64], 140-5.
99. Ibid., 138 [1], 140 [12], [17] are only three of many, see Workbooks, BL, Add. Mss 37793-802; list in H.M. Colvin, *A Biographical Dictionary of British Architects 1600-1840,* Yale U.P., 2008, 867-8.
100. RIBA [note 64], 143 [8]; reproduced, G. Worsley, *Architectural Drawings of the Regency Period*, Andrea Deutsch, 1991, 149, entrance front perspective; *Specification* (Birmingham, 1830), copy in RIBA Library at E.g. 712 (12).
101. RIBA [note 64], 144 [14]; *Specification* (Birmingham, 1830), copy in RIBA Library,

at E.g. 712 (13).

102. BL, Add. MS 52587, ff. 33-4.

103. BL, Add. MS 37799, f. 27.

104. T.M. Rickman [note 9], 45.

105. Ibid., 45-6, 48.

106. Rickman, Diary, 15, 24 Mar. 1831.

107. T.M. Rickman [note 9], 50, 54.

108. Rickman, Diary, e.g., 29 Sep. 1826.

109. *Recollections of Thomas Graham Jackson 1835-1924*, Oxford U.P., 1950, ed. B.H. Jackson, 58-9.

110. Harry Hems, a carver, in *Builders' Journal and Architectural Record*, 30 May 1900, 309, quoted by A. Saint, *The Image of the Architect,* Yale U.P., 1983, 68.

111. Hems [note 110], n. 51.

112. RIBA [note 64], 138-9 [4], reproduced in Worsley [note 100], 111; Rickman, Diary, 19 Feb. 1820, quoted, Baily [note 2], 229.

113. Rickman, Diary, 26 Feb. 1821.

114. Ibid., and Sun., 3 Mar. 1821.

115. See BL, Add MS 37793, under dates mentioned.

116. Rickman, Diary, 7, 8 Nov. 1822.

117. T.M. Rickman [note 9], 39.

118. Rickman, Diary, 27 Sep. 1826. 'The drawing table was *the* most important piece of furniture in the office', J. Lever, 'Architects' Offices', *Georgian Architectural Practice,* Georgian Group, 1991, 60.

119. BL, Add. MS 37800, f. 96.

120. Keythorpe, Normanton, Carleton Scroop, Ancaster, Wilsford, Kelby, Heydour, Culverthorpe and Sleaford. He noted of Kelby 'the window as well as one at Ancaster is a good authority for the Window to the ground so often wanted in mod[ern] Work', BL, Add MS 37795, f. 11.

121. Rickman, Diary, 30 Dec. 1823.

122. Ibid., 7 and 10 Jan. 1824. In the 3rd edition of the *Attempt* [note 19], Rickman devotes a page and a half to Heckington, about the same length as his description of Lincoln Cathedral, 233-5, 245-68.

123. BL, Add. MSS 37794, f. 218; 37795, f. 2.

124. *Attempt* [note 19], 245.

125. Rickman, Diary, 18 Jan. 1822.

126. Ibid., 8 Feb. 1824.

127. See Colvin [note 99].

128. Diary, 11 and 14-16 Feb. 1824.

129. RIBA [note 64], 139 [10]; Strathclyde Archives , D-TC 13/603 A-U, St David's Church.

130. See Macaulay [note 5], 268-9. The T-plan is 'peculiarly Scottish', evolved from the addition of a transeptal aisle to a pre-existing building; see G. Hay, *The Architecture of Scottish Post-Reformation Churches 1560-1843,* Oxford U.P., 1957, 52.

131. For Cleland, see Colvin [note 99]; E. Williamson, A. Riches and M. Higgs, *BoE: Glasgow,* Yale U.P., 2005, 157; Ramshorn Theatre website: 'Before building works commenced, … Dr James Cleland took Rickman's drawings … to a secret retreat

– cut himself off from the world for three days – then returned with modified drawings. He had added a crypt, and steps to the front door which folk said threatened life and limb.'The steps are steep and on to the pavement.

132. Hay [note 130], 120-1.

133. Macaulay [note 5], 270 (with illustration).

134. Rickman, Diary, e.g., 27 Feb. 1824.

135. BL, Add. MS 37795.

136. Ibid., f. 143.

137. Williamson *et al.* [note 131], 157.

138. Ibid.

139. RIBA [note 64], Thomas Rickman [10].

140. Colvin [note 99], 865.

141. A. Fairfax-Lucy, *Charlecote and the Lucys,* Oxford U.P., 1958, 311-12.

142. Rickman, Diary, 25, 26 Feb. 1822.

143. Ibid., 25, 27 Jul. 1822, 17, 28-9 Jan. 1823.

144. BL, Add. MS 37794, 11-16, 18 Aug. 1823; MS 37795, 31 Jul.-6 Aug. 1824, 5 Jan., 2 Dec. 1825; Rickman, Diary, 13 Jul., 4 Aug. 1824; 7 Jul., 2 Aug., 2 Dec. 1825.

145. BL, Add. MS 37797, 17, 26 Aug., 13, 24 Oct. 1826.

146. *St Peter ad Vincula* leaflet in church.

147. N. Pevsner and A. Wedgwood, *BoE: Warwickshire,* Yale U.P., 1966, 305. See also Fairfax-Lucy [note 141], 311.

148. *BoE: Warwickshire* [note 147], 305.

149. *Attempt,* 84.

150. Rickman, Diary, 9 Oct. 1824, 24 Feb. 1825; BL, Add. MS 37795, 15, 24 Dec. 1825. Rickman frequently spent much time on design of glass in his churches. This window was replaced in 1837 by Willement's finest (shown as the frontispiece of his book of 1840), which was divided for re-insertion in Scott's apse, and damaged in the Second World War.

151. *Attempt* [note 19], 245.

152. Cp with his designs in BL, Add. MS 37803.

153. Rickman, Diary, 14 Feb., 1, 3 Mar. 1821.

154. Ibid., 8 Jun. 1821; 25 Oct., 5 Nov. 1822; 23 Dec. 1824; 6 Jan. 1825; BL, Add. MS 37795, 6-8 Jan. 1825.

155. The arrangement was that the marchioness was to be the contractor for the new church, receiving £7,000 from the trustees as well as the materials of the old church. Rickman's estimate was £6,546, exclusive of commission, &c. (BL, Add. MS 37796, f. 57).

156. BL, Add. MS 37796, 3-4, 22, 24 Jun. 1825.

157. BL, Add. MS 37798, 18 Jun., 16, 22 Aug., 1, 9, 10, 17 Sep. 1828.

158. A. Brooks and N. Pevsner, *BoE: Worcestershire,* Yale U.P., 2007, 507; and see note 80.

159. Cp illustration, Port [note 63], 154.

160. Rickman, Diary, and BL, Add. MS 37797, under dates given.

161. BL, Add. MS 37798, *sub* dates given.

162. Worsley [note 100], 120. Plan, elevation and section are reproduced on pp. 120-1, from RIBAD.

163. Illustrated, Port [note 63], 158.

164. Oulton flower festival leaflet, 2009, kindly communicated by the Revd Andrew Pearson.

165. There is a copy in RIBA Library. It is not clear from this whether the groined ceiling is of brick; it is very detailed about the construction of the wooden ribs of the roof.

166. CC file 21687.

167. BL, Add. MS 37800, *sub* dates given.

168. Rickman, Diary, 28 Feb. 1832.

169. BL, Add MS 37801.

170. Ibid., f. 35v.

171. CC file 21687.

172. BL, Add. MS 37802.

173. *Victoria County History: Warwickshire*, 6, University of London, 1951, 243-4.

174. *BoE: Warwickshire* [note 147], 421. This was surely one of two cases referred to by his son in which Rickman had to bear the cost of extras: see T.M. Rickman [note 9], 53.

175. RIBA [note 64], 139 [6] perspective.

176. BL, Add MS 37801; Rickman, Diary, 9 Aug. 1833. Higgs and Goodwin had been 'so peculiarly prompt' at the house built for Rickman's Bristol friend E.B. Fripp (BL, Add. MS 37801, 20 Jun. 1833).

177. Drawings are in RIBAD, *Catalogue*, 139 [7]. Nos 1-4 are for the rejected design without clerestory; nos 5-12 for that with clerestory, as built. The printed specification is in RIBA Library, press-mark E.g. 712 (16).

178. N. Pevsner and E. Williamson, *BoE: Leicestershire and Rutland,* Penguin, 1992, 284; the printed specification, signed by Hussey, is in RIBA Library, pressmark E.g. 712 (19).

179. Plan in LPL, ICBS file 00739.

180. N. Pevsner and E. Williamson, *BoE: Nottinghamshire,* Penguin, 1979, 250.

181. BL, Add. MS 37802.

182. J. Newman, *BoE: North East and East Kent*, Penguin, 1969, 360.

183. Archbishop Howley signed the drawings on 2 June 1831, and Rickman spent 17 hours in the succeeding week on sketches for the 'new Plan'; the specification he drew up 27-9 Jun., BL, Add. MS 37799; Rickman, Diary, 10 Jun. 1831: 'Today done my finished sketches for Hardress.'

184. 'Regency Gothic, with its shallow mouldings, ogival arches, flat, cusped panels, and balanced design, is, however, a style in its own right.' T.S.R. Boase, *English Art 1800-1870*, Oxford U.P., 1959, 67.

185. BL, Add. MS 37796, 11 Mar. 1825. Cp G. Worsley, 'The Architect as Surveyor' in *Georgian Architectural Practice* [note 118], 39.

186. He refers to houses at Liverpool for five clients, BL, Add. MS 37800, 29-30 Jun. 1832.

187. See W. Hutchinson, *History of the County of Cumberland,* Carlisle, 1794, II, 437-8 and plate; J. Wilson, *Rose Castle,* Charles Turnham, 1912; C.M.L. Bouch, 'Rose Castle', *Transactions of the Cumberland and & Westmorland Antiquarian and Archaeological Society,* 1957, 140; J.M. Robinson, 'Rose Castle', *Country Life*, 183 (1989), no. 47, 70-5.

188. BL, Add. MS 37800, ff. 31-2.
189. Potential net annual rental of £7,000 in 1859 (D. Keene (ed.), *St Paul's The Cathedral Church of London 604-2004,* Yale U.P., 2004, 338.)
190. RIBA [note 64], 144 [22] plans.
191. BL, Add. MS 37798, 16-17, 20, 24-5 Oct., 20 Nov. 1828; 15, 25 Jun., 28 Oct., 20, 24 Nov., 10, 14, 15, 17, 24, 26 Dec. 1829; MS 37799, 29 Jul. 1830; MS 37800, 15-19 Dec. 1831, 10 Feb., 30 Mar. 1832.
192. Rickman, Diary, 24 Jan., 3 Mar., 28 Nov. 1832; 12 Jul. 1833.
193. Northumberland Archives, Ashington, ZBL 257, Rickman to Blackett, 3 Sep. 1832.
194. Rickman, Diary, 21-7 Sep.; BL, Add. MS 37801, 22, 24-7 Sep. 1832.
195. Of Trowbridge, advocate of a ventilation system combined with warming. See J. Gwilt, *Encyclopaedia of Architecture* (revised by W. Papworth), Longmans, 1899, 742.
196. 'Sir E B was fidgeting about the Plan with E Swinburne for a long time.'
197. Northumberland archives, Ashington, ZBL 257, Rickman to Blackett, 10 Dec. 1832; see also, same to same, 15 Apr. 1833, about height of windows from floor, calculated to enable persons seated in drawing room to see the view.
198. Rickman, Diary, 13, 26 Oct., 19-22 Nov., 10, 17 Dec.; BL, Add. MS 37801, 19-22 Nov. 1832.
199. BL, Add. MS 37801, 12-15, 19-20, 26 Dec. 1832.
200. Northumberland Archives, Ashington, ZBL 257, Rickman to Blackett, 13 Feb. 1833.
201. Rickman offered a similar roof in his Fitzwilliam Museum competition entry, see below. Pugin drew something similar in 1833 or 1834 in one of his volumes of imaginary buildings, and repeated it in the entry to the Houses of Parliament competition that he drew for Gillespie Graham, see M.H. Port (ed.) *The Houses of Parliament,* Yale U.P., 1976, 55-7, 68; those at Alton Towers and Scarisbrick were high, open roofs. But Salvin at Bayons Manor built a hammerbeamed hall, *c.*1837 (M. Girouard, *The Victorian Country House,* Yale U.P., 1979, 28, pl. 68).
202. Rickman, Diary, 3-5 Sep. 1833.
203. Northumberland Archives, Ashington, ZBL 257, Rickman to Blackett, 13 Feb. and drawing '6mo.1833'.
204. BL, Add. MS 37801, *sub* dates cited; and ff. 286v-7; MS 37802, f. 54v.
205. Ibid., MS 37802, 8-12 Nov. 1834; ff. 100v-101.
206. Northumberland Archives, Ashington, ZBL 257, Blackett to Sir Matthew W. Ridley, Bt., MP.
207. RIBAD, *Catalogue,* 140 [14] sketches.
208. BL, Add. MS 37798.
209. BL, Add. MS 37799, 17 Jan. 1831, 'examining his [Brunel's] design for Clifton Bridge & contriving Buildings for Ends'; also 21, 24, 26-9 Jan., 3-5, 7, 8, 15 Feb., 9, 11, 23, 24, 28, 29 Mar. 1831.
210. R. Willis and J.W. Clark, *Architectural History of the University of Cambridge,* Cambridge U.P., 1886, III, 102-3.
211. BL, Add. MS 37798, 25 Jul.-26 Oct. 1829. Rickman may have submitted only his cheaper, Ionic design ('Design A' in RIBAD, *Catalogue,* 144 [13]. Willis states that Rickman and Hutchinson were 'content with a single design', *University of Cambridge* [note 210], III, 106.

212. *University of Cambridge* [note 210], vol. 3, 109-21. The contention in the Senate provoked a pamphlet warfare, G. Peacock of Trinity attacking Rickman's plans in *Observations on the Plans for the New Library,* Cambridge, 1831; Rickman's friend, W. Whewell published *Reply to Observations,* Cambridge, 1831, defending them; and Rickman and Hutchinson published their own *An Answer...* Birmingham, 1831.

213. Whose son was a fellow. See Colvin [note 99].

214. *University of Cambridge* [note 210], II, 277-8; A.C. Crook, *From the Foundation to Gilbert Scott,* Cambridge U.P., 1980, chap. vii, a reference I owe to Dr M. Underwood. Wilkins did not compete.

215. Whittaker also arranged for Rickman to design the three new churches allotted to his parish by the Commissioners, Mellor, Over and Lower Darwen (see Port [note 63], 94, 158).

216. Rickman, Diary, 31 Mar., 4, 9, 12, 13, 14, 22, 23 Apr. 1825.

217. Rickman, Diary, 31 May, 23 June; 17, 24, 30 Nov. 1826; *University of Cambridge* [note 210], II, 278. These are doubtless the geometrical drawings in the college archives. I am deeply grateful to Dr Malcolm Underwood, the archivist, for showing me the drawings and related archive material. There are minor differences between the drawings and the court as built (notably in the lantern), and they show the earlier version of the bridge, not Hutchinson's.

218. Rickman, Diary, 5 Apr. 1826; 8 Feb. 1827, cited by Willis, 279.

219. *University of Cambridge* [note 210], 278-9.

220. N. Pevsner, *BoE: Cambridgeshire,* Penguin, 1954, 128. Rickman ingeniously provided cellars with a door on the river for coal delivered direct by barge, Crook [note 214], 78-80.

221. D. Howard, 'Thomas Rickman, Architect of the New Court', *Eagle,* 67, 1974-7, 19-21. I am grateful to Professor Howard for a copy of her article.

222. He saw the vice-chancellor on 13 Aug. 1834, with a long list of queries about what was required, BL, Add. MS 37802, f. 84v.

223. BL, Add. MS 37802, f. 212v lists attacks of illness from 9 Apr. 1834.

224. Ibid., from 5 Feb. 1835 to early Mar.

225. RIBA [note 64], 142 [1], 1-11. Although these are catalogued under 'Rickman and Hussey', and the firm was now designated as such, the workbook does not specify 'With RCH' in Fitzwilliam entries, which would follow Rickman's habit, but does specify 'With JAB' on 2 Feb. 1835 and subsequently.

226. See *University of Cambridge* [note 210], vol. 3, 198-205; C. Winter, *The Fitzwilliam Museum, Cambridge,* Fitzwilliam Museum, 1958; J. Cornforth, *Country Life,* 132, 1962, 1278-81, 1340-3 (illustrations of four designs); A. James, 'Rickman and the Fitzwilliam Competition', *Architectural Review,* Apr. 1957, 270ff. (illustrated).

227. A. James, *Architectural Review,* Apr. 1957, 270ff.

228. BL, Add. MS 37802, many entries from 27 June to 28 Nov. 1835.

229. RIBAD [note 64], 142, 1-4. That from the south-west is reproduced in Port [note 201], 39.

3

'Foremost among those who successfully promoted the ancient style of architecture': the churches of Thomas Taylor (1777/8-1826)

Christopher Webster

To satisfy the growing interest in England's Gothic past, the first half of the nineteenth century witnessed a significant number of books on the subject, largely aimed at the antiquarian market and the church visitor. The trend started modestly at the beginning of the century, but quickly gathered momentum, especially in the 1840s, following the impetus given to the subject by the Cambridge Camden Society and the diocesan architectural societies it spawned.[1]

Certainly by the opening years of Victoria's reign there was almost universal acceptance that Gothic was the most appropriate style for church building,[2] and by the 1840s there was no shortage of books illustrating the best historical examples which could usefully serve as models for new churches. However, almost all authors ended their accounts with the Reformation; the contentious issue of precisely *which* of the more recent Gothic churches were worthy of emulation was thus carefully avoided.[3]

A very rare foray into this minefield comes from Andrew Trimen, architect, and author of *Church and Chapel Architecture from the Earliest Period to the Present Time with an Account of the Hebrew Church* ... , first published in 1849.[4] His approach to ancient history is somewhat idiosyncratic,[5] but at least Trimen didn't shirk when it came to assessing the recent past and his views are fascinating. He wrote confidently that 'the 19th century opened with bright prospects for architecture' and following the passage of the 1818 Church Building Act, 'in every part of the country, [churches] have arisen as with a magic spell … and an impulse has been given to the study of architectural science, which promises to make this century celebrated' for its 'imitation' of the 'glorious fanes [temples] of the middle ages'.[6] And who does he conclude has led this welcomed development? Certainly not A.W.N. Pugin whose Lambeth Cathedral 'exhibits the most lamentable deficiencies [and whose details] furnish no correct specimen of either English, French or German characteristics. The tracery of the windows is flat and flimsy … ',[7] and the vitriol doesn't stop there. And not Pugin senior or Thomas Rickman either, despite measured praises for the latter's *Attempt*.[8] The crown, he assesses, rests on an unlikely head: 'Foremost in the rank of those who successfully promoted … the ancient ecclesiastical style … was the late Mr Taylor, of Leeds.'[9] Trimen even sees James Savage (designer of St Luke, Chelsea, 1820-4) and John Shaw (designer of St Dunstan-in-the-West, 1831-3) as among the 'others … who followed his [Taylor's] examples'. This is an extraordinary conclusion and Trimen's assessment will repay attention.

Few today would even put Taylor in the same league as Rickman, although it is likely his first Gothic ecclesiastical design was several years ahead of Rickman's. Perhaps the real importance of examining Taylor's career is that it provides another valuable piece in the far from complete jigsaw of the evolution of the nineteenth century Gothic church. Both Rickman and Taylor arrived at a position where they could deal exceptionally successfully with the complexities of Gothic, not as a result of a conventional architectural education, but through an alternative route: Rickman *via* his antiquarian interests and Taylor as an accomplished artist, adept at recording medieval buildings in their topographical setting. His development as an eminent church designer reveals another seminal facet of the Gothic Revival story, the importance of patronage, an issue to which we will return.

Early career

Thomas Taylor came to Leeds from London in about 1805, and remained in the town until his death, some twenty years later. Remarkably, he was the subject of a monograph as early as 1949[10] – an almost unique occurrence for a provincial, late-Georgian architect at that time – and more recently his career in Leeds has been examined.[11] It is thus sufficient that the biographical details of his life are dealt with briefly. In 1811, he placed the following advertisement in the *Leeds Intelligencer*:

THOMAS TAYLOR, *ARCHITECT FROM LONDON*, begs leave to inform the Nobility and Gentry of the County of York, that his Designs having been approved for the New Court House, in Leeds, this, with his other Engagements in the County, will render him stationary in Leeds, where he will be happy to receive the Commands of those who may have Occasion for his Professional Services, in which he flatters himself enabled to give every Satisfaction, as during a Period of Eight Years Practice under Mr James Wyatt, the present Surveyor-General, he was in the Habit of making Plans, Elevations and Sections, for executing some of the most distinguished Buildings in the Kingdom, and from Five Years Practice under Mr Andrews, builder of eminence in London, previous to being with Mr Wyatt, he is enabled to calculate Estimates upon an unerring Principle. And farther trusts from having made careful Studies of all the superior French Buildings, he is enabled to arrange Architectural Decorations in a superior Style; Specimens of which may be seen in several distinguished Mansions in this Neighbourhood ... [executed] during the Six years he has been in Yorkshire.[12]

At first sight, this seems to suggest that, contrary to the statement earlier, he had indeed arrived on the Yorkshire architectural stage through an entirely *conventional* route – building site experience, office training and foreign travel. However, it appears that Taylor's puff gives only a partial account of his professional activities thus far and its publication – intended to promote a career reorientation for its subject – includes a degree of obfuscation.[13] He might well have produced *some* buildings – although there is scant evidence of it – but there is abundant corroboration that he had enjoyed a successful career as a painter. It is this writer's opinion that in 1811 Taylor chose to launch an architectural career and was intent on producing a resumé of his earlier experience that would be most advantageous for his new venture.

A rather more objective account of Taylor's activities appear in the Royal Academy's *Exhibition Catalogues* and reveal his prolific output over a 20-year period in which he always referred to himself as 'painter', not architect. The *Catalogues* also record his subjects – and thus his interests – as well as his addresses. Between 1792 and 1811 he exhibited annually (except 1807), showing a total of 58 pictures; in 1799 alone he had an impressive 14 works chosen. There are some landscapes, occasionally what appears to be a 'fancy picture' in the George Morland tradition, but the vast majority are topographical scenes of major medieval structures.

Certainly Taylor had been in James Wyatt's office as his 1792 and 1793 exhibits were sent from there, but what, precisely, was he doing there during the century's last decade? The RA *Catalogues* provide some answers. His 1792 RA piece was a 'Design for a mausoleum', no doubt a typical student exercise, but the following year's entry – when Taylor would only have been 15 or 16 years old – is more unusual: 'View of the church of All Saints, Stamford', a fine medieval structure and an indication of Taylor's precocious talent. By 1794 he was living independently in London and over the next three years exhibited views of Rochester Cathedral, Westminster Abbey, Burleigh House and more views of Stamford's churches. In 1797 and 1798 – still living in London – he showed landscapes, but in 1799 he sent – from an Oxford address – a mixture of landscapes and topography, including several scenes of the Isle of Wight as well as ones of Winchester and Canterbury. He was back in London by 1800 and for the next ten years submitted work from various addresses in the capital. These included views of the Isle of Wight, Canterbury, Warwick, Oxford and, from 1803, north Wales and Shrewsbury. He must have visited northern France early in the century – no doubt taking advantage of the Treaty of Amiens, signed 27 March 1802 – as he exhibited 'Entrance to the City of Amiens' in 1803 and 'Interior of the Chapel Royal, Versailles' in 1804. His first Yorkshire views came in 1808 (of Fountains Abbey and various York locations) although they were sent from his London address. Only in 1810 did he send work from Leeds – more views of York and Paris. So far as his employment with Wyatt is concerned, it seems safe to conclude – from the subjects and their locations – that he cannot have been shackled to an office drawing board, as was the lot of most architectural assistants.

Wyatt had an exceptionally busy practice, but was, apparently, disorganised and unbusinesslike, and relied on a large number of staff who just about managed to keep the business from disaster. He had spent five years studying in Italy and his early work can be located in the mid-Georgian Classical tradition, but later he was equally engaged with Gothic, and designed some of the earliest Gothic Revival mansions. He was also an early restorer of cathedrals. While Taylor was associated with Wyatt, the latter was engaged on restorations at Salisbury, Hereford, Durham and Ely cathedrals, St George's Chapel, Windsor, and was erecting the seminal Gothic palaces at Belvoir Castle, Leicestershire; Ashridge, Hertfordshire; and Fonthill Abbey, Wiltshire. Antony Dale, Wyatt's first biographer, notes the master, as a young man, 'acquired an elaborate knowledge' of the great examples of the Classical tradition, 'but when he came to turn his attention to Gothic, the occupations of his professional life rendered a personal repetition of this process impossible … Instead, he was forced at great expense to employ draughtsmen to visit the celebrated monastic and baronial structures of England and to make detailed drawings of their decoration.'[14] It is known that William Porden was engaged to draw York Minster and in 1785 and J.T. Smith was sent to record

St George's Chapel, Windsor;[15] Taylor's talents too must have been exploited in this way. It thus appears reasonable to conclude his principal role while in Wyatt's employment was to provide a steady supply of Gothic details, taken from the best medieval sources, for use in the master's numerous Gothic compositions.

Once settled in Leeds, Taylor stopped exhibiting at the RA – 1811 was his last London show – but not because he had given up painting; he had merely transferred his association to the Leeds-based Northern Society for the Promotion of the Fine Arts. Its first exhibition was organised in 1809 and others followed at irregular intervals.[16] From the beginning Taylor was a loyal supporter showing large numbers of paintings as he had done at the Royal Academy.[17] Again they included landscapes, but the biggest group was architectural. There were more views of northern France,[18] but they were primarily of British medieval buildings, including views of Yorkshire abbeys and major churches. From what little information survives concerning sales, it seems Taylor was held in high esteem.[19]

It is surely significant that, at the start of 1810, when Taylor joined a Masonic lodge in Leeds, he chose to record his profession as 'artist' rather than architect.[20] It is thus likely that much of the first few years in Leeds was spent in this capacity. Revd T.D. Whitaker chose Taylor as the principal supplier of illustrations – others came from J.M.W. Turner – for his magisterial books on Leeds, *Loidis and Elmet* and *Ducatus Leodiensis*, both of which were published in 1816 and are known to have been the product of many years' preparation.[21] Although some of Taylor's fine plates show modern buildings, many more illustrate the area's medieval churches in a series of outstanding atmospheric perspective views – most engraved by John Le Keux, generally regarded as the finest of the period's practitioners – comparable with those that appeared in John Britton's many superbly illustrated volumes. Especially impressive are his views of Kirkstall Abbey (**3.1**) and the interior of the Saville Chapel at Thornhill, near Dewsbury, both in *Loidis*.

Taylor even had ambitions to publish his own book of illustrations of Yorkshire's rich medieval past. In a pamphlet he published in 1813[22] he included the following:

> In [Liversedge church] I have ... followed the most simple Gothic style to be met with in Churches and Monastic Buildings in this county; and, I believe, the County of York can, in this respect, vie with any other district in the United Kingdom. I offer this observation with a degree of confidence and pride; as being the result of visits and numerous architectural drawings, which I have made of these buildings during the eight years I have been in Yorkshire. These drawings are intended for a

3.1: Kirkstall Abbey, Leeds, engraved by Le Keux from a drawing by Taylor. (*T.D. Whitaker*, Loidis and Elmet, *Robinson, Son and Holdsworth, 1816, opp. p. 118.*)

> publication of the Monastic Architecture of this county [and] of course have been attended to in an architectural way, in preference to the *tout ensemble* which has been the general mode of portraying these valuable relics of our ancient, and certainly original style of architecture.[23]

The passage implies Taylor had exceptional knowledge of these buildings, but even more interesting is his proposed mode of delineation. It is assumed that by '*tout ensemble*' Taylor meant perspective views where landscape was an important ingredient, and that by intending to show them in 'an architectural way', he implied they would be in plan, elevation and section. The project must have been abandoned, but had the book appeared it would have been groundbreaking. Britton had already published several volumes in his *Architectural Antiquities* series (1807–26) and had in preparation the *Cathedral Antiquities* set (1814–35), all of which had a number of architectural drawings alongside the perspective views. However, Britton's market was clearly antiquarian rather than the architectural and only in later volumes does he appear to identify potential sales to architects. Closer to what Taylor had in mind were Frederick MacKenzie and Augustus Pugin's *Specimens of Gothic Architecture ... at Oxford*, of 1816[24] and in the 1820s, Pugin's solo effort, *Specimens of Gothic Architecture*,[25] but Taylor would have been well ahead of these writers. Yorkshire's monastic remains had to wait another 31 years until Richardson and Churton illustrated them comprehensively.[26]

An intriguing advertisement appeared in the *Leeds Mercury* in 1816 promoting 'Three Novel, Interesting and Popular LECTURES on the ARCHITECTURE and other REMAINS of England and Wales as connected with the earliest periods of our National History, illustrated with a considerable number of large Drawings, from Aboriginal, Roman, Saxon, and Norman remains in Britain.'[27] They were organised by Edward Baines, the paper's energetic editor, but the lecturer is not recorded. Could it have been anyone but Taylor, especially as the advertisement mentions Welsh buildings, a topic largely overlooked by the period's antiquaries,[28] but something that featured in several Taylor paintings?

What had brought him to Yorkshire? The 1811 advertisement is silent on the issue and in the absence of any documentation, we can only speculate. Perhaps Wyatt had sent him to record Yorkshire's rich medieval heritage. And it has been suggested[29] that Jonathan Taylor, a land surveyor with an office in Commercial Street, Leeds, from around 1800,[30] was Thomas's brother. And what employment did he receive in his early years in Leeds? Of the 'several distinguished mansions in this neighbourhood' in Taylor's 1811 advertisement, nothing specific can be linked to him, although it is likely he was the architect of Thomas Nicholson's impressive house in Roundhay (Leeds).[31] Indeed, before Leeds Court House (1811-13), his only known architectural project was the rebuilding of the south side of the medieval Leeds Parish Church (1808-12).[32] On the latter's completion, the *Intelligencer* noted: 'The South Side has been in a great degree new-built. The large South window exhibits a beautiful specimen of Gothic architecture from the designs of that ingenious artist, Mr Taylor of this place ... '[33] Again he is referred to as 'artist' rather than architect, and seems to confirm he was known primarily at this time for his paintings. And if Taylor had launched his Leeds architectural career by 1808, when he started the Parish Church job, why did he not appear in the 'Architects' list in the 1809 *Leeds Directory*? Furthermore, in May 1810 – half way through this project – following 'a degree of alarm having been excited' about the condition of the substantial tower over the church's crossing, 'an application has been made to the vicar

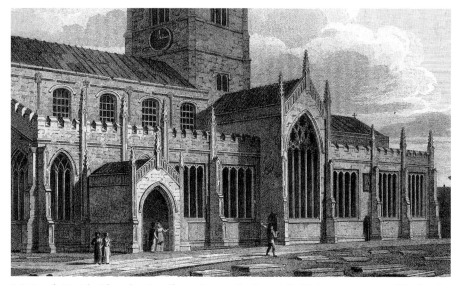

3.2: Leeds Parish Church, view from the south. Certainly Taylor was responsible for the south transept and its window; he might also have been responsible for much of the south elevation. Engraving, by Le Keux, from a drawing by Taylor, detail. (*R. Thoresby, revised by T.D. Whitaker,* Ducatus Leodiensis, *Robinson, Son and Holdsworth, 1816, opp. p. 39, detail.*)

to appoint some respectable architect to examine and survey the steeple … and report to him',[34] and Charles Watson (*c.*1770-1836), an eminent York architect, was engaged. But why was Taylor passed over? An obvious explanation is that the cautious churchwardens did not consider a complex structural assessment could be entrusted to a 'mere' painter.

It is not clear just how much of 'the South Side' Taylor rebuilt, but the detailed print based on one of Taylor's own drawings (**3.2**) reveals his striking new window in the south transept, an accomplished Decorated essay, and a remarkable product for its date. This engraving shows many changes from the illustration produced by Francis Place of 1715[35] and perhaps Taylor's project was extensive.

However, his move into the mainstream of architectural practice was confirmed by his appointment to build the new Leeds Court House in 1811. It was a handsome building distinguished by a tetrastyle Corinthian portico and plainer wings,[36] but architecturally it was a building of little originality that might suggest it was an early work of its author (**3.3**). The 'extra' (lower) storey of the side elevation is not satisfactorily resolved with the two-storey principal façade, an issue highlighted by the awkwardly detailed, apparently baseless, corner pilasters. Nevertheless, it was an important statement of

Leeds' aspirations as a regional centre, it was enthusiastically reported in the newspapers, and it announced Taylor's ambitions as a professional architect. There followed a succession of modest jobs – a bank and several schools, and he would, surely, have been responsible for some of the substantial town houses and suburban villas in Leeds – but the century's second decade was not a propitious moment for anyone seeking fame via big-budget secular projects.[37] If Taylor's earlier experience had not equipped him to undertake structural surveys or virtuoso Classical compositions, it had, nevertheless, given him a quite exceptional knowledge of Gothic. But there was one more component needed to ensure his emergence as one of the most accomplished and prolific church architects of the age: patronage, crucially that of Revd Hammond Roberson (1757-1841). Roberson and Whitaker were united in their concerns about the future of the Established church, and the architectural forms best suited to buildings for worship.

Patronage and the Gothic Revival

At this point, we need, temporarily, to leave Taylor to consider the role of the paymasters in the evolution of northern Gothic church building. Despite its diligent supervision of the projects it helped finance – what might be termed 'micro management' in twenty-first-century jargon – the Church Building Commission, established to administer the 1818 Church Building Act, made no stylistic prescriptions and was content to leave the issue to the 'local committees'.[38] With few exceptions, in the north of

3.3: Leeds, the Court House, by Taylor, 1811-13. (*T. Allen*, A New and Complete History of the County of York, *I. T. Hinton, 1829-31, vol. 2, opp. p. 529.*)

England they wanted Gothic. In the opinion of R.D. Chantrell, a Soane-trained Classicist and one of Taylor's contemporaries in Leeds, West Yorkshire had, by 1820, 'submitted to the county mania for plain Gothic … I should wish to present a Grecian or Roman design, but the objections to them made by local committees would be so strong that I fear my labour would be entirely lost.'[39] Many years later, Chantrell concluded it was the clergy who had led the fashion and 'where they had sufficient influence, induced local committees to adopt [Gothic] for their new churches'.[40] Indeed, the northern preference for Gothic was well established before 1818. The dominant figure in this stylistic innovation was Roberson and his reasoning is crucial to our understanding of Taylor's output; it is also central to our understanding of the role played by the clergy in the wider promotion of the style.

Roberson was a remarkable character, widely seen as the model for the Revd Matthew Helstone in Charlotte Brontë's *Shirley*, 'inflexibly Anglican and immovably Tory'.[41] From his own published work – as well as Brontë's – comes a picture of a man who believed passionately in arresting profanity and the spread of Nonconformity in his locality by the presence of a vibrant Established church, and who adhered firmly to the liturgy and rubrics of the *Book of Common Prayer*.[42]

Roberson grew up in Norfolk and after studying at Magdalene College, Cambridge, was ordained in 1779 and began his first clerical appointment as a curate in Dewsbury.[43] He stayed for nine years and was 'active, energetic and ready to promote every good cause'. He was especially concerned about education and the welfare of the young, and in 1783 established in the town what he believed was 'the first Sunday school in the North of England', commenced 'in spite of difficulties of all kinds'. He was also deeply troubled that 'the Sabbath was profaned, and the duties of religion entirely neglected' by the majority of the population. His moves to prosecute those who organised bull-baiting – just one of several 'brutal vices' commonplace among townsfolk – were among his more redoubtable acts. In 1788, he resigned from his curacy to concentrate his efforts on education and in 1795, moved a few miles west to Healds Hall, Liversedge, which he ran as a private school. While Dewsbury might have been memorable for its vices, it did at least have a parish church; Liversedge, in the parish of Birstall, was several miles from any outpost of the Establishment.

In the new century, he organised the distribution of bibles and prayer books to the poor, encouraged the formation of a volunteer corps – of which he was honorary chaplain – to stand against the threat from Napoleon, and in 1818 he published *The Select Vestry or Parish Committee* dealing with the efficient conduct of parish business. His standing among the local Anglicans is confirmed by the 1835 appeal, accompanied by the signatures of no less than 194 of the local clergy, urging him to convene a meeting 'for the purpose of endeavouring to form a Society for building and endowing churches'. His address to the ensuing meeting was published in 1836. There followed two further published *Addresses to the Clergy and influential laity of the West-Riding on … Church accommodation and pastoral superintendence.*[44]

Despite the best endeavours of the Ecclesiologist to suggest the late-Georgian church was moribund, their assessment was highly subjective. While Roberson might have been among the most vigorous of those that sought to revive Anglicanism in the region – 'the father of Church principles in the West Riding', according to the vicar of Leeds[45] – he was far from alone. Roberson's associates Christopher Sidgewick in Skipton, the author the Revd Dr Whitaker, and Dr Walter Farquhar Hook in Leeds were just three of many who shared his aims.[46]

So far as architecture is concerned, Roberson is of seminal importance in Taylor's career because it was he who commissioned Taylor's first new church, Christ Church in Liversedge. As early as 1806 he had in mind such a project, but it was not until December 1811 that he circulated a printed prospectus,[47] with a plan, accompanied by an argument that was soon to become familiar: not only were the dissenters well ahead in providing for worshippers, but many who would seek to worship in the Established church were excluded either through want of accommodation, and because much of the accommodation that did exist was appropriated and thus denied to the poor. He bought the site, paid for the necessary Act of Parliament (obtained in March 1812) and funded the church too. The foundation stone was laid in December 1812 and the consecration took place in August 1816. At the time, it was widely believed to be 'the first church in the Gothic style erected in the [nineteenth] century',[48] and while others might lay claim to this designation, it was certainly among the earliest. When did Taylor become involved in the project? It seems unlikely that Roberson would have bought the hilltop site without establishing that a church could be built on it, and could be completed within the (limited) funds at his disposal. Taylor was thus probably engaged by 1811 but perhaps much earlier. But why a *Gothic* church?

Roberson's many publications rarely address the issue of architectural style directly; his concern was the heritage of Anglicanism. He was building at Liversedge so that 'members of the Established Church … might enjoy the privileges of attending her most sound instruction and devotional services'.[49] It was erected 'for the celebration of Divine Worship according to the rites and forms subscribed by our excellent national Church Establishment'.[50] For Roberson, one of the objections to Nonconformity was the lack of structure and consistency in its services, while the Church of England offered clear principles. It also offered a sense of continuity and history. 'The numerous [churches that] our pious ancestors … left us demonstrate their knowledge of nature, their judgement, their skill, their tastes and their devotion.' They are much more conducive to piety than modern buildings of 'just symmetry and proportion where everything is neat, decorous and solemn'. Conversely, he believed Taylor's Liversedge design 'forces upon our recollection the judicious piety of our fathers. This style of building is perfectly distinguished from everything that is mean or insignificant. When executed with simplicity, it is chaste and decorous, and yet conveys suitable ideas of grandeur.'[51] Only once, at the end of the 62-page pamphlet, does Roberson use the word 'Gothic', but it is clear he saw the style as the perfect confederate for the form of service he worked tirelessly to promote. He wanted Gothic for the continuity with the roots of Anglicanism that it represented, but it is also discernable that he would not have been content with a Gothic preaching box: he needed a decent chancel so that the rubrics of his treasured *Book of Common Prayer* could be reverently followed. There is no indication how often the communion service was celebrated in Liversedge – and thus the chancel used to its full potential – although, in reflecting on the great benefits the new church had brought to the village, Roberson wrote 'We have a considerable increase of people at holy communion', whereas a comment on general church attendance might have been more usual at this time.[52] Subsequently, he was more explicit discussing the 'value of our National Establishment to individuals and society. A part of the beneficial influence depends upon the style of architecture and the arrangements in churches.'[53]

What made Roberson choose Taylor? We shall never know precisely, but most likely he had visited the latter's substantial repairs to Leeds Parish Church – the adjacent parish to Birstall – or had seen Taylor's watercolours at the 1809 or 1810 Northern Society shows in Leeds. And it is likely that Taylor was already known to Roberson's clerical friend Whitaker. There were professional architects in York (30 miles to the north-east), and Leeds had Thomas Johnson (*c*.1762-1814), but all were Classicists; Manchester (30 miles south-west) would soon have its own architects, but could offer nothing around 1810. Rickman, in Liverpool, had not yet launched his career. Taylor was the obvious choice.

There is one more interesting aspect of Roberson's church and the *Account* of its foundation-stone laying which he published to ensure the widest circulation of his agenda: the discussion of the relative costs of the

3.4: Christ Church, Liversedge, West Yorkshire, 1811–16. The finished building has simple pitched-topped pinnacles instead of those shown here. (Engraving after a drawing by Taylor in H. Roberson, *An Account of the Ceremony of Laying the First Stone of Christ's Church, now building in Liversedge*, privately printed, 1813.)

Classical and Gothic styles. 'Being desirous to ascertain the truth of the commonly received opinion respecting the extraordinary *expense* of the Gothic style of Architecture when applied to Churches, above the common [i.e. Classical] mode of executing such buildings, I requested Mr Taylor to give me his opinion.'[54] There follows Taylor's 'Letter on the Comparative Expense of Gothic Churches'. He begins by stating that the design is the result of his careful studies of

> the Churches and Monastic Buildings of this county ... [those] valuable relics of our ancient, and certainly original style of architecture. A style, of which every English Amateur must be proud, and consequently wish to see adopted in preference to the total want of character with which structures have of late years been erected as places of worship.

111

This disgraceful want of taste and judgement is particularly observable in those parish churches to which repairs and additions have been made, composed of walls and a covering resembling dwellings, warehouses or manufactories; in fact like any building but a place of Worship. I am persuaded these circumstances have occurred from an erroneous idea of the *expense* [of employing a Gothic specialist].[55]

He then proceeds to explain that Gothic is actually *cheaper* than the Classical alternative: 'A Gothic cornice need be only ¼ of the size of a modern [Classical] one; the trod-down battlements, which is a striking feature of Gothic buildings, cost less, in most cases, than the coping used upon other buildings … Buttresses add nothing to the cost of a thicker wall with no buttress … ' He then gives a detailed costing of a church window with 50 square feet of glass and shows the 'Modern one at £19/14/4 whereas a Gothic one may be had for £17/16/0.'[56]

In considering the stylistic alternatives, did Roberson influence Taylor, or vice versa, or was their relationship a perfect one in which each had come to the same preferences independently, though from rather different starting points? Probably the latter.

3.5: Christ Church, Liversedge. There have been several re-orderings since Taylor's time, but the structure remains as first built. The tracery in the east window is post-Taylor (*Ruth Baumberg.*)

3.6: St Swithun, East Grinstead, Sussex, by James Wyatt, *c*.1790. (*Postcard, 1908, West Sussex Record Office, PH1613.*)

Liversedge and other early churches

Roberson's account book reveals Liversedge had cost him £7,474 11s. 10¾d.[57] The church has a clerestoried nave with aisles, a west tower and chancel of exceptional length for the period (**3.4, 3.5**). The basic form and many of the details can be traced back to James Wyatt's St Swithun, East Grinstead, Sussex (1788-92),[58] a rare new church for Wyatt (**3.6**), but a project perfectly timed for Taylor's arrival in his office. East Grinstead's battlements and buttresses – especially the cappings of the latter – reappear constantly in Taylor's early churches.[59]

The Liversedge plan is of considerable interest (**3.7**). It contained no galleries,[60] and no big box pews to denote their owner's status. Indeed, although it included both appropriated and free seats, unusually there was no discernable difference between them. In place of the usual three-decker pulpit, Taylor designed a neat pulpit and matching reading desk which were placed at either side of the chancel arch. In the spacious chancel, the altar was railed on three sides, and traditionally arranged stalls faced north and south, although they appear to be for congregational use. It might even have had some sort of chancel screen, although the plan only hints at one. It was, without doubt, an arrangement well ahead of its time.

It was the nineteenth century's first new Gothic church in the region – indeed the first in any style – and with the dynamic Roberson keen to promote it, its importance was guaranteed. However, it would be quite wrong to see Roberson seeking his own fame; his concern was with the wider issue of church provision. He had merely given a lead, but it was a lead that had been long awaited and was eagerly celebrated. Roberson had

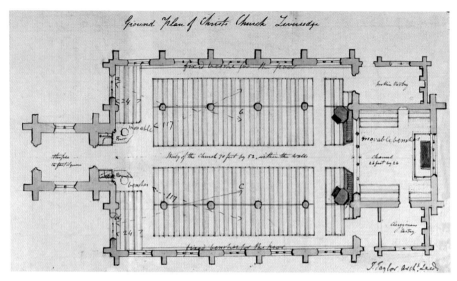

3.7: Liversedge, plan of *c*.1820 drawn by Taylor. (*Lambeth Palace Library*.)

persuasively argued that if church room could be provided, profanity and the spread of Nonconformity would be arrested, and he had demonstrated that the ideal building was one that reminded worshippers of the traditions and continuity of the Establishment – Gothic. Once Taylor had produced figures to show that a Gothic church might be built for *less* than a Classical one, the stylistic course of the northern Anglican revival was set. And the success of Taylor's new career was assured; commissions for other new churches and substantial reconstructions of older ones soon followed.

In addition to his almost unique familiarity with medieval Gothic and the invaluable support of Roberson, Taylor had another significant factor in his favour. At a time when architects' estimates were widely believed to be wholly unreliable, Taylor's ability 'to calculate estimates on an unerring principle' – noted in his 1811 advertisement[61] – was likely to have much enhanced his status. His methodology can be seen in the surviving archives of the Church Building Commission: whereas most architects' estimates comprise only global sums for (say) carpentry or masonry, Taylor's include huge amounts of detail. Usually he enumerates the quantity of each component, its unit price and thus the actual cost of every single item of the labour and materials in a particular project involving many pages of manuscript. It was an ability that surely endeared him to building committees just as much as his skills at the drawing board.

A remarkable number of commissions reached Taylor even before the

1818 Act, and many more came after it. However, his early inventiveness was not maintained. It seems that having established a viable modern design at Liversedge, he was content to repeat its key components in his churches over the next ten years. A design was never reproduced in its entirety – they differ in size, and some have clerestoried naves with aisles while others are without aisles – but all use substantial blocks of stone, have a massive quality and are easily identified. And not surprisingly for churches that pre-dated Rickman's *Attempt to Discriminate the Styles of Architecture in England* (first edition, 1817), Taylor's early works defy easy categorisation as Early English, Decorated or Perpendicular, although they have a quality that differentiates them from 'Carpenter's Gothic'.

Despite the explicit aim of 'economy' rehearsed in some detail by both Roberson and Taylor in the Liversedge *Account*, the details are by no means thin. The buttresses, each with several offsets, are plain but substantial, and often diagonal at corners; it is their cappings that are the Taylorian signature, simple pitched crowns with their gables parallel to main walls. Medieval precedents – although usually with more decoration – are easily identified. Among the Yorkshire examples Taylor might well have 'met with … in his visits … and drawings [during] eight years'[62] in the county are those in the south transept of York Minster – a building he had certainly seen[63] – and at Beverley Minster. The pinnacles he specified for his towers are interesting: steeply pitched pyramids with what appear to be well-detailed crockets. At least that is how they appear from the ground. In reality, the 'crockets' are nothing more than crudely carved knobs lining the angles with only limited resemblance to a medieval one.[64] Was this simply economy again or ignorance? There was no excuse for the latter; by 1812 there existed a number of books illustrating carefully recorded medieval examples, for instance the early volumes of Britton's *Architectural Antiquities* series.

Finally, there is Taylor's signature Y-tracery. It is a feature widely used in the Middle Ages,[65] and a particularly good example from about 1300 is at Great Gonerby, Lincolnshire, on the Great North Road that Taylor would surely have stopped to note in the 1790s as he travelled north following his paintings of Stamford. Crucially, in the early nineteenth century, it was a form that could be found even more widely in medieval churches: economical post-Reformation replacements of more elaborate originals. Perhaps Taylor believed them to be authentic as many certainly did at this time (**1.19**).[66] Again, Britton and other authors could have provided reliable contrary evidence, but Taylor's preferred type had two advantages: it was cheaper than the more complex medieval forms and, probably, it was the nearest thing to authentic Gothic with which the local stonemasons had much familiarity.

115

3.8: Holy Trinity, Huddersfield, 1816–19. (*Ruth Baumberg.*)

Perhaps Taylor believed he had little choice, although he had already shown at Leeds Parish Church that more sophisticated tracery was achievable.

Taylor's second new church was Christ Church, Bradford (*c*.1813–15). It was demolished in 1878 and inadequately recorded. Although many of Liversedge's details reappear, the composition lacks the latter's elegance: it had a large body and more modest chancel. Then came two small churches in the vast parish of Halifax, at Luddendon (1815–17) and Southawram (1815–18), both low-budget rebuildings of earlier chapels. His reputation quickly spread over the Pennines to Lancashire and in 1815–16 he carried out substantial and complex repairs to the large medieval churches in Colne and Rochdale, discussed below. In the latter parish, he also rebuilt the chapel of ease at Littleborough (1816–20).

His next major new church was Holy Trinity, Huddersfield (1816–19) (**3.8**). This is a large, stately building, erected as a proprietary chapel in an affluent suburb of this rapidly expanding town at a cost of £12,000. The driving force behind the project was Benjamin Haigh Allen whose mansion was nearby; significantly, he was a close friend and former pupil of Roberson.[67] He was also a friend of William Wilberforce and one of the founders of the local branch of the Church Missionary Society Association. Its campaign for more church room echoed Roberson's: 'The state of the

116

Church here is truly painful. We have a population of 8,000 and only one church and every seat in it is private property. The consequence is that the body of Dissenters and Methodists is very great.'[68] It provided 1,500 sittings, 500 of which were free. It is an impressive composition, a larger version of Liversedge, and significantly loftier, designed from the outset for galleries. The details are broadly similar, but unlike Liversedge, it retains its original Y-tracery throughout.

Post-1818 churches

By the time of the 1818 Act, Taylor had started – although not entirely completed – six new Gothic churches. It was, quite simply, a level of experience without parallel in the country; not surprisingly, the Commissioners in London entrusted him with more projects. The first was St Lawrence, Pudsey (1819-24) (**3.9, 3.10**), an even bigger version of Huddersfield, intended to accommodate 2,000 at a cost of £13,475, although it, like his other Commissioners' churches, has only a modest chancel. Its interior remains impressive and might have been awesome had the groined ceiling that Taylor proposed halfway through execution been accepted by the Commissioners. Sadly, they balked at the extra £1,050.[69] However, the building certainly pleased their surveyor; after his 1822 visit, he noted the exceptional foundations: 'very deep … 12 [feet] in places …

3.9: St Lawrence, Pudsey, West Yorkshire, 1819-24. (*Ruth Baumberg.*)

3.10: St Lawrence, Pudsey. (*Ruth Baumberg.*)

3.11: St John, Dewsbury Moor, West Yorkshire, *c.*1820-7. (*Author.*)

All seems too substantial.'[70] A year later he recorded, 'With reference to the strength of this building, it exceeds many others which have been inspected, particularly in the mason's and carpentry works.'[71] The blocks of stone from which it is built are indeed massive.

An interesting variation on the Liversedge/Huddersfield theme came at St John, Dewsbury Moor (?1820-7).[72] Holding a mere 600, the scale is much smaller, there is no clerestory or galleries, but the Liversedge details remain (**3.11**). Two years after starting the Pudsey job, he secured further work from the Commissioners in Sheffield: St Philip (1821-8) (**3.12, 3.13**) and Christ Church in the suburb of Attercliffe (1821-6). Both were 2,000-seaters and both have been demolished with only limited records of their appearance. St Philip followed the Pudsey model – although with pinnacles instead of pitched caps on the aisle buttresses – but Christ Church represented quite a departure. Although its plan differs little from St Philip's, apparently there was no clerestory; in place of the wider 'Y'-traceried aisle windows of St Philip's, it had lancets, and in place of St Philip's open roof, it had a groined ceiling. Subsequently, Taylor regularly exploited Early English, no doubt for its economy.

3.12: St Philip, Sheffield, 1822-8, demolished.

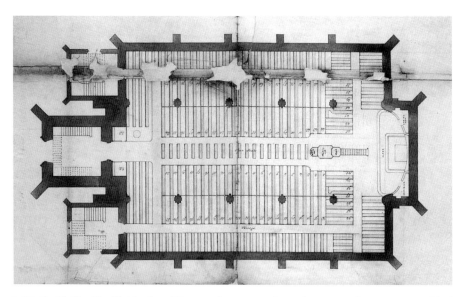

3.13: St Philip, Sheffield, plan. The north-west and south-west staircases were added during construction to give better access to the galleries. There is no vestry, but a space to the north of the altar, little bigger than a cupboard, is marked 'robing room'. (*Church of England Records Centre.*)

3.14: Christ Church, Woodhouse, Huddersfield, 1823-4. (*Leeds University Library, Special Collections.*)

In around 1823, Taylor developed a substantially different model design which, like the Liversedge predecessor, was then used in a number of different contexts. Its first appearance was at Christ Church, Woodhouse, Huddersfield (1823-4), another privately funded project (**3.14**). It was paid for by John Whitacre, who lived in Woodhouse, and was the brother-in-law of Benjamin Allen whom we encountered earlier as the builder of Holy Trinity. The design has little in common with Taylor's earlier churches: its features – especially its lancet windows – place it firmly in the Early English style; it has a tower with broach spire; it is cruciform in plan. The latter feature warrants further examination. Not only was the rectangular body derived from Gibbs's St Martin-in-the-Fields – perfectly illustrated by Pudsey – by far the most common model in the early nineteenth century, but it was also the Commissioners' favoured arrangement; Woodhouse

3.15: St John, Roundhay, Leeds, 1824-6. (*Leeds Library and Information Services.*)

represented a radical alternative. However, it had certain things in its favour, primarily that the transepts allowed additional seating where it was most useful: close to the pulpit. On the other hand, it precluded the easy addition of galleries and if the Commissioners' prescription of eastern-facing seats was to be followed, those occupying the eastern-most rows in the transepts would stare at a blank wall. Perhaps its most compelling advantage was the visual attractiveness of the model when seen from the outside. Taylor went on to develop it further at St John, Roundhay, Leeds (1824-6) (**3.15**), St Peter, Earlsheaton, Dewsbury (1825-7) (**3.16**) and Holy Trinity, Ripon (1826-7) (**3.17, 3.18**). Both Roundhay and Ripon were privately financed.

Illustrations suggest these four churches shared a near identical design, but in reality they differ considerably in size: Roundhay is tiny, built to hold just 320, while Ripon had room for 1,000.

Alongside these new churches were numerous repairs, extensions and new galleries for others including: St Bartholomew, Colne, (repairs, 1815); St Chad, Rochdale, (repairs, 1815-16); Holy Trinity, Littleborough (new gallery, 1822-3); and St Luke, Heywood (enlargement, probably unexecuted, 1824), all in Lancashire. In Yorkshire there was: Holy Trinity, Ossett (extension, 1821); Gildersome Chapel, Leeds (new gallery, 1821-2); St Peter, Birstall (alterations, 1824). Taylor's commitment to these sorts of alterations is underlined by his 1816 proposal to publish *AN ADDRESS to the CLERGY of Great Britain,* to be dedicated to the Archbishop of York and the Bishop of Chester. It was intended to discuss

> the possibility of repairing Ancient Parochial Churches and Chapels in their original Style in Preference to the incongruous Matter generally introduced in the Repair of ancient Edifices and frequently at much greater Expense than would attend the Restoration of decayed Parts – Exemplified by an Account of the Repairs of the Churches of Leeds and

3.16: St Peter, Earlsheaton, Dewsbury, 1825-7, demolished. The chancel is a later addition. (*Earlsheaton Local History Group*.)

3.17: Holy Trinity, Ripon, North Yorkshire, 1826-7. (*Anon.*, The Tourist Companion … Ripon, *Langdale, 1833*.)

> Rochdale, and particularly of Colne, where the Foundations of Ten Pillars have been completely removed without disturbing the Superstructure.[73] With Plates descriptive of the progress necessary in the most perilous Circumstances. The whole will be illustrated with perspective Sketches, exterior and interior, of Seven Churches erected or now executing in the Counties of York and Lancaster.[74]

The book seems not to have been completed, but even this astonishing prospectus places Taylor in a unique position in the fledgling movement to establish Gothic as the most appropriate style for Anglican worship, a movement, in 1816, largely independent of the architectural profession.

Taylor's architectural achievement

We can only speculate on what Taylor would have achieved had he not died, apparently in his late forties, in March 1826,[75] following exposure to a cold wind while inspecting progress at St Mary, Leeds (1822-6) (**3.19, 3.20**).

Certainly he would have completed a huge new church in Travis Street, Manchester – where he was appointed in 1823 – the ultimate Liversedge derivative: a massive structure, but with the addition of a spire atop the already lofty tower to create a monumental edifice.

During his lifetime, he enjoyed an enviable reputation, especially among those who shared Roberson's vision of Gothic as a necessary adjunct to a revival of Anglicanism. Dr Whitaker, writing at the time of Liversedge's consecration, noted:

> It is no small gratification, in the midst of deformity and barbarism, which is every day obtruded on the public eye under the name of Gothic, that the founder has had the good sense (I almost said the fortitude) to adopt a plan which even a severe judge must, with a few and trifling exceptions, pronounce to be really such. It has … every constituent part of a church of the fifteenth century … the whole was designed by Mr. Taylor of Leeds, who, with a perfect conception of old English models, has the modesty to adhere to them, and by that means has the merit of producing beautiful copies instead of monsters. Such too has been the advantage of working for an individual who was willing to take advice, above the irksomeness of submitting to the improvements of committees and parish vestries.[76]

3.18: Holy Trinity, Ripon. (*Anon.*, The Tourist Companion, *Langdale, 1833.*)

3.19: St Mary, Quarry Hill, Leeds, 1822–6. (*Leeds University Library, Special Collections.*)

3.20: St Mary, Quarry Hill, 1822–6.

Edward Vernon, Archbishop of York, who consecrated Taylor's Holy
Trinity, Huddersfield and St Mary, Southowram in 1819, considered them
'perfect examples of what we need ... nothing can be better or more truly
church-like than their external appearance or their internal arrangements
in every way'.[77] Thus Vernon 'confidently ... recommended [Taylor]
to the attention of the Commissioners' and urged them to employ him
for Pudsey's proposed new church. R.D. Chantrell, writing to his former
master John Soane in 1821, noted 'the designs of Thomas Taylor have given
great satisfaction to the Archbishop and other exalted ecclesiastics'.[78] Much
later, Chantrell wrote of Liversedge that it was 'one of the best formed
modern churches of plain character, having a spacious chancel, nave, and
side aisles, vestries on each side of the chancel, a western tower, and open
roofs'.[79] But the most remarkable aspect of Taylor's reputation is that, to a
significant degree, it survived the proselytising of the Ecclesiologists. We
have already encountered Andrew Trimen's extraordinary 1849 assessment[80]

and at the end of the century praise came from another unlikely source: J.T. Micklethwaite. Discussing church arrangements, he noted the efficiency of Wren's plans and continued, 'A few exceptional buildings, such as All Saints, Derby and the church which Mr Hammond Roberson built at Liversedge, show us that at all times there were men who looked to a higher ideal.'[81] Praise indeed.

Acknowledgements

I am most grateful to Terry Friedman for reading the typescript and making many helpful observations. I would also like to record my appreciation of assistance from Geoffrey Forster, Pamela Maryfield, Alan Petford, John Martin Robinson and others mentioned in the notes.

Notes

1. Typical of the prefaces of these books is that of G.A. Poole, *The Churches of Yorkshire*, T.W. Green, 1844, 2: 'Perhaps one of the most interesting features of the present day, is the revived zeal manifest in the study of ecclesiastical architecture. That there is such a zeal, let the different Societies formed for its study and extension, and everywhere the rising embattled tower, and heaven-directing spire, bear witness.'
2. However, Classical churches were still being built. Brighton, for instance, had a long attachment to the style – see St John the Evangelist, by George Cheeseman, 1838-40 (Lambeth Palace Library, papers of the Incorporated Church Building Society, file 2310: henceforth ICBS) – and early-Victorian examples can be found elsewhere.
3. Following the Cambridge Camden Society's strident lead, there was a tacit understanding that anything produced by the Georgians was likely to be contemptible and probably most authors felt the issue was best avoided.
4. Published by Longman *et al.* which issued a second edition in 1856.
5. Towards the back of the book is a 'Table of Architectural Writers, Architects and the Principal Edifices Erected during the Different Centuries', which begins with the Tower of Babel and ends just five compact pages later with Chambers' Somerset House. Interestingly, this was almost exactly the scope of J.E. Goodchild's 'Comparative heights of some of the principal buildings of the world' (*c.*1842), itself based on the 'drop scene' which accompanied C.R. Cockerell's RA lectures in the 1840s. See A. Bordeleau, '"the Professor's Dream": Cockerell's *Hypnerotomachia Architectura?*', *Architectural History*, 52, 2009, 117-45, especially 123-6.
6. A. Trimen, *Church and Chapel Architecture*, Longman *et al.*, 1849, pp. 81-2.
7. Ibid., 87-8.
8. Ibid., 86. T. Rickman, *An Attempt to Discriminate the Styles of Architecture in England*, Longman *et al.*, 1817 and later editions.
9. Ibid., 83. How did Trimen come to know of Taylor's work? The likely answer is as

follows: Trimen was associated with the amateur Saddleworth (Lancashire) architect George Shaw who, in the late 1820s, had visited several Taylor churches as a means of forming his own ideas about church design. His diaries are in the Oldham Local Studies Collection. I am grateful to Alan Petford for this information. See also M. Hyde and A. Petford, 'George Shaw of St Chad's: the Making of a Provincial Architect' in C. Hartwell and T. Wyke (eds), *Making Manchester*, Lancashire and Cheshire Antiquarian Society, 2007, 36-52.

10. F. Beckwith, *Thomas Taylor, Regency Architect, Leeds*, Thoresby Society, 1949. Beckwith produced an impeccable piece of research, trawling a huge range of sources for the facts of Taylor's life and work. However, writing at a time when little work had been done on this, then unfashionable, period of architectural history, not unreasonably he struggled to contextualise adequately Taylor's work, and seemed to lack the confidence to make more than very limited praise of his subject's achievements.

11. C. Webster, 'Thomas Taylor', in C. Webster (ed.), *Building a Great Victorian City: Leeds Architects and Architecture 1790-1914*, The Victorian Society in collaboration with Northern Heritage Publications, 2011, 79-98.

12. *Leeds Intelligencer*, 9 Sep. 1811.

13. For instance, far from having been in Yorkshire for the previous six years, Taylor was using a London address on other documents as recently as the previous year. The inconsistencies in this account of Taylor's career are discussed in Webster [note 11].

14. A. Dale, *James Wyatt, Architect 1746-1813*, Blackwell, 1936, 84-5.

15. I am grateful to Dr J.M. Robinson for this information.

16. For the Northern Society, see T. Fawcett, *The Rise of English Provincial Art*, Clarendon Press, 1974, 168-70.

17. Taylor exhibited at the exhibitions in 1809, 1810, 1811, 1822, 1823 and 1826. Copies of the Society's *Catalogues* are held in Leeds Central Library.

18. In 1809 he showed 'View of Paris' (no. 174), in 1810 'Sketch of the City of Amiens' (no. 190), in 1811 ''Sketch of the Pantheon, Paris' (no. 193) and in 1822 'View of the Pantheon at Paris' (no. 179).

19. Taylor's 1822 exhibit, no. 205, 'Interior of the Cathedral at York showing the Screen and Choir' was bought by one of the country's leading collectors, John Sheepshanks. (For Sheepshanks, see F. Davis, *Victorian Patrons of the Arts*, Country Life, 1963, 74-9.) Taylor's 1823 exhibit, no. 54, 'York Cathedral, view of Transept', was sold for £20, putting it among the most expensive works on show. By way of contrast, the architect Anthony Salvin's 'Bambrugh Castle', no. 33, sold for just 4 gns.

20. Taylor joined the Lodge of Fidelity in Leeds on 29 Jan. 1810. A. Scarth and C.A. Brown, *A History of the Lodge of Fidelity*, Beck and Inchbold, 1894, 210.

21. Beckwith [note 10] refers to them as 'published at long last', 39. Taylor's watercolour of the Leeds Library, the basis of the engraving in *Loidis* (now in the possession of the library) is dated 1812. It is the only known survivor from the many Taylor produced for Whitaker's books. Whitaker produced several important volumes of Lancashire and Yorkshire history and in them is revealed as a knowledgeable antiquary. Interestingly, they also record his belief that Gothic is the most appropriate style for churches. For Whitaker's publications, see P. Maryfield, 'T.D. Whitaker, 1759-1821: Historian of Yorkshire and Lancashire', *Yorkshire Archaeological Journal*, 75, 2003, 165-80.

22. Taylor's pamphlet formed part of Revd Hammond Roberson's *An Account of the Ceremony of Laying the First Stone of Christ's Church, now building in Liversedge*, privately printed, 1813, 63-71.

23. Ibid.

24. Published by J. Taylor.

25. Two volumes, 1820-2, published by Nattali.

26. W. Richardson and E. Churton, *The Monastic Ruins of Yorkshire*, 2 vols, Robert Sunter, 1843.

27. *Leeds Mercury*, 10 Feb. 1816. The lectures were to take place on 20, 21 and 22 of that month.

28. However, John Britton had published *North Wales* (1812) and *South Wales* (1815) in his *Beauties of England and Wales* series.

29. I am grateful to Geoffrey Forster, librarian at the Leeds Library, for this information. The topic arose in a conversation he had with the usually reliable Professor Maurice Beresford.

30. He appears in the 1809 *Directory*, but is not in that for 1807. However Beresford notes him in Leeds by 1802. M. Beresford 'The Birth of Commercial Street' in *The Dial: The Leeds Library Magazine*, 3, 1993, 7.

31. Now 'The Mansion', Roundhay Park, Leeds, currently a catering establishment. See Webster [note 11].

32. These dates appear in T. Allen, *A New and Complete History of the County of York*, vol. 2:1, T. Hinton, 1831, 498. *Leeds Intelligencer*, 31 July 1809, states the churchwardens had been 'actively engaged in the … work for some time past'.

33. *Leeds Intelligencer*, 11 May 1812.

34. Ibid., 7 May 1810.

35. In R. Thoresby, *Ducatus Leodiensis*, 1715.

36. A detailed description can be found in *Leeds Mercury*, 9 Oct. 1813, and repeated more or less verbatim in the 1817 *Directory … of Leeds*, reprinted Beckwith [note 10], 20-1.

37. For a discussion of Taylor's secular work, see Webster [note 11].

38. The subject is fully discussed in M.H. Port, *600 New Churches: the Church Building Commission 1818-1856*, Spire Books, 2006, Chapter 5.

39. Sir John Soane's Museum, London, Private Correspondence, XV.A, 32.

40. *The Builder*, 5, 1847, 300.

41. Beckwith [note 10], 25.

42. In his 'Account' at the Liversedge foundation stone laying [note 22] Roberson announced his church would be 'built for the celebration of Divine Worship according to the rites and forms prescribed by our excellent national Church Establishment' (p. 6). And in the *Prospectus* for the new church which he published in 1811, he refers to the importance of 'the Doctrines, the Sacraments, the Rites and Ceremonies of the Established religion be[ing] faithfully and duly administered.' (Quoted in Beckwith [note 10], 94.)

43. He secured the post with a recommendation from Revd Samuel Hey of Leeds, and Revd Henry Venn of Huddersfield. This, and other biographical details of Roberson's life come from F. Peel, 'Old Liversedge' in *Heckmondwyke Herald and Courier*, 7 Apr. 1887.

44. These were published in Huddersfield in 1837 and 1838 respectively.

45. Quoted in Peel [note 43].

46. And further afield, one can point to men such as Henry Handley Norris and Joshua Watson in Hackney who, quite independently of Roberson, worked towards similar ends.

47. Beckwith [note 10], 26.

48. Peel [note 43].

49. *Account* [note 22], iv.

50. Ibid., 6.

51. Ibid., 24, 29.

52. This comes in a letter from Roberson, written in Jan. 1821, quoted in Peel [note 43]. In *Account* [note 22], 9-10, he included 'In the Church of England, we enjoy incalculable privileges, inestimable blessings … By her institutions, the sacraments ordained by our Lord Jesus Chris are duly preserved; and in her communion, the advantages of a true Christian Church are fully enjoyed.'

53. This comes in an 1819 letter from Roberson to the ICBS when he sought, unsuccessfully, a grant to increase accommodation. (ICBS, file 114.)

54. *Account* [note 22], 61-2.

55. Ibid., 63-4.

56. Ibid., 65-7.

57. The details come from Beckwith [note 10], 26.

58. The tower of the medieval church collapsed in 1785 destroying the rest of the building. See T. Friedman, *The Eighteenth Century Church in Britain*, Yale U.P., 2011, 616-17, pl. 739. I am grateful to Nicholas Antram and John Allen for answering questions about this church.

59. However, it is claimed that 'the original design of [St Swithun] has never been completed; the side buttresses were to have had pinnacles', although no further explanation, or source is given. (G.M. Smart (ed.) *Guide to East Grinstead Parish Church*, Uckfield Press, 1975, 3.)

60. Although three years after the consecration, an unsuccessful application was made to the ICBS for funds to erect a gallery.

61. Quoted above (*Leeds Intelligencer*, 9 Sep. 1811).

62. *Account* [note 22], 63.

63. He exhibited a number of drawings of York at various Northern Society exhibitions. See notes 17 and 19.

64. The author was able to salvage one from Taylor's St Mary, Leeds, during the church's 1978 demolition.

65. The use of Y-tracery is discussed, with examples, in S. Hart, *Medieval Church Window Tracery in England*, Boydell Press, 2010, 70, 72-3.

66. See Chapter 1 of this book.

67. Beckwith [note 10], 38-9, which gives more information about Allen.

68. The Revd John Coates, the curate of Huddersfield, writing to the Church Missionary Society in 1813, quoted in R. Brook, *The Story of Huddersfield*, Macgibbon and Kee, 1968, 129.

69. Papers of the Church Building Commission (CBC), Building Committee Minute Book 7, 275. (Church of England Records Centre).

70. Papers of the CBC, Surveyor's Report Book 1, 86.

71. CBC [note 69], 178.

72. Papers of the CBC, Board Minute Book, 3, meeting of 29 Feb. 1820, refers to 'Taylor's … plans for … Dewsbury … ' It is not clear to which of Taylor's three Dewsbury churches this refers, although Dewsbury Moor is the most likely.

73. A detailed account of Taylor's work at Colne appears in T.D. Whitaker, *History of the Original Parish of Whalley*, 3rd ed., Nichols, Son and Bentley, 1818, 392. Strangely, the author does not name Taylor, but refers to him as 'an architect whose skill and courage were adequate to the task of restoring the [church]'. Whitaker – whom we encountered above – had been Taylor's patron for illustrations for his two 1816 books about Leeds, and continued to take a keen interest in his career.

74. *Leeds Mercury,* 13 July 1816.

75. *Leeds Intelligencer*, 30 Mar. 1826.

76. T.D. Whitaker, *Loidis and Elmete*, Robinson, Son and Holdsworth, 1816, 249-50.

77. Letter to the Church Building Commission, 26 Oct. 1819, CBC, Pudsey file, 16,039.

78. Sir John Soane's Museum, Private Correspondence, XV.A. 32.

79. *The Builder*, 5, 1847, 301. Open roofs had been an aspect of church design that Chantrell had championed.

80. Trimen [note 6], 83.

81. J.T. Micklethwaite, *Occasional Notes on Church Furniture and Arrangements*, ICBS, 1908, 18. This was a reprinting of a series of pamphlets originally published between 1899 and 1905. I am most grateful to Peter Howell for this information.

4

R.C. Carpenter (1812–55): the Anglicans' Pugin

John Elliott

Richard Cromwell Carpenter achieved considerable prominence as a result of the churches he designed before his early death at the age of only 42. An essential ingredient in his fame came from the support he received from the Ecclesiologists. However, the early part of his career was dominated by commercial work – railways and property development – precisely the sort of employment the Ecclesiologists felt was incompatible with the role of a church architect. The story of his career reorientation is a remarkable one.

Carpenter was born on 21 October 1812 and baptised at the Pentonville Chapel a month later.[1] His father, also Richard, was from Clerkenwell and had married Sophia Page from the adjacent parish of St Luke eight years before. He was educated at Charterhouse, where he attended as a day boy from 1825 until 1827 or 1828.[2] On 6 October 1840 he married Amelia Dollman whose father, the Revd Francis Dollman, was perpetual curate of St Mark's church in Myddleton Square from 1839 until 1848.

Carpenter's father kept cattle but went on to become a successful entrepreneur involved in the more lucrative business of property development.[3] This shift of emphasis had important consequences for both father and son. The former became, amongst other things, a magistrate, a deputy lord lieutenant, and a director of numerous railway companies, whilst the latter was launched upon an architectural career. Carpenter senior maintained a house at 62 Myddleton Square in a development which he most probably built, and also another at 24 Lonsdale Square which he also built and owned until 1846. He was living at 19 Old Steine, Brighton in

1845, had a house at 4 Eagle Terrace, St Helier, Jersey, where he was living in 1847, and died at Dinan in France on 15 August 1849.[4] The death duty records suggest that his estate was worth £14,000.[5]

Richard Cromwell Carpenter spent his youth living in Myddleton Square and it has been suggested that he may have contributed to the design of the west tower of the adjacent St Mark's church which was added 1825-7, though he would only have been an adolescent at the time.[6] He later 'served his articles with Mr John Blyth, a gentleman of great practical experience'[7] who 'early discovered in the mind of his pupil a strong inclination towards the study of ecclesiastical architecture, a bias which he encouraged by releasing him from the trammels of "office routine", and afforded him full liberty and means for following the natural bent of his mind'.[8] Blyth and Carpenter remained close. In 1836, when writing to his friend and future patron, Nathaniel Woodard (who became the founder of schools for middle-class boys), Carpenter refers to 'the marriage of Jonathon Bly [sic]', which he would 'attend ... as a Bride's man',[9] and in 1855 he named 'my friend John Blyth of Aldersgate Street in the City of London' as an executor of his will. Blyth's name appears regularly in letters and he acted as estimator and quantity surveyor for the work Carpenter undertook for Nathaniel Woodard. Blyth repaired St Bartholomew's, Smithfield, in 1830, designed the Northampton Tabernacle in Clerkenwell around 1836, and the City of London Literary and Scientific Institution at 165 Aldersgate Street in 1838. Although there is no direct evidence, it is possible that Carpenter may have had a hand in some or all of these commissions.

The first unequivocal record of Carpenter as an architect comes in 1830 with a design entitled 'Transepts for a Cathedral'. This was exhibited at the Royal Academy where he showed another ecclesiastical work the following year, 'The Shrine: Design for a Cathedral'.[10] Neither was subject to review nor appears to have survived. Carpenter's next offering came in 1832 when the Revd Thomas Mortimer, minister of the episcopal chapel in Gray's Inn Road, commissioned Carpenter to design a church 'in the early English style' which would hold 3,000 people.[11] In 1835 it was noted that if the design had been executed the 'Church contemplated would have been a commanding structure', and though 'assiduously devoid of ornament, [it was] peculiarly effective in its general character'.[12] A later comment appeared in *The Ecclesiologist* where Beresford Hope cited the design as 'An interesting memorial of ... [Carpenter's] early application of ecclesiastical architecture', designed 'seven years before our Society was founded' when Carpenter 'himself, [was] only nineteen.'[13] According to Beresford Hope the design was 'for a large church in First-Pointed, with double aisles, two western towers and spires, clerestory, low central lantern and transepts, defined chorus cantorum, and apsidal sanctuary'.[14] In 1855 Beresford Hope commented: 'Judged by our present standard, the design and the arrangements would be thought very mediocre; but for its time of day, the case was far otherwise.'[15] However, the vicar of Islington blocked the scheme as the intention was 'to celebrate Service ... with an attention to ritual much beyond the standard' thought acceptable in 1832.[16]

The year 1832 was also notable for the emergence of Carpenter's first secular designs which were exhibited at both the Royal Manchester Institute and the Royal Academy. At Manchester in 1832 he exhibited a remarkable design in the Gothic style which he described as a 'Town Hall & Exchange Buildings designed in the Style prevailing towards the close of the 15th century'. At the Royal Academy in 1833 he exhibited (from the same set) 'No 2 of a series of designs for City Buildings – The Guildhall'.[17] His 'Italian Villa' was exhibited at the Royal Academy in 1832,[18] and again as 'An Italian Villa designed for John Bentley Esq of Theobalds, Herts – lawn front' at Manchester in 1833. 'The Retreat – design' appeared in Manchester in 1833,[19] and at the Royal Academy in 1834 where it was titled the 'Design for a Cottage'.[20]

Exhibition designs aimed at improving his future prospects were one thing, fee-paying commissions were quite another, and for Carpenter the first significant change came in 1839-40 with his father's development of what was to become Lonsdale Square in Islington. As early as 1831 Carpenter senior and his brother Thomas had entered into an agreement with the Drapers' Company to lease the 'Gossey Field ... as a Cattle Layer for the term of seven years from Lady Day next at the rent of £100 per ann over and above the Land Tax and all other Taxes'.[21] Almost instantly the agreement was extended to last fourteen years because – as the company's minutes put it – of 'the Expenditure they will have to make on the Field' which the surveyor estimated would amount to 'upwards of £300'.[22] In 1836 there was the first hint of a housing development on this land when – in response to Carpenter's application that the lease be extended from fourteen to 70 years – the Drapers' Company surveyor reported that 'the field contains nearly 7 acres which ... computes to be applicable to 74 houses ... worth £280 per annum', and suggested that Carpenter senior might take advantage of this potential.[23] He declined the offer, however,[24] and nothing happened for two years.[25] But then agreement was reached and what followed was a development comprising Lonsdale Square together with both sides of Upper Barnsby Street and the northern side of St George's Terrace – 45 houses in Lonsdale Square, 38 in Upper Barnsby Street and 19 in St George's Terrace.

What may be Carpenter's initial designs survive as part of the agreement which was made between his father and the Drapers' Company on 12 April 1839, though they are unsigned.[26] They comprise a site plan, plus two Classical elevation sketches. Carpenter changed these initial designs, with a switch to a mild and romantic Tudor. According to Hitchcock the result was 'rather a pleasant Late Georgian kind of Tudor ... [which] looks back to the flimsy Gothic terraces of Regency times rather than forward to the characteristic Early Victorian Gothic of the church mode'.[27] Christopher Hussey declared that the 'design, for all its romantic trimmings, is essentially practical, providing large high windows on three floors ... The halls ... [being] lit by groups of quatrefoils taking the place of fanlights above the front doors.'[28] The specification required the 'Houses to be full sized third rates arranged agreeably'; the brickwork to be of 'hard well burned grey Stocks'; the fronts to be of 'second Marl Stocks'; the mortar to be of well-burnt Marstham or Dorking lime; the roofs of Countess slates; the cills, copings and front openings to be of Portland Stone with Yorkshire stone at the rear.[29] The result is a range of terraced houses with three main floors, plus basements and attics (**4.1, 4.2**).[30]

Overall Lonsdale Square exudes images of Georgian order, with ranges of identical buildings set in straight lines around a central garden. However, closer examination reveals that the order has variety. Lonsdale Square is not a square but a rectangle with the houses on the longer sides having wider bays. It is entered through entrances arranged asymmetrically at the top and

4.1: London, Lonsdale Square, Islington, showing the development of 1839-42. (*Islington Public Library.*)

4.2: Lonsdale Square, general view in 2011. (*Geoff Brandwood.*)

bottom of the Square; these entrances are forced to align with the public house in Upper Barnsby Street and Barry's church in Cloudesley Square, with the result that the houses on the south-west side are wider than those on the south-east. Two different coloured bricks provided a degree of variety, something which is enhanced by the diaper patterns which adorn certain walls, particularly the eastern end wall at the northern entrance to the Square – all very different from the ecclesiastical work for which Carpenter was to became renowned, and a 'youthful sin' for which – according to Hitchcock – Carpenter would have 'doubtless paid later by hours of ecclesiological penance'.[31]

The Carpenters were also involved with the development of Great Percy Street nearby about the same time. The Percy Arms was designed by R.C. Carpenter with an Italianate design that was based on the West End clubhouse model, and specifically on Barry's designs for the Travellers' Club of 1829-32. They also acquired building plots on Great Percy Street and Carpenter junior was almost certainly responsible for the designs of nos 1-8 in Percy Circus which were built in 1841-8 (**4.3 & 4.4**).[32]

A less rewarding project – and something Beresford Hope would have considered a distraction – also had the stamp of Carpenter's father on it – namely the construction of Victoria Street from a point north of Holborn Bridge to Clerkenwell Green.[33] An Act of 1840 enabled the Improvement Commissioners to facilitate 'opening a Street to Clerkenwell Green ... [being] a continuation of the new Street from Farringdon Street'.[34] The route which the new road was intended to follow was occupied by numerous streets which 'are extremely narrow, and almost impassable for Carriages, and many of the Houses and Tenements therein are in a very ruinous and dilapidated Condition', being inhabited 'by many Persons of a vicious and immoral Character'.[35] The area was also 'intersected by a very long Common Sewer called the Fleet Ditch, at many parts uncovered, and thereby causing Malaria, productive of Fever and Epidemics'.[36] The Commissioners were authorised to 'make a spacious and convenient street' not less than 60 feet wide,[37] and one of those commissioners was Carpenter senior.[38]

Carpenter junior was 'employed by a Committee of Gentlemen, who are anxious for this improvement'. He surveyed 'the property which will be required to be taken for the intended line of [the] Street',[39] and ultimately marked out the route.[40] The local inhabitants objected and the matter led to a House of Commons Select Committee enquiry.[41] Under examination Carpenter referred to the area as 'Of the most wretched description', occupied by 'Immoral and poor people', 'Many of them the worst description of people in London'.[42] He estimated the cost of building the street at £91,500, but that the sale of building land would recoup £62,112, to which the Government would contribute £25,000 by way of the coal duty, leaving a deficit of £4,388 which the Commissioners needed to raise.[43] Two further Parliamentary Acts followed in 1842 and 1845,[44] the former extending the period over which compulsory purchase could be undertaken, while the latter enabled the construction of three further connecting streets at Clerkenwell Green, and extended the period of

4.3: London, Percy Circus, Islington, 1839-42. (*Geoff Brandwood*.)

4.4: London, Percy Circus, Islington, 1839-42. (*Geoff Brandwood.*)

compulsory purchase by a further five years. By 1848 half the street which had originally been planned was completed, but further progress had been halted by the opposition of one landowner, and this led to a further Select Committee Enquiry.[45] Giving evidence, Carpenter said that £58,000 had already been spent, and that while he did not expect the original estimate to be exceeded, the land auctions had been discontinued because their start had coincided with City failures which threatened the supply of capital.[46] Later that year another Act was passed to overcome difficulties which 'have arisen in raising sufficient Money for the Completion of the said street', and this 'enabl[ed] the Clerkenwell Improvement Commissioners to make any Agreement or Arrangement required in case any Sum of the public Money should be set apart for them on Loan or otherwise in order to enable them to complete the said Street'.[47] Despite these provisions the problems rumbled on and the street was not completed until 1862.

Equally distracting was the railway work with which Carpenter became involved in the second half of the 1840s: an involvement which again bore the influence of Carpenter senior and his new-found interest in railway speculation. His initial stockholding was with the Taw Vale Railway and Dock Company, an organisation which had been formed in 1838 to construct a non-tidal dock at Fremlington in north Devon, and a short, two-and-three-quarter mile horse-drawn railway to connect it with the market town of Barnstaple.[48] The company was restructured in 1845 as the Taw Vale Railway Extension and Dock Company which had plans to connect the line with the Exeter and Crediton Railway, and Carpenter' father was cited as a director of both the old and new companies. Carpenter senior's railway investments mushroomed, and by the first half of 1845 he had become a director or part of the provisional committee for the Trent Valley Continuation and Holyhead Junction Railway,[49] the Staffordshire and Shropshire Junction Railway,[50] the Leicester and Bedford Railway,[51] as well as being a deputy chairman of the London and Birmingham Extension Railway,[52] and of the Warwick and Worcester Railway.[53]

By the second half of 1845 railway mania had gripped the nation and Carpenter senior's name appeared as a member of the provisional committee for some seventeen railway companies whose prospectuses were published in *Bradshaw's Railway Gazette*. While none of these companies managed to gain the approval which was a necessary precursor to construction, this intense activity did result in his son holding paid positions with at least three railway companies and possibly more.

Such were the early years of Richard Cromwell Carpenter, a man who owed many of his early architectural opportunities to the entrepreneurial spirit of his father. Yet having gained his first experience of substance with the secular commission of Lonsdale Square, he turned his back on entrepreneurial success to serve the Tractarian cause, and to become what Goodhart-Rendel called 'the Puseyites' man ... their Pugin'.[54] The seeds of this change had been sown in the early 1830s and found expression in his 1830 and 1831 designs for a cathedral, his 1832 designs for a church in Islington, and his 1836 proposals for the Newtown Chapel which, he told Nathaniel Woodard, was 'going to be Episcopalized' and where he had 'made the designs &c for the same'.[55] However, throughout most of the 1840s the influence of his father is much stronger: at Lonsdale Square, at Victoria Street and in the railway work, and hence the period from 1840-7 is one where the two sources of commissions compete for dominance. Then in 1847 Carpenter senior retired, gave his son £2,000, moved to Jersey and subsequently died in France during 1849, so ending the pressure towards commercial affairs, and making the pursuit of church architecture a practical and all-consuming proposition for his son.

Carpenter joined the Cambridge Camden Society on 1 May 1841 and throughout his church-building career his ideas mirror those propounded by that body. Pugin had charted the architectural way forward but his conversion to Roman Catholicism in 1835 made him generally unacceptable as an architect within the Established Church. Hence there was an opportunity for a talented Anglican who could deliver the same architecture, and this is a role Carpenter filled. As such, his contribution to the early stages of the Gothic Revival and to Anglican church building should never be underestimated. In considering his special contribution it is convenient to examine separately his output of churches suitable for town and city parishes, and the smaller ones considered suitable for country parishes.

Carpenter's town and city churches

Both the Evangelical and Tractarian wings of the Church of England were united in recognising the massive problem of ministering to the masses of the rapidly expanding industrial towns where the provision of church accommodation nowhere near satisfied demand. The model hitherto usually adopted for new town churches was that of a large, galleried auditorium, a design which the Camdenians found contemptible. No matter how archaeologically accurate, adopting the exemplar of a medieval country church for use in a modern town also presented philosophical problems. Much credit should therefore be bestowed on Pugin and Carpenter for identifying and adopting the Austin Friars' church in London as a suitable model for the new urban churches: it had impeccable medieval credentials and was capable of accommodating a large congregation without recourse to galleries. The significance of this development should not be minimised. This was an important innovation by both Pugin and Carpenter, and made a major contribution to the pressing debate on the issue of town church design which was to find its fulfilment in later decades.

In 1840 the Austin Friars' church had provided the precedent for Pugin's St George, Southwark,[56] and in 1849-52, it also provided the inspiration for Carpenter's principal London church, St Mary Magdalene in Munster Square. Just as the church suited Pugin's needs, so also it met all the Camdenian requirements. The linkage was confirmed by Carpenter's son in 1881 when, in a talk for members of the St Paul's Ecclesiological Society, he said 'the principle aimed at in the church was spaciousness', and that as a precedent the 'ancient City church of Austin Friars was taken as an example, and worked out with necessary modifications'.[57] Specifically, the 'wide aisles and lofty arcades, with the absence of a clerestory, were like Austin Friars', while the separate high-pitched roofs for the nave and aisles were 'improvements on the flat aisled roofs of the older church'. The aim, Carpenter junior explained, of wide aisles as well as of a wide nave, was to make the arcade the chief feature, in contrast to contemporary churches which often had a wide nave and narrow aisles, an arrangement which made the arcade insignificant.[58]

At Munster Square the chancel arcades were copied from Exeter Cathedral – 'one of the finest examples of this Geometrical Decorated date' – while the roofs were taken from Sherborne Abbey.[59] The window tracery was 'based

4.5: London, St Mary Magdalene, Munster Square, 1849-52, from the west. (*Geoff Brandwood.*)

on geometrical forms', the mouldings being 'very carefully proportioned to the larger and smaller mullions and tracery.' The west window at Exeter Cathedral formed the precedent for part of the window at the eastern end of the south aisle (**4.5 – 4.8**).

It was the Revd Edward Stuart, a curate at Christ Church, Albany Street, and a man with private means, who commissioned the church in Munster Square around 1848. The foundation stone was laid on 10 July 1849 and the church was consecrated on 22 April 1852. Both Carpenter and Stuart had been involved with the reordering of Christ Church some five years earlier when they had produced a conversion which was both architecturally and liturgically something of a compromise. Hence the aim in Munster Square was to achieve the perfect union of both without the constraints of an existing building, and as Basil Clarke so aptly put it, to create a church which was 'as near perfection as the handicraft of men, the skill of architects, and the experience and ingenuity of ecclesiastical art could make it'.[60]

Carpenter's original design – illustrated in *The Ecclesiologist* of February 1850 – was in the Middle Pointed style, and comprised a chancel, nave, two separately gabled aisles, plus a tower and spire at the south-western corner; which also contained the entrance (**4.7**).[61] Of the design *The Ecclesiologist* reviewer wrote:

4.6: St Mary Magdalene, Munster Square, interior looking east. (*Geoff Brandwood*.)

The style we need hardly say, is Middle-Pointed, of exceedingly good, but not [of a] very enriched character … The interior will be very satisfactory, we expect, the arcades being excellently proportioned; the arches of two orders, the columns clustered of four, with filets on each, and with good capitals, far better indeed than the bases.[62]

143

4.7: St Mary Magdalene, Munster Square, lithograph. (*The Ecclesiologist, 10, 1850, 352.*)

A shortage of funds required economies, and building of the north aisle, tower and spire were deferred. This was a decision which *The Ecclesiologist* regretted, as it called into question the practice of building 'very large churches in neighbourhoods like this, when 'had the founders of S. Mary Magdalene been content with a smaller church, they might at once have finished the fabric, instead of leaving anything so imperfect as the part it is now proposed to raise in the first instant'.[63] However, by the time the church was completed in 1852, all signs of serious criticism were gone, *The Ecclesiologist* complimenting Carpenter on 'this noble church', whose 'architectural ornamentation generally is particularly good', and whose structure had 'fully succeeded in producing an imposing effect of height and space', the 'graceful arcades of five arches offer[ing] scarcely any encumbrance'.[64] The sanctuary was 'very spacious', surrounded by 'an arcade of beautifully carved arches, resting on detached shafts of S. Anne's marble', while a dossal with 'rich diaper of gilding' topped the altar and was itself 'emblazoned [with] a floriated cross'.[65] Overall they declared that this was 'the most successful modern architectural',[66] and 'artistically correct new church yet consecrated in London'.[67] More recently Basil Clarke described it as 'one of the best illustrations of the revolution in church building that the Ecclesiologists accomplished'.[68]

St Mary Magdalene differs in several respects from the ideal model that the Cambridge Camden Society had recommended. For instance, the porch is not on the south side and there are no buttresses, yet despite these structural variants the design received considerable praise, most probably because its interior was arranged to facilitate the proper observance of the liturgy, and, for Ecclesiologists, this was the most important consideration. The church also provides a stark contrast to the Society's model church – All Saints in Margaret Street – which was built at much the same time to Butterfield's design. Both were started in 1849, and it would be hard to imagine two more different examples of Ecclesiology, yet both met with Camdenian approval. Carpenter used stone and relied upon the architectural detail for its effect, Butterfield used coloured brick and tiles to achieve a riot of coloured surfaces: one is an understatement, the other an overstatement.

Two churches in Brighton had preceded that in Munster Square, both modelled on the Austin Friars' plan and both the product of the patronage of one of Victorian England's great church-building dynasties, the Wagners. St Paul was built in West Street between 1845 and 1848, while All Saints was

4.8: St Mary Magdalene, Munster Square, lithograph. (Illustrated London News, *XX (19 June 1852), 480.*)

erected nearer to the railway station between 1847 and 1852. The Wagner family had a varied career before its members became enmeshed in the religious life of Brighton. A lengthy family history appears in *The Wagners of Brighton*[69] which shows that in the seventeenth century they were tailors in Silesia, while a hundred years later they were hatters in Pall Mall servicing the Hanoverian Court, the army and much of the aristocracy.[70]

Henry Mitchell Wagner was born in 1792, the second and youngest

4.9: Brighton, St Paul, 1845-8, viewed from West Street.

son of Melchior Henry Wagner, hatter to George III and the army, and himself the grandson of Henry Mitchell, the rector of Maresfield and vicar of Brighton. H.M. Wagner married Elizabeth Harriott Douglas, and they had one son, Arthur Douglas Wagner,[71] before she died in 1829. In 1838 Wagner remarried, this time to Mary Sikes Watson,[72] and they had two sons prior to her 1840 death. H.M. Wagner was appointed vicar of Brighton in 1824, and throughout his incumbency, which lasted until his death in 1870, he remained vicar of what he insisted be kept as a single, undivided parish.[73]

Arthur Douglas Wagner (1824-1902) represented a generation much taken with Tractarianism. He returned from Cambridge University to a Brighton dominated by Evangelical Protestantism, all very different in ethos from Trinity College and the ideals of the Cambridge Camden Society. He became perpetual curate at St Paul's in 1850, founding the Community of the Blessed Virgin Mary in 1855, and remaining there until his death.[74]

Both Wagners were prolific church builders, especially in the more deprived parts of Brighton, where they spearheaded the Anglican mission towards the poor. However, they held different liturgical views, the father being a robust High Churchman in the eighteenth-century tradition,[75] while his son was equally strong in his Tractarianism.

In 1839 H.M. Wagner had planned to build a church near the railway station, and in 1840 he appealed to the Incorporated Church Building Society, saying 'having completed St John's Church only within these few days and Christ Church not two years ago, I dare not venture upon a fresh appeal to my parishioners on behalf of another church until strengthened by considerable encouragement from within'.[76] The result was a promise of £1,000 providing the church had 1,200 sittings, of which at least half were to be free. However, a cluster of public houses rapidly appeared in the same area and the church plans were shelved and the land was sold off. An alternative site was selected in West Street, close to the seafront in the midst of where the fishermen lived, and the budget was increased to £5,000.[77] The site was occupied by a Bethel Chapel, and as 'many as 20 Houses or "sheds" passing as Houses', all of which H.M. Wagner purchased for about £3,025. The building of St Paul's, which commenced in February 1846, was finished by February 1848. The church opened on 18 October that year, and was consecrated exactly a year later (**4.9, 4.10**).[78]

The Ecclesiologist approved and in 1846 declared: 'We give this design our warm approbation.'[79] Then in 1848 it said: 'we must express how very much gratified we are on the whole with the structure, which is decidedly one of remarkable beauty and correctness, and placed as it is in such a town as Brighton, cannot fail to do much good'.[80] The same message was

4.10: Brighton, St Paul. (The Ecclesiologist, 5, 1846, 156.)

repeated in 1850 when it announced that the church 'seems just suited for the Anglican ritual to be solemnly and statelily celebrated in the presence of such a congregation as its nave could contain'.[81]

The Tractarian outpost of St Paul's was soon joined by another even larger church – All Saints – which was also commissioned by H.M. Wagner, designed by Carpenter and erected closer to the railway station.[82] *The Ecclesiologist* glowed with anticipated satisfaction saying:

> We congratulate our readers on the news that the extremely important
> town of Brighton is about to be enriched with a second satisfactory

church. We cannot conceal our satisfaction at the fact, since Brighton has become a species of suburb to London. A new church having been determined upon near the terminus, the committee were so satisfied with S. Paul's church, that they put this into Mr Carpenter's hands ... We are conscious that the very high opinion which we have of Mr Carpenter's talents makes any praise on our part of his works suspicious in many quarters; we shall not therefore attempt a general analysis of the present church, but simply express our anxiety to behold the actual building.[83]

Both St Paul's and All Saints were of knapped flint with Caen stone dressings; both were in a Middle Pointed style and, as initially designed, both comprised a two-bay chancel, a nave whose arcades were supported on compound columns, two aisles, plus a tower and spire.[84] In both there were marked dimensional similarities with what was to follow in Munster Square: the nave widths being 28ft 6ins at All Saints, 23ft 6ins St Paul's, and 26ft in Munster Square, while the north aisles were almost identical 20ft 6ins at both Brighton churches and 21ft 5ins in London. In German hall-churches the nave and aisles were of similar widths so as to avoid any suggestion that the latter were subsidiary spaces, and the ratio of space between the nave and north aisles of these three churches comes close to the German 50/50 model, with the nave accounting for 58 per cent of the combined width at All Saints, 53 per cent at St Paul's and 55 per cent in Munster Square.[85] It was in the south aisles that the main variation occurred, with a width of 21ft 6 ins in London, 17ft 3ins at All Saints and just 14ft at St Paul's. The cause of this was almost certainly Carpenter's desire to orientate St Paul's toward the east, and so towards West Street. Convention also required that the worshippers enter the church at the south-west corner and so a long passageway was built along the south side of the church, occupying part of what would have been the south aisle. The alternatives were to scale down the whole design, to omit the south aisle or to orientate the church towards the west. These were all unacceptable possibilities for a follower of the Ecclesiologists, though Somers Clark later argued that by 'wedging [the church] in between adjoining houses' and following the medievalising ideas advocated by *The Ecclesiologist*, Carpenter had 'screwed himself into a medieval coffin'.[86] Carpenter also built a prototype of St Mary Magdalene, Munster Square and – in a somewhat reduced and simplified scale – at Chichester where in 1847 he designed the church of St Peter the Great. In 1847 the parish church of Chichester was located in the north transept of the Cathedral. According to the Cathedral Restoration Committee, this was an arrangement which made the transept 'not only unsightly and sordid in its actual condition, but ... [one which was] incapable under any circumstances of being made a suitable place for Worship for its large Parish'. A thorough restoration of the cathedral was planned, and the restoration committee decided that a part of this process should include the building of a separate parish church. They minuted how 'it is hoped that the erection of such a church will form an integral part of the present plan and proceed simultaneously with the restoration of the Cathedral'. A site had been identified which would cost £1,200 and the building would cost a further £6,000 or £7,000.[87]

In November 1847 Carpenter presented his designs. The church would hold 700,[88] and have a four-bay nave, a two-bay chancel, aisles – the south of which was to become a two-bay chancel aisle – plus a tower and spire at the south-west corner.[89] Demolition of the existing building and clearing the site began in January 1848,[90] and the foundation stone was laid on 17 August. By January 1850 the walls and roof were complete, though shortage of funds had caused some prevarication over the tower which was never built, and the church was finally consecrated on 1 July 1852, when the total cost had risen to £5,450 8s. 5d.[91] The result was a sizeable Middle Pointed church of Caen stone ashlar (**4.11**). The four-bay nave and south aisle were of similar dimensions and separately gabled, while, because of a shortage of space, that on the north was narrower and roofed with a lean-to. There was a two-bay chancel which was signified by a lower roof-line, and a prominent chancel arch. Like the Brighton and Munster Square churches, the compound columns and nave arcade mouldings were copied from the Austin Friars' church, as was the curvilinear window tracery. According to Basil Clarke: 'The whole church is one of the best of its kind that we have seen. There is a graciousness about it that is often entirely missing from Victorian churches. The outside will one day be indistinguishable from a 14th century church: the inside is more definitely Victorian – but good Victorian.'[92]

Despite the wider north European influences that were starting to be felt as architects and critics began to abandon their previous fidelity to English precedents – not least because the railways made Continental travel much easier – the domestic precedents remained undiminished. Likewise the Camdenian ideals were also usually executed in full and so St Paul, Brighton (1845-8) was 'correctly' orientated with the chancel at the eastern end despite the problems this caused and, as Eastlake so aptly put it, it was 'one of the first modern county-town churches erected with a palpable recognition of those changes of ritual which were now openly encouraged by a certain section of the clergy'.[93]

4.11: Chichester, St Peter the Great, 1848-52. (Anon.)

It is now hard to appreciate how revolutionary these churches were in the 1840s, both in their architectural style and their internal arrangement. Architecturally they contrasted with the rather 'mean and lean' Commissioners' churches which had been built in the previous two decades and with the Classical buildings that had recently been popular. Internally the changes were equally striking. When Goodhart-Rendel compared two of Brighton's churches – the Evangelical St Peter's with the Tractarian St Paul's – he noted that 'At St Peter's there were galleries, a high pulpit, and rented pews ... [but] at St Paul's [there] were stalled chancel, rood-screen, sedilia, [and] piscina.'[94] Without any doubt Carpenter was one of the very first architects to perfect the Camdenian ideas of church arrangement and style. His churches at Brighton, Chichester and Munster Square are all perfect examples of newly developed Ecclesiology.

Country churches

Carpenter produced just four churches in rural locations, but their importance was no less marked than the urban ones. The architectural precedents were also less complex. In the early years of the Cambridge Camden Society much attention had been paid to medieval churches close to Cambridge. It was hoped that some of these would provide the

4.12: Cookham Dean, Berkshire, St John the Baptist, 1844-5. (*Geoff Brandwood.*)

precedents for new churches which would echo the architecture and liturgy of medieval Britain. In 1843 *The Ecclesiologist* carried a report on the abuse which had been inflicted on St Michael, Long Stanton, Cambridgeshire: a 'very beautiful little Early-English chapel' whose chancel was being 'used for a school'.[95] In 1845 it reported that tracings of this church had been sent to the United States so that they could be used as the basis of designs there, and this was almost certainly the precedent for St James the Less Episcopal Church in Philadelphia (1846-8).[96]

Pugin also used Long Stanton as the model for his Roman Catholic church in Cambridge, St Andrew (1842-3), and for many other of his church designs. It is thus not surprising that Carpenter should also use the same model in the four rural churches for which he was responsible. Likewise he sought inspiration from medieval precedents as the basis of the designs for wooden and iron churches which were published in *Instrumenta Ecclesiastica* and intended for poorer areas and especially for parts of the Empire. Similarly copies of his rural and urban church designs were taken overseas by the clergy and replicated in Australia and the United States. These designs had a major influence on the development of Anglican ecclesiology overseas and Carpenter's contribution was pivotal. The first of these was at Nutley, near Maresfield in Sussex where, in 1842, an application was made to the ICBS for assistance with a church for 250.[97] *The Ecclesiologist* reviewed the proposal in 1843, declaring it 'an excellent design', for a 'beautiful chapel'; a design which displayed 'extreme simplicity of composition', and yet 'the beauty ... of the outline full shews that the most severe simplicity is consistent with the truest architectural effect'.[98] Some changes occurred between design and execution: the south aisle was omitted,[99] stone rubble walls with rubbed dressings were replaced by ones of undressed stone.[100] The Early English precedents were emphasised by slender single lancet lights on the north and south: 'EE of the plainest kind – strictly orthodox'.[101]

About the same time similar developments were taking place at Cookham Dean near Maidenhead, Berkshire (**4.12**), an area 'abutting on and being part of Maidenhead Thicket', which had a population of 'Nine hundred or thereabouts [who were] ... almost exclusively ... Agricultural Labourers among whom ignorance and immorality have prevailed for some time past': Carpenter's proposal was for a building of knapped flint with Bath stone dressings; a four-bay nave, a two-bay chancel, south aisle, porch, and western bell-cote.[102] The foundation stone was laid on 15 July 1844, and the church consecrated on 22 May 1845, *The Ecclesiologist* reporting:

> A church is just completed at Cookham Dean, near Maidenhead, dedicated in honour of S. John Baptist. It is a most satisfactory design; very simple, and yet not mean or starved; of unpretending but solemn character. The chancel is of a good size, with windows of excellent workmanship. The style is of the fourteenth century. The pitch of the roof is proper, and all the details are appropriate. The nave has a western bell gable, very ably treated, holding one bell. The aisles have lean-to roofs, low side walls, and square windows; the eastern windows of the aisles are like the side windows in the chancel. The south-western porch is of wood, well carved, and rather elaborate. The church holds 300 persons: the cost is about £1300.[103]

It was not until 1850 that Carpenter had an opportunity to repeat this design, and then for one of the sponsors of the church at Cookham Dean – Henry Skrine – who was anxious to find a parish for his second son Wadham Huntley Skrine. This was to be a church for 'about one hundred and twenty persons residing at a place called "The Cross Roads"' plus a further 'three hundred persons residing ... in proximity to the locality of Stubbing[s]',[104] which is also on the outskirts of Maidenhead (**4.13, 4.14**).

The plan was largely a replica of what had gone before, with a four-bay nave, an elevated two-bay chancel, a south porch and a western bell-cote. However, the detail was somewhat different with a chancel arch terminated by corbels, and circular nave columns, which like the arcade mouldings emphasised mass rather than form. Like its neighbour at Cookham Dean,

4.13: Stubbings, Berkshire, St James the Less, 1849-50. (*Geoff Brandwood.*)

the exterior was of knapped flint, and buttresses provided both structural and symbolic permanence. Overall the sheer simplicity of the design provided a charm which was often missing from the more elaborate offerings available elsewhere.

The final country church that Carpenter designed was that dedicated to St John the Evangelist and erected at Bovey Tracey, Devon, for the Revd Charles Leslie Courtenay, a nephew to the Earl of Devon (**4.15**). This is an excellent church, one where there was no pressure from a limited budget. *The Ecclesiologist* correctly summed it up when they reported that it was 'very beautiful … though modest and unpretending'. Carpenter's design was for a building with multi-coloured undressed ashlar blocks, with a four-bay nave, a two-bay chancel which was lower but not narrower than the nave, a south aisle with a lean-to roof, a northern vestry, and a south-west porch. *The Ecclesiologist* was 'pleased with the buttresses',[105] and especially with that at the western end which was terminated by a double bell-cote. Their review concluded: 'We have rarely seen anything better than this, and we hail with especial delight the use of good sculpture in the decoration of a small village church.'[106]

There is a great similarity in plan and style between the churches Pugin designed and those produced by Carpenter. For Pugin such stylistic similarity

4.14: Stubbings, St James the Less. (*Geoff Brandwood.*)

between two different brands of Catholicism was not surprising, as 'in the present revival of Catholic architecture, the authorities for which can only be found in the ancient edifices of the country, it is very possible and even probable that two architects may erect precisely the same edifice', as 'When

4.15: Bovey Tracey: St John the Evangelist. (*Author.*)

buildings are derived from a common source, it is very natural that they should greatly resemble each other'.[107] Hence, the fact that both Carpenter and Pugin designed country churches with the same plan and in the same architectural style, that both alternated 'two-light traceried Decorated windows with the Early English lancets',[108] that both placed 'belfreys, in the form of perforated gables' atop the western wall,[109] was not plagiarism but simply the consequence of such features being found in ancient churches.

The similarities with Pugin's churches are striking. Compare Carpenter's St James, Nutley (1842-4), St John the Baptist, Cookham Dean (1844-5), St James the Less, Stubbings (1849-50), and St John the Evangelist, Bovey Tracey (1852-3) with Pugin's St Mary, Southport (1837-8), St Anne, Keighley (1838-9), St Mary, Warwick Bridge (1840), St Lawrence, Tubney (1844-7), and even St Alphonsus, Barntown, Co. Wexford (1844-51), where, as at Bovey Tracey, the bell-cote emerges from a western buttress. In all these designs the nave and chancel are separately articulated and the aisles have lean-to roofs and are subsidiary spaces; each church has a bell-cote but no clerestory. The buttresses are as much symbolic as structural and in all cases the materials are local. Inside the chancels are elevated above the nave with the altar raised even more. The style is First or Second Pointed, and, taken together, these churches share much in common, the basic design of which may be traced back to Pugin.

Death and succession

In the mid-1830s Carpenter had become associated with William Slater (1819-72), who joined the architectural practice as its first pupil. Carpenter, his wife Amelia and Slater all lived at 99 Guildford Street[110] where they remained until about 1850. During the 1840s three children were born to the Carpenters, and all were baptised by Amelia's father at St Mark, Myddleton Square. In 1849 the practice moved to Carlton Chambers at 4 Regent Street, an address from which it continued to operate for the rest of the century.[111] About 1851, the Carpenters moved again, and the census of that year shows the family, with William Slater, two students and three servants, living at 40 Upper Bedford Place.[112] By 1855 the Carpenters had also acquired Poplar Cottage on Hornsey Road.

Some time between 1851 and 1854, the Carpenters had a fourth child, Amy, who died around the end of June 1854. As *The Ecclesiologist* noted, this was 'a blow from which ... [Carpenter's] spirits ... never completely recovered'.[113] On 2 July 1854 he purchased a plot at Highgate Cemetery[114] and Amy was buried there.[115] Within nine months, aged just 42, Carpenter himself died on 27 March 1855[116] at 40 Upper Bedford Street from

'Tubercular disease of Lungs and Bladder'.[117] He was buried at Highgate Cemetery, in the same plot as his daughter, on 2 April. The service was conducted by Nathaniel Woodard and Benjamin Webb.[118] *The Builder* and *The Ecclesiologist* both carried lengthy obituaries, the latter being provided by Beresford Hope. Carpenter's will is dated 2 March 1855, less than four weeks before he died which, together with its brevity and simplicity, suggests his death was expected. He left the entirety of his estate to his wife, appointing John Blyth and his brother-in-law, Francis Dollman of Fenchurch Street, as his executors.[119] The value of the estate was estimated at something less than £6,000.[120]

Before Carpenter died, Slater had set out on his own, or in partnership with another of Carpenter's pupils, William Smith (1830-1901: he changed his name to Bassett-Smith, *c*.1882). Loughborough Town Hall (1852-5), the parsonage at East Haddon (1855), and the restoration of churches at Weldon (1853-4), Islip (1854), Stanwick (1854-7), all in Northamptonshire, and Wisbech, Cambridgeshire (1856-7), are all by Slater. However, this was to be a short-lived development and Slater's architectural ambitions were sacrificed when Carpenter died. Without a breadwinner Carpenter's wife and children faced destitution unless some new arrangement could be secured. The solution, which was engineered by Nathaniel Woodard, meant that Slater abandoned his own plans, and instead took over the Carpenter business, providing an income for Amelia and her children, plus in the fullness of time, an architectural apprenticeship for Carpenter's eldest son.

Over the next seventeen years Slater designed thirteen new churches – including two cathedral-like structures for the Church of Ireland (at Kilmore, Co. Cavan, and Bray, Co. Wicklow) – and a cathedral in Honolulu. He restored many more churches (particularly in his native Northamptonshire and the adjacent parts of Leicestershire); created grand houses for Lord Salisbury, Lord Goschen and several others; was responsible for a varied and extensive range of buildings commissioned by – or supported by – the Digbys of Sherborne, while continuing to produce designs for the new schools that Woodard was determined to create including Lancing College Chapel. However, that is another story.

Notes

1. On 25 Nov. See the baptism register for the Pentonville Chapel at the London Metropolitan Archives, X27/19. According to strong traditions he was born in or near Russell Square. For a fuller account of Carpenter's career see J. Elliott, *The Architectural Works of Richard Cromwell Carpenter (1812-55), William Slater*

(1819-72) and Richard Herbert Carpenter (1841-1893), unpublished PhD thesis, Royal Holloway University of London, 1995. It includes a comprehensive list of Carpenter's executed and unexecuted projects.

2. See Anon., *Charterhouse Register 1769-1872*, 68. At this time Charterhouse School was located in Finsbury.

3. In 1819 he was recorded as a watch-case-maker in Islington Road. By 1822 he was involved in the development of the New River Estate and specifically the building of Arlington Way near Sadler's Wells and houses in Myddleton Square. Information from Peter Guillery based on research for *The Survey of London: Islington*.

4. This is the address given on the death duty records at the National Archives, IR 26 f1832, 828.

5. National Archives, PROB 11 2102 f830, 237-8.

6. Information from Peter Guillery based on research for *The Survey of London: Islington*.

7. *The Ecclesiologist*, 16, 1855, 137. For Blyth, see H.M. Colvin, *A Biographical Dictionary of British Architects 1600-1840*, John Murray, 1978, 120.

8. *The Builder*, 13, 1855, 165.

9. See letter 27 Feb. 1836, Lancing College archive.

10. The 1830 exhibit was no. 1059 and that of 1831 no. 1099 (see A. Graves, *The Royal Academy of Arts: A Complete Dictionary of Contributors and their work from its foundation in 1769 to 1904*, George Bell and Sons, 1906).

11. Samuel Lewis junior, *The History and Topography of the Parish of St Mary Islington in the County of Middlesex*, J.H. Jackson, 1842, 362. Mortimer had been the first incumbent of St Mark's, Myddleton Square, and so would have known the Carpenter family.

12. Thomas Cromwell, *Walks Through Islington*, Sherwood, Gilbert & Piper, 1835, 192-3.

13. *The Ecclesiologist*, 16, 1855, 138-9.

14. Ibid., 139.

15. Ibid.

16. Ibid. which notes that about the same time Carpenter also produced designs for 'a sumptuous church, show[ing] very fair Middle-Pointed tracery'.

17. See Manchester Central Library, M6/1/53/18, 208; M6/1/49/1, 28; M6/1/53; exhibit no. 979 at the Royal Academy.

19. Manchester Central Library, M6/1/54/14.

20. Exhibit no. 977.

21. Drapers' Company, minutes 11 Mar. 1831.

22. Ibid., 15 Apr. and 13 May 1831.

23. Drapers' Company, minutes 12 Mar. 1836. Clearly in 1836 Carpenter was a reluctant entrepreneur, as he declined the offer and nothing happened for two years.

24. Ibid., 7 Apr. 1836.

25. Ibid., 6 Dec. 1838.

26. The designs (unsigned), dated 17 Nov. 1841, are in the Drapers' Company archive.

27. H.-R. Hitchcock, *Early Victorian Architecture in Britain*, Yale U.P., 1954, 129-30.

28. Christopher Hussey, 'Georgian London: Forgotten Squares', *Country Life*, 4 Mar. 1939, 228.

29. The wall plates were to be 5ins x 4ins, the rafters 5ins x 2¼ins, the joists 9ins x 2¼ins and the lintels 4ins. The upstairs floors were to be covered with 1in. deal, with 1¼ins downstairs. See Drapers' Company archive.

30. It is possible that Carpenter also designed the houses, shops and pub erected in Upper Barnsby Street and St George's Terrace though there is no proven link.
31. Hitchcock [note 27], 420.
32. Information from Peter Guilllery based on researches for *The Survey of London: Islington.*
33. R.C. Carpenter was District Surveyor for Clerkenwell. The street is today part of Farringdon Road.
34. Act 3° & 4° Victoria Cap cxii 23 July 1840, 2557.
35. Ibid.
36. Ibid.
37. Ibid., 2566, 2600-7.
38. Ibid., 2558.
39. Evidence given to the House of Commons Select Committee, 11 June 1840 (House of Lords Records Office).
40. Ibid., 7 Apr. 1848.
41. On 11 June 1840.
42. As note 39.
43. Ibid.
44. Act 5° Victoria Cap xlvii and Act 8° & 9° Victoria Cap xvii.
45. On 7 Apr. 1848. The landowner was Henry Charles Englefield.
46. Evidence given to the House of Commons Select Committee, 7 Apr. 1848 (House of Lords Records Office).
47. Act 11° & 12° Victoria Cap clxii.
48. E. Carter, *An Historical Geography of the Railways of the British Isles*, Cassell, 1959, 78; National Archives, RAIL 524, 1. For a full list of the railway projects with which Carpenter senior was involved, see Elliott [note 1], 568.
49. *Railway Times*, Jan.-July 1845, 513.
50. Ibid., 636. He is not mentioned in earlier prospectus e.g. *Railway Times*, Jan.-July 1845, 291, 370.
51. Ibid., 638, 686, 717, 770, 957.
52. See *North Devon Journal,* 18 Sep. 1845, 1 and the *Railway Times* Jan.-July 1845, 1107. He is not listed in a prospectus which was published in the *Railway Times* a little earlier in 1845 (p. 1059). This was a scheme to connect Northampton, Daventry, Leamington and Warwick with the main London line.
53. *Bradshaw's Railway Gazette*, Jan.-July 1845, 1059; Jul.-Oct. 1845, 435. None of these schemes obtained Parliamentary sanction.
54. MS letter Goodhart-Rendel to B. Handford, 29 Dec. 1945 (Lancing College archive).
55. He did the designs jointly with Brooks (letter 27 Feb. 1836, Lancing College archive). Correspondence between Carpenter and Woodard at Lancing College suggests that in 1836 Carpenter was in business with somebody called Brooks. Specifically, a letter of 23 Dec. 1836 from Brooks and Carpenter uses Carpenter's address in Myddleton Square. Brooks is also mentioned in another letter from Carpenter to Woodard, 27 Feb. 1836.
56. Pugin also used the same arrangement at St Mary, Newcastle upon Tyne, and St Thomas of Canterbury, Fulham (information from Dr R. O'Donnell).

57. By naming the area Munster Square those responsible were openly declaring the source of the German precedents.
58. *Building News*, 6 May 1881, 513.
59. Ibid.
60. Basil Clarke, *Parish Churches of London,* Batsford, 1966, 142.
61. *The Ecclesiologist*, 10, 1850, facing 352-4.
62. Ibid., 354.
63. Ibid., 353. The north aisle was added in 1882-3. The tower and spire were never built.
64. *The Ecclesiologist*, 13, 1852, 167.
65. Ibid.
66. Ibid., 286.
67. Ibid., 168.
68. Clarke [note 60], 142.
69. A. Wagner and A. Dale, *The Wagners of Brighton*, Phillimore, 1983.
70. See J.M. Crook, *William Burges and the High Victorian Dream*, John Murray, 1981, 209.
71. He was born at Windsor Castle on 13 June 1824 and baptised at Winkfield, Berkshire on 6 Aug. 1824.
72. She was the daughter of Joshua Watson, who according to Nicholas Taylor was 'the principal pillar of the Church Building Commission and "the greatest lay churchman of his day"' (N. Taylor, 'Wagnerian High Church', *Architectural Review*, 1965, 218).
73. Crook [note 70], 210.
74. He was educated at Eton from 1835, and went to Trinity College, Cambridge between 1842 and 1845. He was ordained a deacon in 1848 and a priest in 1849. He became perpetual curate of St Paul's in 1850 and vicar in 1873. He achieved national prominence through the Constance Kent case in which he refused to reveal the secrets of the confessional. He died in Brighton on 14 Jan. 1902, and was buried at the Lewes Road Cemetery on 18 Jan.
75. Nicholas Taylor describes him as 'a High Churchman of the old school ... a pre-Oxford Movement hierarchy of great private wealth and administrative ability, a masterful and intolerant upholder of the Establishment'. (Taylor [note 72], 214.
76. Letter 7 Feb. 1840 (ICBS file 2648, Lambeth Palace Library).
77. Letter from Teignmouth to the Bishop of Chichester, 24 June 1845 (Church Commissioners' file 16470, Church of England Record Centre); letter 16 July 1845 from Wagner to the Secretary of the ICBS says that the site was bought for 300 guineas and sold for £300 (ICBS file 2648).
78. The initial intention was to convert the Bethel Chapel 'into a Chapel of Ease for the use of Fishermen', while the school buildings would be 'altered or pulled down, and ... two three or more rooms built on its site', including a 'reading room ... [which would] be furnished with books and papers for their instruction and entertainment' (letters 4 July and 18 June 1844 from Cooper and Williams on behalf of H.M. Wagner to the Church Commissioners (Church Commissioners' file 16470). The cost was £9,036 3s. 11d.: the Commissioners gave £1,000 (file 16470) and the ICBS £500 (file 2648). The church had 1,117 seats of which 653 were free.

79. *The Ecclesiologist*, 5, 1846, 155-6.

80. Ibid., 8, 1848, 188-9.

81. Ibid, 10, 1850, 204-7.

82. The church was built on Terminus Road and was estimated to cost £8,956 and held 1,217 (ICBS file 4078). It was consecrated on 29 Sep. 1853 and demolished in 1957. The first incumbent was the Revd Thomas Coombe.

83. *The Ecclesiologist*, 8, 1847, 55-6.

84. See ibid., 5, 1846, 203 and a letter from Carpenter which says the spire of St Paul's should be 283 feet tall. The collapse of Chichester Cathedral spire in 1861 unsettled the church authorities, and ensured that the original design for St Paul's was never executed. Instead, between 1873-5 Herbert Carpenter designed a wooden lantern tower. The tower and spire of All Saints were not finished (A. Dale, *Brighton Churches*, Routledge, 1989, 102.)

85. Figures for All Saints taken from ICBS file 4078 and those for St Paul's from drawings held in the RIBA Drawings Collection.

86. See 'Correspondence' in *Architectural Review*, 1919, 37; 1918, 109. *The Ecclesiologist*, 5, 1846, 156, commented upon 'The plan, [which] necessarily [is] somewhat irregular from the exigencies of orientation and the difficulties of the site.' There is also a letter from Carpenter in the same issue (p. 203) where he says difficulties connected with the site 'oblige me to place my principal entrance at the east end, there not being sufficient space on either the north or south sides for approaches'.

87. West Sussex Record Office, Cap I/11/, 3-4. The site eventually cost £1,480.

88. Ibid., 37.

89. Ibid., 75-6.

90. Ibid., 44.

91. West Sussex Record Office, 1/11/1, 135.

92. Clarke, Notebooks 7, 2, held by the CCB Library, Church House, Westminster.

93. J.M. Crook (ed.), C.L. Eastlake, *A History of the Gothic Revival*, Leicester U.P., 1970, 224.

94. H.S. Goodhart-Rendel, 'The Churches of Brighton and Hove', *Architectural Review*, 1918, 27.

95. *The Ecclesiologist*, 2, 1843, 171.

96. Ibid., 4, 1845, 23.

97. See ICBS file 3026.

98. *The Ecclesiologist*, 2, 1843, 94, 137.

99. A north aisle was added in 1871.

100. See ICBS file 3026.

101. Goodhart-Rendel Index, RIBA Library.

102. Carpenter's drawings dated 23 Jan. 1844 are in the Berkshire Record Office, D/B 43B/6/1/1-6.

103. *The Ecclesiologist*, 4, 1845, 138.

104. Oxford Record Office, c747 f. 121-4.

105. *The Ecclesiologist*, 14, 1853, 453.

106. Ibid.

107. A.W.N. Pugin, *The Present State of Ecclesiastical Architecture in England*, Charles Dolman, 1843, 108.

108. R. O'Donnell, 'Pugin as a Church Architect', in P. Atterbury & C. Wainwright (eds), *Pugin: A Gothic Passion*, Yale U.P., 1994, 67.

109. Pugin [note 107], 19.

110. See 1841 census, HO107 Bk 5, fol. 15.

111. See editions of the *Post Office Directory* from 1849.

112. See the *Post Office Directory* for 1851 and the census, HO107 1507, f. 187, 42. The students were William Smith and Edward Mathews.

113. *The Ecclesiologist*, 16, 1855, 137.

114. This is grave 5902 in square 13. It cost £15 15s. See Highgate Cemetery records.

115. *The Ecclesiologist*, 15, 1854, 267 refers to a 'domestic calamity'.

116. Ibid., 16, 1855, 49, referred to Carpenter being seriously ill.

117. See the death certificate.

118. See *The Ecclesiologist*, 16, 1855, 137. A memorial tomb was designed by William Slater, reviewed in ibid., 311, 400, and erected at Highgate Cemetery before the end of the year.

119. National Archives, PROB 11 2215 f336.

120. IR 26 2060 f676.

5

George Edmund Street (1824-81): An Architect on Holiday

Neil Jackson

A great and long-lasting controversy followed the publication of George Edmund Street's designs for the Royal Courts of Justice (the Law Courts) in 1871. It was ironic, therefore, that some of the agitators would have promoted the continental town hall model, and particularly those of Ypres, Louvain, Oudenaard and Brussels, as a solution to what they perceived as the shortcomings of Street's picturesque design for the Strand elevation.[1] No leading mid-nineteenth-century architect, they should have realised, had travelled as much on the continent, and had been as prolific in their observations, as had Street. These were buildings which he knew well and to which he had referred before, specifically in the Foreign Office competition of 1856-7. But blind historicism, then as now, was not Street's practice; his architecture was to be synthetic, eclectic and, in its way, wholly original. For six months Street held his tongue 'under great provocation' and when he did eventually launch his defence in a pamphlet on New Year's Day, 1872, he wrote that if anyone 'can find any feature in my design which is copied from any thing else anywhere, I shall be happy to change it'.[2] In his enquiry into *The Dilemma of Style*, J. Mordaunt Crook suggests that the Law Courts is as much Italian as Nikolaus Pevsner thought it English and Henry-Russell Hitchcock, French.[3] This chapter will examine the basis for Street's eclecticism, how he worked, where he travelled, and what he looked at. Even though the difficulties which eventually faced him at the Law Courts are strangely prescient of our times, his story is still, in a way, a very modern, cosmopolitan one: 'In these days of railways and rapid travelling,' he was to write in 1855, 'there is scarcely any excuse for stopping quietly at home.'[4]

Few English architects are as well memorialised as George Edmund Street (**5.1**). At the Law Courts he sits in the second bay of the Great Hall, bearded and balding, with dividers in hand and a plan unrolled across his knees. In the frieze which wraps around the plinth, he is shown again, more than once, supervising tradesmen and craftsmen who carry on with their work apparently oblivious to their architect's spectral death mask which hovers above them. When he died on 18 December 1881, following a stroke at the age of 57, he was without doubt the country's pre-eminent architect. He was President of the Royal Institute of British Architects (RIBA) and had been awarded the Institute's Royal Gold Medal for Architecture in 1874, allowing his name to be later engraved on *both* sides of the entrance hall at the RIBA's present headquarters on Portland Place; and at the Royal Academy of Arts on Piccadilly he was both Professor of Architecture and Treasurer. His colleagues at the RIBA subscribed towards a bust of him,[5] to be carved by Henry Armstead RA, the author of the monument at the Law Courts where yet another bust can be found. Had he lived a year longer to see the opening of that building,[6] he would doubtless have been knighted. He instead received the honour of a burial beneath the nave of Westminster Abbey, alongside Sir George Gilbert Scott (d.1878) and Sir Charles Barry (d.1860), and over a century later the Greater London Council memorialised him with a blue plaque on the wall of his house at 14 Cavendish Place.

Pre-eminence in architecture guarantees neither total approval nor lasting fame. In 1877, long after the row over the published design of the Law Courts died down and the building was emerging from the ground, George Cavendish Bentinck MP opined that the tower 'will not be worth the cost of its foundations'[7] – and by the time of its completion the Law Courts was clearly the swansong of the Gothic Revival.[8] It was his assistant Richard Norman Shaw who later commented, 'Street would not compromise anything' adding, perhaps in the same interview, 'We were trying to revive a style which was quite unsuited to the present day. Since 1880, however, we have been gradually awakening to this fact.'[9] It was not that anything was particularly wrong with the building; as a piece of functional design it was to serve its purpose well, but, as Norman Shaw suggested, its picturesque arrangement and polychromy belonged to a passing generation, and taste was moving on. Street's reputation suffered as much as any architect's in the early twentieth century's general rejection of High Victorian architecture,[10] although his buildings largely survived. Following his son Arthur's *Memoir* of 1888 and Georgina Goddard King's publication, in 1916, of his notes and papers, together with a lengthy introduction,[11] little was written of him until H.S. Goodhart-Rendel's interpretation of *English Architecture since the*

5.1: George Edmund Street in about 1850. (*A.E. Street*, Memoir of George Edmund Street RA, 1824–1881, *John Murray, 1888, facing p. 19.*)

Regency (1953).[12] Perhaps this renewed interest prompted Hitchcock[13] to re-evaluate his work in 1960, as did John Summerson[14] a decade later. But by now the Victorian Society, founded in 1957, was encouraging a change in popular taste and soon other architectural historians, such as Basil Clarke[15] and Michael Port,[16] were taking Street's architecture seriously, an interest which peaked again around 1980.[17] Street has never received the full-blown architectural biography given to some of his peers, such as his employer and frequent adversary, George Gilbert Scott, or his assistants, Philip Webb and Norman Shaw; instead, his architecture has been analysed bit by bit, almost by attrition. Foremost amongst these analyses, and, indeed, amongst nineteenth-century architectural studies, is David Brownlee's 1984 monograph, *The Law Courts: The Architecture of George Edmund Street*.[18] Coupled with the fact that his personal papers were destroyed in the bombing of Bath in 1942,[19] the problem with Street, and perhaps the reason why there has never emerged a complete, critical overview, is that his architectural work was so wide-ranging and his writing so extensive that any part of it, as Brownlee has demonstrated, could be a study in itself.[20] Street's foreign architectural tours are just one fragment of that greater picture.

Street in France and Germany

In September 1850 Street crossed the English Channel for the first time. In ten days he visited, Paris, Chartres, Alençon, Caen, Rouen and Amiens, and developed an enthusiasm for foreign travel which he sustained throughout his life. His tours were always well planned and hastily conducted, a great number of buildings being seen in a very short time. He sketched almost unceasingly, attentive to detail yet sparing of line, recording what he needed and no more. Thus each year he would go, as he said, 'sketchbook in hand, with some ancient town or thrice noble cathedral set before him as his goal'.[21] Over the next 32 years he crossed the Channel as many times if not more, visiting and revisiting countries until he knew their architecture well. Only the Franco-Prussian war of 1870, it seems, thwarted him and in that year he went to Scotland. The result of these travels was not just a pluralist yet always Gothic architectural style, but books, lectures and papers in which he expounded the glories (and failures) of the foreign architecture he had seen as well as promoting the idea of architectural tourism. Street's intention was not so much to discover new solutions but to find ways of developing his existing Gothic vocabulary. 'I conceive that one of the most important opportunities for the discovery of the best mode of improving our style,' he told the Oxford Architectural Society in February 1852, 'is the careful study of Continental examples ... We have to go to all those lands to discover in

windows, stair turret and corner tower, betray only Street's experience of French and German architecture. The adoption of the high French roof became a frequent trope in Street's work, as did the other recognisably French feature, the rounded chancel or apsidal east end. Similarly, as his designs for Lille Cathedral (1856) and Crimea Memorial Church (1857)[41] competitions show, transepts might be reduced, in the French manner, but not totally excluded.

In Street's paper on 'The True Principles of Architecture,' read before the Oxford Architectural Society in February 1852, he had noted that 'the wonderful beauty of the apsidal east ends abroad ought to be gladly seized upon'.[42] This he did, for coincident with the two competition churches, came St Andrew, Firsby, Lincolnshire (1856), followed by Cowley church, Oxford (1859, unbuilt); St John, Howsham, Yorkshire (1859-60); St James the Less, Westminster (1858-61); St John the Evangelist, Hollington, Staffordshire (1859-61); All Saints, Denstone, Staffordshire (1860-2); St Philip and St James, Oxford (1860-2, spire 1864-6); St Mary, Fawley, Berkshire (1865-6); St Mary Magdalene, Paddington (1865-8 *et seq.*); All Saints, Rome (first design, 1872); St Paul within the Walls, Rome (1874); St John the Divine, Lambeth (1870-4, tower 1888-9 under A.E. Street); St Andrew, East Heslerton, Yorkshire (1877); St James, Kingston, Dorset (1873-80); All Saints, Rome (final design, commenced 1880). All had apsidal east ends. Although this list is incomplete it is nevertheless representative and shows that whereas Street's early enthusiasm for apsidal east ends waned, he never quite rejected them.

Street frequently used high roofs and a long ridge for his naves; less common was the unbroken ridge-line over both nave and chancel. Where he employed the apsidal east end, he would sometimes make the chancel's roof higher than the nave's, an idea which came from St Mary the Virgin at Stone, Kent. Located about fifteen miles from Sundridge and Brasted, Street would almost certainly have known of this thirteenth-century church even before he was asked to restore it in around 1859-60. His long essay about it published in *Archaeologia Cantiana* in 1860,[43] describes its condition following the fire of 1638 and the subsequent rebuilding (1638-40), and confirms that he raised the chancel walls 'to their old height, so as to admit of the restoration of the groining,' with the result that 'the chancel roof is now much higher than that of the nave'.[44] It was an idea which he tried early on in his 1858 design for St Ursula, the church for the English community at Berne, Switzerland;[45] but that church was never built. However, the arrangement can be seen at All Saints, Denstone (**5.3**), St Mary, Fawley and St Andrew, East Heslerton. Rib-vaulting, as at Stone,[46] was introduced at

5.4: At St John, Howsham, Yorkshire (1859-60), the break between the roof of the nave and that of the rounded chancel is almost imperceptible. (*Author.*)

both Fawley and East Heslerton, but the timber ceiling at Denstone can only suggest that the chancel's high roof was for external effect, height being of 'immense importance'. It was, however, more common for Street to allow the chancel roof to drop down, although the difference in height at the ridge-line was sometimes almost imperceptible, as at St John, Howsham (**5.4**), and St John the Evangelist, Hollington, where only the coping stones and perhaps a cross at the apex marked the change. Whether the roof stepped up or down, at this point, the internal result was the same: the introduction of the chancel arch, beloved by the Ecclesiologists. This may have been another of those 'Anglicanisms'. In some instances, as in the unbuilt scheme for St Dionis Backchurch, London (1857),[47] where space was restricted, or St John the Evangelist, Whitwell-on-the-Hill, Yorkshire (1858-60), where it was not, Street failed to mark the chancel by running the ridge-line through from one gable end to the other, but then cut the east end off square, in the English manner. It is as if he believed that only the large scale of the competition churches permitted the use of both the continuous ridge-line and the rounded east end; he managed both at his great brick church of All Saints, Sculcoates, Hull, in 1866-9 (**5.5**).[48]

The use of brick in the coastal East Riding of Yorkshire was a long-standing practice. A brickyard had been opened in Hull at the start of the fourteenth century and the town's walls, as well parts of the fourteenth-century church of Holy Trinity,[49] were built of brick. Indeed, this church constituted, as the Revd Thomas James had put it in 1847, 'probably the most ancient as well as the most worthy specimen of Ecclesiastical brick building still existing in England'.[50] The proximity of Hull, as a trading port, to the Low Countries and the Hanseatic cities would have further encouraged the use of brickwork,[51] something to which Street applied himself in his tours of Germany and Belgium in 1851 and 1854. 'One of the most important facts which we can learn here,' he told the Oxford Architectural Society in 1855, 'is, that brick is not only good outside, but just as much inside a church.'[52] Yet he was not wholly uncritical of German brickwork, saying that in north Germany the buildings have 'an air of great coarseness',[53] and, more precisely, that German brickwork 'teaches us, distinctly and unmistakeably, that brick is no material for window traceries'.[54] His assessment of German brick building was influenced by what he had seen in northern Italy in 1853, the subject of the book he was then, in 1855, preparing. 'Though the

5.5: North German brick churches influenced the design of All Saints, Sculcoates, Hull (1866-9). The campanile was added later by Samuel Musgrove. (*English Heritage, National Monuments Record, 8871/3909.*)

brickwork of Lübeck,' he told his audience, 'is far inferior, in delicacy and beauty, to that which I have seen in Italy, there is much that can be learned from it.'[55] So although the pilaster strips, which decorate the apex of the west gable at All Saints, Hull, are brick and very Germanic, the plate tracery is carried out in stone.

Street seems to have learned more from German detailing than from the general execution there of medieval buildings as a whole. Some features which he adopted could be described as generic, such as the dormer windows set within the steep roof of the Adderley Park Institute at Saltley, Birmingham (1854-5),[56] or the pilaster strips in the west gable of All Saints, Hull. However, some buildings which he admired, such as the Rathaus at Ratisbon (now Regensburg),[57] visited in 1851, offered particulars soon apparent in his own work, although it cannot be said with certainty that this was their only source. The Rathaus had a first-floor window set beneath a pinnacled canopy and opening on to a balcony supported by a single shaft rising between two arched, ground-floor windows. This idiosyncrasy must have caught Street's eye, for he used just such a composition, developed as an oriel window beneath a hipped roof, at Cuddesdon College, Oxfordshire (1852-4) (**5.6**);[58] and what could be called the memory of the pinnacled canopy is traced in the decorated gable ends of the saddle-roof spire added by his son at St John the Evangelist, Torquay (1861-71, tower 1884-5).

Identifying sources for such details is almost impossible without the evidence of Street's sketchbooks to which he referred long after the journeys which produced them.[59] Only eight sketchbooks survive – six in the RIBA Drawings Collection at the Victoria and Albert Museum, and two at the Royal Academy of Arts, also in London. The RIBA sketchbooks record his trips to Germany of 1851;[60] to northern France in 1858;[61] to France and northern Spain in the autumn of 1861 (in two volumes);[62] and to the south of France and Spain in the spring of the following year.[63] Another was compiled during a visit to Wiltshire, Somerset and Devon in August 1880, and then to Cumberland, Yorkshire (North Riding) and Cheshire the following month.[64] The Royal Academy sketchbooks, both from 1879, record his visit to northern France[65] of that year together with examples of English and Welsh architecture.[66] The drawings are in pencil, with plans, sections, perspectives and details jostling for space on the page. Although sketched quickly, and usually done while he was standing up,[67] the lines are confident and unhesitating, with features such as capitals and windows sometimes drawn with greater pressure, for effect. Where a doorway or window was symmetrical, only one half is fully delineated, the other just blocked out; plans show measurements in feet and inches; margin notes

5.6: At Cuddesdon College, Oxfordshire (1852-4), Street probably based the idiosyncratic design for the oriel window on the Rathaus at Ratisbon (now Regensburg). (*Author.*)

describe what is seen and usually give the place and date. He heeded his own later advice to students at the Royal Academy: 'Draw accurately, firmly, and, as far as may be, with a single stroke …' and to represent 'with a few lines the effect of several.'[68] In the later sketchbooks, a larger proportion of drawings are more complete and more heavily rendered than before, and a number of sketches cover a double-page spread. But this greater attention to detail does not suggest any slowing down on his part: in ten days in August 1879 Street filled 144 pages of his sketchbook. In 1918, soon after Arthur Street had presented some of his father's sketchbooks to the RIBA,[69] Walter Millard, who had been an assistant in Street's office, wrote in the *RIBA Journal*:

> he drew things that he cared about because he cared about them and wanted to know all he could get to know about them … Fastening on the salient points of his subject, and ignoring non-essentials, he would mark down with prompt decision and with precision just what he wished to record, and no more. He seized on what he wished to record, on what to him signified, and drew it — and it alone … Free and fearless might be apt enough terms to apply to his handiwork, perhaps it would be even still better described as incisive and masterly.[70]

175

5.7: The influence of Street's visit to Italy was first apparent at the vicarage at Colnbrook, Buckinghamshire (1854). (*Author.*)

By the time of his visits to Spain in 1861–3, Street was supplementing his hand drawings with photographs, some purchased and others taken himself, when he could. 'I have never yet taken a photograph of Zaragoza, neither in January, May, nor yet July,' he noted in *Gothic Architecture in Spain*, adding, 'you cannot photograph the outside of a building in a streaming rain.'[71]

Street in northern Italy

Street's first visit to northern Italy came in the summer of 1853 and the record of that trip, *Brick and Marble in the Middle Ages*, was published two years later. The influence, however, was apparent much sooner, both in his lectures and papers and in his architecture. The result was such that, as his son remembered, he complained on 'labouring in some quarters under the entirely undeserved imputation of being a blind admirer of everything Italian'.[72] His critical, not blind admiration for Italian medieval architecture was soon evident in way he treated the windows of his smaller domestic buildings. In the vicarages at Boyn Hill, Maidenhead, Berkshire

(1855-7), and at Colnbrook, near Slough, Buckinghamshire (1854) (**5.7**), he inserted heavily mullioned windows beneath a brick relieving arch and recessed tympanum in the Italian manner where, as he told an audience at the Architectural Exhibition in 1859, 'window heads are always arched, and supported on shafts'. The result of this, he explained, was that 'you do not see a crack in every window-head in a building, as you generally do in modern London,' and 'you can put either sashes, French casements, or whatever contrivance for holding the plate glass you happen to prefer'.[73] It was a logical arrangement which he had tried even before his visit to Italy, at the schoolhouse at Inkpen, and one which Butterfield had used at least as early as 1851,[74] but the evidence he saw in Italy authenticated its use.

It was in Italy that he also found evidence for a truly constructional use of polychromy. 'The brick churches of Italy,' he told the Oxford Architectural Society in his lecture of 1855, 'are remarkable in that they owe much of their beautiful effect either to the mixture of stone with brick, or to the exquisite moulding of the brick, and the care and delicacy with which it was built ...'[75] He was to use colour, soon after his return from Italy, in the chancel of St Peter, Chalfont St Peter, Buckinghamshire (1857), and at the Colnbrook vicarage. The energetic banding and diapering of the first, however, is Butterfieldian, while the second is more Italianate, particularly in the use of alternating colours in the voussoirs.[76] At All Saints, Boyn Hill (1855-7 *et seq*) (**5.8**), where both the constructional polychromy and cut brickwork were particularly Italianate, the colouration of the exterior extends throughout the interior of the church. There the red and black brickwork of the windows and the aisle arcade is not only interspersed with white stone, but is also cut in a form of dog-tooth. Such treatment immediately recalls, but does not duplicate, the four chromolithographic plates included in *Brick and Marble in the Middle Ages* (**5.9**), which show yellow, pink and black polychromatic brickwork arches.[77]

In the introduction to *Brick and Marble* Street acknowledges 'the obligations which not only all who travel in Italy, but all who are interested in good architecture, owe to Mr Ruskin'.[78] It was not only Ruskin's writings on Italy, especially *The Stones of Venice*, to which Street was referring but also his *Seven Lamps of Architecture*. From this book it was 'The Lamp of Power' which was most influential in Street's earlier work, for it not only encouraged his use of such French devices as in the continuous ridge-line and the apsidal east end, both of which gave French churches a sense of solidity rarely found in their more aggregative English counterparts, but also in the adoption of the robust Italian campanile. The best example of this is at St James the Less, Westminster, begun the year after Street's second trip to northern Italy

5.8: In 1855-7, Street used Italianate polychromy in both the exterior and interior of All Saints, Boyn Hill, Maidenhead, Berkshire. (*Author.*)

5.9: A chromolithographic plate from *Brick and Marble in the Middle Ages* (1855), facing p. 67, showing the polychromatic archivolts of the Broletto at Brescia.

of 1857. The illustration which appeared in *The Ecclesiologist* of December 1859 emphasised the monumentality and relative isolation of the campanile, attached to the body of the church only by a small arcade.[79] In addressing the Italian campanile, Ruskin had written that 'where the height of the tower itself is to be made apparent, it must be … detached as a campanile' and 'there must be one bounding line from base to coping'.[80] This Street does and in so doing achieves what he, writing in *Brick and Marble*, calls 'breadth of effect; … the very point in which northern architects were most careless to succeed'.[81] It was breadth of effect which aggregative English churches largely lacked, and which Street achieved through the incorporation of these continental features. St James the Less offers his most pronounced example of the free-standing campanile,[82] but at St Dionis, Backchurch, St Mary, Fawley, St Andrew, East Heslerton, St John the Evangelist, Whitwell-on-the-Hill, St Paul within the Walls, Rome, and even in Street's unbuilt designs for both the 1857 Foreign Office competition[83] and for All Saints, Rome, the tower is solid, massive, nearly detached and with one 'bounding line'.

An examination of St James the Less (**5.10**), however reveals many more continental features than the campanile and rounded east end.[84] Indeed, according to Charles Eastlake's *A History of the Gothic Revival* (1872), 'Here

179

5.10: Charles Eastlake thought St James the Less, Westminster (1858-61), to be 'eminently un-English'. (*Author.*)

5.11: The polychromatic belfry window at St James the Less betrays both Italian and French influence. (*Author.*)

the whole character of the building, whether we regard its plan, its distinctive features, its external or internal decoration is eminently un-English.'[85] The most pronounced feature of the dominant tower is its octagonal spire with corner spirelets. Street had seen examples of this type of spire at both Tournai, in Belgium, visited in 1854 – 'the central spire is octagonal with four square slated turrets at the angles'[86] – and at Genoa, visited in 1857.[87] Hitchcock suggests that the generic model for this spire was French,[88] but Street's comments on the spires of Genoa, given in a lecture to the Architectural Exhibition in April 1859, and the fact that he had been to Genoa not long before starting work on St James the Less, would suggest the latter provenance.[89] In that lecture, in which he spoke specifically only of buildings which he had actually seen, he noted that the Genoese campanili 'are more northern in their character than the other, and are plain towers with two pierced stages at the summit, and octagonal stone spires, with pyramidal pinnacles at their feet'.[90] At St James the Less there is only one distinct upper stage, but the elaborate polychromatic belfry window within it provides, on each face of the tower, a variety of specific, and generic, references to both Italian and French architecture (**5.11**). The more curious the feature, the more likely there is to be a precedent for it: for example, the circular discs bearing knob-like roundels which are set both within and on either side of the window-head meet Street's description of the marble incrustation on the façade of the Palazzo Priuli in Venice: 'From the centre of the medallions of marble small balls of marble project, fixed with metal, and giving great life and beauty to the medallions.'[91] The position of these discs within the window-head further recalls the archway above the Ponte Paradiso in Venice where 'The incrusted circles of marble … give great life to the spandrel beneath the arch.'[92] Yet it was more often an understanding of the principle, rather than a reproduction of the precedent, which Street sought to achieve. In the cusping of the belfry windows, for example, he followed the good practice which he had recognised in the campanile at S. Andrea in Mantua.[93] 'The relative proportion of the cusps in this,' he wrote in *Brick and Marble*, 'and in most other Italian buildings is very good. In trefoils, for instance, the upper cusp is by far smaller than the lower; and in all good cusping it must be so.'[94] To do otherwise was to design, he argued, without feeling.

As St James the Less began construction in 1858, Street travelled once again to France[95] and that December noted in *The Ecclesiologist* how, 'A short holiday among French churches, has left so many pleasant recollections of new ideas received, new thoughts suggested, ancient memories revived afresh.'[96] The effect of these pleasant recollections upon the church is clearly

5.12: A Venetian window shaft and a carved French capital influenced the design of the aisle arcade at St James the Less. (*Author.*)

demonstrated through his sketchbook of that tour. On 29 September he sketched the rounded east end of St-Pierre, Montmartre, in Paris, where four tall stepped buttresses separate the lancet windows.[97] Three days earlier he drew the paired columns (the shafts are 7 feet tall and 5 inches in diameter) in the east wall of the cloister at St-Georges de Boscherville, near Rouen,[98] and, in its chapter house — 'an exquisite example of the earliest pointed work, full of delicate and beautiful detail'[99] — the capitals, where human figures intermingle with stiff-leaf carving.[100] At St-Jacques, Compiègne, where he complained how little there was in the church 'to detain an architect beyond the general effect',[101] he sketched the rib vaulting radiating out into the polygonal apse.[102] Each of these features was reinterpreted and then incorporated at St James the Less.

'The brick churches of Germany and Italy,' Street told the Worcester Diocesan Architectural Society in September 1855, 'were alike finished inside and as well as outside with red brick.'[103] This he had done to effect at All Saints, Boyn Hill, and now Street repeated the strategy at St James the Less. The polychromy of the external red and black bricks is extended across the arcade and aisle walls, while in the chancel vaulting white stones, bordered with black brick, add a third colour. In the arcade the brick arises are cut to a spade shape and each arch drops hard onto the abacus of a carved capital which is supported, in turn, upon a dumpy, almost compressed, banded granite shaft (**5.12**). This assembly is a melange of ideas generated by a window-shaft seen in Venice and later illustrated in *Brick and Marble*;[104] but Street has now infused the composition with a robust sense of constructional strength, or what he called a 'principal of truth',[105] such as he recognised in French architecture.

Street in Spain

Street made his first trip to Spain in September 1861, while St James the Less was under construction, and he returned there in 1862 and again in the autumn of 1863. *Gothic Architecture in Spain*, was published two years later. In 1861 most of the superstructure of the church would have been complete and, as far as can be seen, built as it is shown in the perspective in *The Ecclesiologist* in 1859.[106] Visible in that illustration are the paired columns of the short arcade set between the tower and the north porch, an arrangement which Street had already seen, and admired, in the cloister at S. Zenone, Verona, in 1853. Here, 'the arches are very small, and of brick, supported on coupled shafts of red Veronese marble … and rest on a dwarf wall'.[107] In *Brick and Marble* he included a full-page chromolithograph of the cloister arcade and the comment, 'I doubt whether I have ever seen a more lovely cloister than this.'[108] On his Spanish tour of 1860 he was to see comparable arrangements; there he measured and drew similar cloister arcades at San Pablo, Barcelona; at Gerona Cathedral; and at the fortified monastery of Montmajour at Arles.[109]

Spain also provided new ideas and its most immediate influence can be seen in the railings which surround St James the Less. When the church was published in *The Builder* in June 1861,[110] it was shown behind a low wall comprising brick piers and a stone copings. In the event, what was built were cast-iron railings topped with wrought-iron crestings representing lilies. The wall around the boundary would have been one of the last building works at the site, so a late change to its design could have been accommodated. On 25 September that year, Street was sketching just such lily crestings on railings which closed off the chapels within the cloister at Barcelona Cathedral (**5.13**).[111] In *Gothic Architecture in Spain* he wrote:

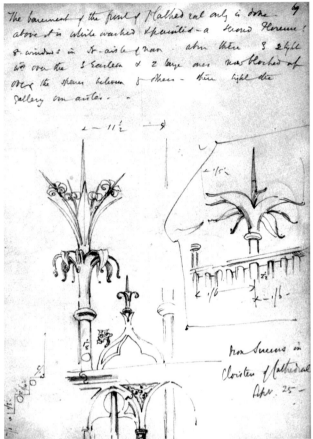

5.13: The cloister railings at Barcelona Cathedral, which Street sketched in 1861, caused him to alter his design for St James the Less. (*RIBA Drawings & Archives Collection, SKB 34/4, p. 69.*)

I have before noticed the excellence of the smiths' work in the Spanish churches. Yet though their work is of the latest age of Gothic, it is never marked by that nauseous redundance of ornament in which so many of the most active metal-workers of the present day seem to revel. Hence it is always worthy of study.[112]

The description which he then supplies might be applied as well to the railings at St James the Less: 'In all the screens here the lower part is very simple, consisting generally of nothing but vertical bars ... The ornament is reserved for the open traceried crestings, with bent and sharply-cut crockets.'[113] However, Street's originality in ironwork, as seen internally at All Saints, Boyn Hill, had already led to the suggestion of copyism,[114] but this is something which he strongly refuted. 'The iron screenwork at Boyn Hill,' he wrote in *The Ecclesiologist* in 1858, 'is not copied from that at Verona.'[115] Similarly, it should not be thought that the ironwork at St James the Less was copied from, rather than inspired by, that at Barcelona.

185

Street's two books on European architecture, *Brick and Marble in the Middle Ages* and the later *Gothic Architecture in Spain*, introduced him to a new readership, the continental traveller. In 1855 Thomas Cook had taken his first group of overseas tourists on a circuit which included Brussels, Cologne, the Rhine, Heidelberg, Baden-Baden, Strasbourg and Paris, where the objective was the great International Exhibition, before returning to London via Le Havre or Dieppe. In his Preface to *Brick and Marble*, published that same year, Street wrote how in recent years he had travelled 'by the noble cities of Belgium, up the church-besprinkled banks of the fair Rhine, over the plains of Bavaria, and through much that was most noble and interesting in different parts of France and Germany'.[116] With the exception of Bavaria, this was the route taken by Cook's tourists. So when Cook led his first tour to Italy in 1864, it is not unlikely that some copies of *Brick and Marble* were amongst the luggage. 'I conceive that I shall be rendering some service,' Street told its readers, 'if I venture to show, by a simple narrative of a tour undertaken in the course of the year before last, how much it is possible to accomplish with pleasure, and, when one has some definite object in view, with profit of no common kind, even in a short holiday.'[117] Cook's first tour to Spain, although he did not lead it himself, was in 1872.[118] Visiting all the principal towns and monuments in the north, centre, south, and south-west of Spain, it was more extensive than Street's travels had been but *Gothic Architecture in Spain* would have played its part. Compared to *Brick and Marble*, this book took a broader view. There were far fewer details of windows, ironwork and suchlike but a great number of plans, which the earlier book's first edition omitted altogether. *The Guardian* (a High Church weekly) thought it 'one of the most curious and valuable architectural works which we have received for some time' while the *Edinburgh Review* judged it 'a useful addition to the very few books with which a traveller may profitable equip himself for the Peninsula'.[119] There survives, however, the tone of the travelogue, which *The Ecclesiologist* had regretted in its review of *Brick and Marble:* 'This handsome and instructive volume would have been, we confess, more to our own taste, had the "travel-talk" been omitted.'[120] Within three paragraphs of the beginning of his book on Spanish architecture, Street was reassuring his readers that 'So far as the inns and food are to be considered, I do not think there is much need ordinarily for violent grumbling.' That is all right then; but, 'All ideas of English manners and customs must be carefully left behind; and if the travelling-clothes are donned with a full intention to do in Spain as Spain does, there is small fear of their owner suffering very much.'[121] Although such advice might today seem out of place in a book on architecture, it would have been appreciated by architectural tourists who, searching for medieval architecture abroad, had little else to guide them.

The first John Murray *Handbook for Travellers* had been published in 1836; it covered Holland, Belgium, Prussia, northern Germany and Switzerland. The volume on northern Italy, written by Sir Francis Palgrave came out in 1842, with a second edition following four years later.[122] It is likely that it was this later edition to which Street referred when he wrote in the Preface to *Brick and Marble*, 'I cannot speak too highly of the assistance afforded to the architectural student by Murray's Handbook of Northern Italy.'[123] Murray's first volume on Spain, written by Richard Ford, appeared in 1845 and sold well; Street probably used Ford's fourth edition of 1858.[124] Of it he wrote,

> Mr Ford's *Handbook of Spain* has been of great service to me, not only because it was the only guide to be had, and on account of the charm of his style, but because it had the rare excellence (in a Guide-book) of constantly referring to local guides and authorities, and so enabling me to turn at once to the books most likely to aid me in my work [125]

In 1855 Murray's *Handbook to Portugal*[126] joined that on Spain and, together with Street's *Gothic Architecture in Spain*, probably formed the basis of Karl Baedeker's first edition of *Spain and Portugal,* published in 1898.[127] Georgiana King, in her Introductory Note to the 1914 edition of Street's *Gothic Architecture in Spain*, observed that '*Baedeker* is for the best part carved out of Street, and for the rest inaccurate as well as inadequate.'[128]

Street's 'travel-talk' is often transferred directly from the pencilled notes in sketchbooks which serve as diaries and account books as well as architectural records. Thus we learn that in September 1858 the cost of the ferry to Le Havre was £1 8s. 9d.[129] It was also by steamboat that he travelled, in September 1861, from Valencia to Barcelona:

> Arrived at 11.30 and after nearly an hours delay first roasting in a boat with a crowd of other passengers & luggage then jostling with a crowd on the quay whilst the *douaniers* finished their several bundles of cigarettes, we walked off to our Inn the Fonda del Viente on the Rambla [*sic*]. After a much later breakfast — neither of us having tasted anything since leaving Valencia — we started for a ramble'.[130]

The Spanish sketchbooks contain many more anecdotal entries than the others, which make for a colourful account. On 19 September 1861 Street rose early to inspect the cathedral at Toledo:

> Went to the Cathedral at 7-0 am — but found it too dark to sketch the subjects on the N. side of the Choir. One must not complain of this for one of the great beauties of the churches is the suceeding [*sic*] beauty of

5.14: St Mary, Holmbury St Mary, Surrey (1879). Pevsner thought it to be enigmatic: it shows little of Street's earlier enthusiasm for foreign architecture. (*Author.*)

light & shade which is provided by the deep gloom of some parts & the brightness of others. I never saw a church in which this was so much the case as Toledo Cathl.[131]

Yet at Toledo he has cause to complain that 'Dogs are perpetually running about and fighting in Spanish churches'[132] while in Barcelona it is '… sundry melancholy cats who are perpetually howling & prowling about both church & cloister & making vigorous efforts to occupy stalls in the choir during service whence they are chased by little choir boys and large priests with much energy!'[133] In finding their way into *Gothic Architecture in Spain*, these observations were sometimes augmented by other memories: 'there are some geese cooped up in one corner,' he wrote of the cloister at Barcelona Cathedral, 'who look as if their lives were being sacrificed in order to provide *patés* for the canons'.[134] Even so, as an assimilated account of three tours of the country, *Gothic Architecture in Spain* does not provide quite the same sense of immediacy as does the first edition of *Brick and Marble in the Middle Ages*.

In 1874 the second and enlarged edition of *Brick and Marble* secured, if that was necessary, Street's reputation as a writer on architecture. In that year John Ruskin declined to accept the award of the Royal Gold Medal for Architecture and the RIBA, under George Gilbert Scott's presidency, transferred the award to Street.[135] Because it was the custom to award the medal every fourth year to a (British) architectural *litterateur*,[136] such as Ruskin or, in 1871, James Fergusson, Street's award was seen to be for his literary achievement. 'Mr Street is an author,' Scott said in making the presentation, 'of no mean eminence, and his book on the *Brick and Marble Architecture of North Italy*, and his *Gothic Architecture in Spain* will always stand forth as practical evidence of this fact, not to mention the more fugitive productions of his pen.'[137] Yet Street was not there to hear the address or to receive the medal: his wife Mariquita, who had accompanied him on many of his continental travels, had died fewer than three weeks earlier.[138]

During the next few years, while the Law Courts' construction ground on, Street also busied himself with a memorial church, built near his home and at his own expense, at Holmbury St Mary, Surrey (**5.14**). 'It sums up very well,' Pevsner writes unenthusiastically, 'the enigma of Street's later architecture, presented at such enormous length by the Law Courts … the perfect example of form without content.'[139] The church, completed

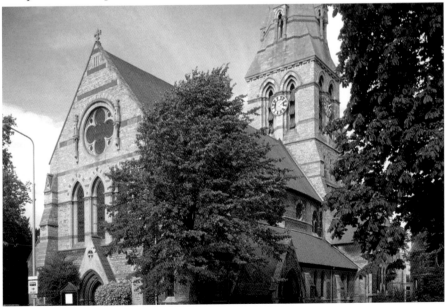

5.15: St Philip and St James, Oxford (1860–2; 1864–6). Goodhart-Rendel thought the church to be 'a test for taste': by incorporating English, French and Italian features, it boldly challenged the precepts of mid-nineteenth-century church design. (*Author.*)

in 1879, was to be a monument not to just one wife but to two: his second wife, Jessie, whom he married in 1876, became ill while they were on honeymoon in Rome and died two months after the wedding. There was, perhaps not surprisingly, little in this stone-built church, apart from the continuous ridge-line, to remind Street of his foreign tours. Apse, plate tracery and polychromy were all done away with; the result was English, picturesque and parochial.

If there was not much about the church at Holmbury St Mary to challenge contemporary and later viewers, a earlier church, St Philip and St James, Oxford (1860-2) (**5.15**), was according to H.S. Goodhart-Rendel, writing in 1953, 'a test for taste – it was admired extremely by the sensitive and roundly condemned by the obtuse. Some may think that it remains a test for today.'[140] As a test, it well demonstrates the polyglot nature of Street's architecture: for its transepts are English, its chancel French, its polychromy Italian. Pevsner observes how the clerestory windows bear no axial relationship to the widely spaced aisle arcade and comments, 'A man like, say, Scott, would not have done that, nor the unconventional arcade spacing.'[141] Goodhart-Rendel, in quoting Scott, explains why: '"Mr Street works by drawings," Gilbert Scott once said, "I by influence."'[142] Street's was a very personal architecture, often drawn from his sketchbooks and passed through the filter of his mind and his pencil: he would not let his pupils design as much as a keyhole.[143]

It was never, as has been shown, the direct adoption of foreign, medieval devices and details which interested Street, but the adaption of their solutions to the shortcomings of High Victorian Gothic architecture, as he had done in the vicarage windows at Boyn Hill and Colnbrook. His son twice reminds us in his *Memoir*,[144] how, while in Brescia, Street wrote of medieval architecture that '*Very* Italian is not so good as *very* English.'[145] Nevertheless, *Brick and Marble in the Middle Ages* was timely and pre-empted a burgeoning fashion for what has become known as Ruskinian Gothic.[146] Although the contemporary *Blackwood's Magazine*, in its review of the book, had asked 'Mr Ruskin! Mr Ruskin! what have not your teachings to answer for?',[147] it is more likely, as Goodhart-Rendel has suggested, that the architecture of Street's 'more susceptible contemporaries'[148] was due to him rather than Ruskin. *The Builder* later recalled how *Brick and Marble* 'had a considerable influence in developing architectural taste in that direction in England,' adding, 'probably a little too much so'.[149] The transmutation of Italian medieval architecture into English was never Street's intention and, in the second edition of *Brick and Marble*, he retracts what must have appeared to be his earlier position, emphasising that he was 'not by any means a blind enthusiast about Italian architecture'.[150] Here he asks rhetorically, whether anyone who has studied, 'on the spot', the number of English, French, Spanish and German Gothic buildings that he has could not 'profess his trust and allegiance to be due to the truthful beauties of his own national variety of the style?'[151] This is no longer the fighting talk of a young man freshly returned from a hot summer on the continent but one now, at 50, middle-aged, and increasingly set about with the responsibilities of building the Law Courts.[152] For in that ultimately tragic year, 1874, when the contract was finally issued for the building's superstructure and the first bricks laid,[153] Gladstone's Liberal party,[154] despite winning the popular vote, was replaced by Disraeli's Conservatives,[155] and the country moved further into a long recession.[156] It was both personally and professionally an unhealthy background against which to build a major public building.

Notes

1. For this reaction, see D.B. Brownlee, *The Law Courts: The Architecture of George Edmund Street*, MIT Press, 1984, 243 *et seq.*, and specifically, 'Flemish Town Halls and the New Law Courts', *Graphic*, 28 Oct. 1871, 418.
2. G.E. Street, *The New Courts of Justice: Notes in Reply to Some Criticisms*, 2nd edn, Rivingtons, 1872, 21, quoted in Brownlee [note 1], 250.
3. J.M. Crook, *The Dilemma of Style: Architectural Ideas From the Picturesque to the Post-Modern*, John Murray, 1987, 90.
4. G.E. Street, *Brick and Marble in the Middle Ages, Notes of a Tour in the North of Italy*, John Murray, 1855, vii.
5. A.E. Street, *Memoir of George Edmund Street RA 1824-1881*, Benjamin Blom, 1972, 296.
6. Queen Victoria opened the Royal Courts of Justice on 4 Dec. 1882.
7. 'The Decline and Fall of British Architecture', *The Builder*, 3 Mar. 1877, 203, quoted in Brownlee [note 1], 372.
8. H.R. Goodhart-Rendel uses this term in *English Architecture Since the Regency, an Interpretation*, Constable, 1953, 145.
9. W.R. Lethaby, *Philip Webb and his Work*, Raven Oak Press, 1979, 71, 76. Lethaby attributes the latter quote to an interview printed about 1902; perhaps the first quote is from the same source.
10. Even Summerson, in writing a short summary for the British Council, ignored Street: 'Of the many architects of the "Gothic Revival" few are entitled to a place in this compressed review, whose purpose is to point to men of effective and innovating genius. But William Butterfield must certainly be mentioned.' J. Summerson, *Architecture in England since Wren*, The British Council, 1948, 13.
11. G.G. King (ed.), *George Edmund Street: Unpublished Notes and Reprinted Papers*, Hispanic Society of America, 1916. King, who was a professor of Spanish at Bryn Mawr College, Pennsylvania, also edited the 1914 edition of *Some Account of Gothic Architecture in Spain*.

12. See Goodhart-Rendel [note 8]. On 9 Feb. 1953, Goodhart-Rendel read a paper on Street to the RIBA. See 'George Edmund Street' in the Goodhart-Rendel Biography File, RIBA Library.

13. H.-R. Hitchcock, 'G.E. Street in the 1850s', *Journal of the Society of Architectural Historians*, Dec. 1960, 145-71.

14. John Summerson, *Victorian Architecture: Four Studies in Evaluation* (New York, 1970) and also 'The Law Courts Competition of 1866-67', *RIBA Journal* (Jan. 1970), 11-18.

15. B.F.L. Clarke, *Church Builders of the Nineteenth Century*, David and Charles, 1969; also, with J. Piper, 'Street's Yorkshire Churches', in J. Summerson (ed), *Concerning Architecture*, Penguin, 1968, 209-25.

16. M.H. Port, 'The New Law Courts Competition, 1866-67', *Architectural History*, 11, 1968, 75-93.

17. See: S. Humphrey, 'St Dionis Backchurch: Victorian Proposals', *London Topographical Record*, 24, 1980, 131-45; M.H. Port, 'From Carey Street to the Embankment — and Back Again!' *London Topographical Record*, 24, 1980, 167-90; N. Jackson, 'The Un-Englishness of G.E. Street's Church of St James the Less', *Architectural History*, 23, 1980, 86-94; J. Hutchinson and P. Joyce, *George Edmund Street in East Yorkshire, A Centenary Exhibition*, University of Hull, 1981; H.A. Millon, 'G.E. Street and the Church of St Paul's in Rome' in Helen Searing (ed.), *In Search of Modern Architecture: A Tribute to Henry-Russell Hitchcock*, MIT Press, 1982, 85-101; and more recently, J. Elliott and J. Pritchard (eds), *George Edmund Street: a Victorian Architect in Berkshire*, University of Reading, 1998.

18. See Brownlee [note 1]. This book received the Alice Davis Hitchcock awards of the Society of Architectural Historians in both Britain and the USA.

19. I believe that they were in his son Arthur's house in Somerset Place (or Crescent) at the time. Some of these papers, it must be presumed, had been included in King [note 11].

20. Goodhart-Rendel writes: 'To convey any adequate realisation of all that Street meant, an enormous album would be needed, containing picture after picture of his infinitely varied and numerous works. Far *too* numerous, that was the trouble!' [note 8], 144-5.

21. Street [note 4], viii.

22. G.E. Street, 'The True Principles of Architecture, and the Possibility of Development', *The Ecclesiologist*, 13, 1852, 250-1.

23. County names are here given as they were in Street's time and as they appear in Pevsner's Buildings of England series.

24. 'A very unaffected parsonage is building by Mr Butterfield, at Coalpit Heath, near Bristol. We think he has quite succeeded in giving the peculiar character required for such a building' (*The Ecclesiologist*, 4, 1845, 189).

25. See 'All Saints, Margaret Street, London', *The Ecclesiologist*, 10, 1850, 432-3. 'The founders and the architect of this church are anxious to make it a practical example of what we are very anxious to see tested, viz., constructional polychrome' (432).

26. Street might well have had in mind Scott's church of St Giles, Camberwell (1844), built of Kentish ragstone, when he wrote: 'a great number of churches have been built in London and its suburbs, and of these nearly all are built of rough stone. Mr

Butterfield, in All Saints', Margaret Street, has shown with incontestable success, what may be done with the costliest, and in S. Matthias, Stoke Newington, what may be done with the meanest kind of brick.' See Street, 'Kentish Rag and Black Pointing', *The Ecclesiologist*, 18, 1857, 9.

27. G.E. Street, 'All Saints' Church, Margaret-Street, Regent-Street', *The Builder*, 17, 1859, 376. When living at Russell Square and later, after 1870, at Cavendish Place, Street was to worship and serve as a churchwarden at nearby All Saints, Margaret Street.

28. See A.E. Street [note 5], 13.

29. Street 'argued against the Destructive theory, that you must not destroy entirely, if at all: but few would go as far as this. He thought that Eclecticism might sometimes even require the destruction of Middle-Pointed work', 'Eighth Anniversary Meeting of the Ecclesiological Late Cambridge Camden Society', *The Ecclesiologist*, 7, 1847, 233-40. Hitchcock also points out that Street published a letter on lychnoscopes (low side-windows) in 1849 [note 13] 146, n. 11.

30. Street's first major publication in *The Ecclesiologist* was 'On the Proper Characteristics of a Town Church', 11, 1850, 227-33.

31. *Instrumenta Ecclesiastica* was first published by the Ecclesiological Society in 1844-7. Street contributed a design for a village or parochial hospital to the second series of *Instrumenta Ecclesiastica* of 1850-6. See, The Ecclesiological Late Cambridge Camden Society (ed.), *Instrumenta Ecclesiastica*, John Van Voorst, 1856, pls 63-4. In his paper read to the RIBA in Feb. 1953, Goodhart-Rendel said that Butterfield's 'design for a school-house, included in *Instrumenta Ecclesiastica* may profitably be inspected before turning to Street's design for a village hospital in the same publication'. [note 12], 50.

32. See A.E. Street [note 5], 13, 22.

33. In 1851 Street visited Mainz, Frankfurt, Würzburg, Hamburg, Nuremberg, Ratisbon (Regensburg), Munich, Ulm, Freiburg, Strasbourg, Heidelberg and three or four Belgium towns.

34. In 1852 Street visited Troyes, Sens, Auxerre and Dijon.

35. Street [note 30], 227-33

36. Ibid., 232.

37. Ibid.

38. Ibid., 233.

39. This was Butterfield's first commission from Alexander Beresford Hope who was also to be his patron at All Saints, Margaret Street.

40. G.E. Street, *An Urgent Plea for the Revival of True Principles of Architecture in the Public Buildings of the University of Oxford*, J.H. Parker, 1853. See also 'Oxford Architectural Society', *The Ecclesiologist*, 14, 1853, 283 and *The Builder*, 11, 1853, 403-4.

41. Street came second to William Burges and Henry Clutton at Lille, and to Burges, again, at Constantinople.

42. Street [note 22], 257.

43. G.E. Street, 'Some Account of the Church of St Mary, Stone, Near Dartford', *Archaeologia Cantiana; Being Transactions of the Kent Archaeological Society*, 3, 1860, 97-134. I am very grateful to Michael Hall for drawing this church to my attention.

44. Street [note 43], 115.

45. In 1857 a site in Hirschengraben was offered to the English community for a church. A drawing of the church is in the possession of Paul Joyce. For Street's perspective drawing, see: http://www.stursula.ch/history1858.html

46. 'I should mention that the new groining ribs are of the same section as the old.' See Street [note 43], 124.

47. This was the rebuilding of a Wren church of 1670-4 and incorporated much of Wren's original masonry.

48. The free-standing and prominent campanile at All Saints, Hull, was added by Samuel Musgrove in 1883.

49. It was the earliest parts of the building which were of brick: the transepts (c.1300-20); the chancel (c.1320-70); and the lowest stage of the tower (early fourteenth century). The nave came later (c.1389-1425). The interior, however, is stone throughout. See N. Pevsner and D. Neave, *Buildings of England: Yorkshire: York and the East Riding*, Penguin, 1995, 505-6.

50. T. James, 'On the Use of Brick in Ecclesiastical Architecture, *Fourth Report of the Architectural Society of the Archdeaconry of Northampton*, Northampton, 1847, 28-9. Pevsner says that this 'is the earliest major case of the use of brick for a church in England'. See Pevsner and Neave [note 49], 505.

51. The largely fifteenth-century St Mary, Lowgate, was also of brick. See Pevsner and Neave [note 49], 498, 505.

52. G.E. Street, 'The Churches of Lübeck', *The Ecclesiologist*, 16, 1855, 35.

53. Street [note 52], 34.

54. Ibid.

55. Ibid., 35.

56. Adderley Park, the first public park in Birmingham, was laid out in 1855 and named after Charles Adderley who also built the Institute, demolished in 1966.

57. 'I may give the Middle Pointed portion of the old Rath-haus at Nuremberg, or the still finer Middle Pointed work in that at Ratisbon ... as convincing examples of its truth.' G.E. Street, 'On the Revival of Ancient Styles of Domestic Architecture', *The Ecclesiologist*, 14, 1853, 79.

58. A similar composition was used by Street's assistant Philip Webb for William Morris (who had also worked for Street) at Red House, Bexley Heath, Kent, 1859.

59. Although Street's sketchbook for the German trip does not record this actual window, it contains many sketches of the Rathhaus and what is probably the cathedral at Ratisbon. See RIBA Drawings Collection, SKB 335/1, 30-2 and 24-7.

60. RIBA Drawings Collection, SKB 335/1. The sketchbook contains drawings of Nürnberg, Ratisbon and Lake Constance.

61. RIBA Drawings Collection, SKB 334/4. Between 25 Sep. And 8 Oct. 1858 Street visited: Fécamp, Rouen, Nantes, Paris, Beauvais, Compiègne, Soissons, Reims, Chalons and Toul.

62. RIBA Drawings Collection, SKB 335/2 and SKB 335/4. Between 5 and 19 Sep. 1861 (volume 1) Street visited: Paris, Bordeaux, Bayonne, Burgos, Palencia, Valladolid, Madrid, Toledo; and between 20 Sep. and 6 Oct. 1861 (volume 2): Valencia, Barcelona, Lérida, Gerona, St Elne, Narbonne, Toulouse, Carcassonne, Arles and Amiens.

63. RIBA Drawings Collection, SKB 336/1. Between 22 May and 3 June 1862 Street visited: Perpignan, Gerona, Barcelona, Tarragona, Granollers, Tarrasa, Manresa, Lérida, Huesca, Zaragoza, Tudela, Olite and Pamplona.

64. RIBA Drawings Collection, SKB 335/1. In Aug. 1880 Street visited Bradford-on-Avon, Frome, North Cadbury, Preston Plunkett, Brympton, Montacute, Barrington Court, Ilminster, Forde Abbey, Ottery St Mary and Bristol. In Sep. 1880 he visited Lanercost Abbey, Bolton Castle, Mount Grace Monastery, York, Cheadle, Runcorn, Warburton and Arley Hall.

65. Between 10 and 20 Aug. 1879 (RA Library, 08.1953) Street visited: Caen, St Etienne-le-Vieux, Chenonceau, Tours, Mont St Michel, Bayoux, Novey and Dol; and between 20 and 27 Aug. 1879 (RA Library, 08.1943): Loches, Amboise and Bourges; on 8 Sep. 1879 he visited Arundel church; on 24 Sep., Monmouth church; and on 25 Sep. Llanidloes and Llandinam-on-the-Severn.

66. RA Library, 08.1943. There is no obvious reason why Street might have visited Arundel at this time but his being in Wales, where he sketched Monmouth church (now cathedral), would have been in relation to his work on St Mary's Priory church at Monmouth (1881-2) and possibly also All Saints at Ffynnon Grouw or Ffynnongroyw (1881), Flintshire. See previous note.

67. Millard says that Street 'must almost certainly have sketched standing, as an architect would': Walter Millard, 'George Edmund Street's Sketches at Home and Abroad', *RIBA Journal*, Mar. 1918, 100.

68. G.E. Street, 'Lecture 1: The Study and Practice of the Art of Architecture' to students of the Royal Academy, 14 Feb. 1881. See A.E. Street [note 5], 81, 323.

69. Millard refers to sketchbooks 'recently presented to the Institute by his son': Walter Millard, 'Some Records of the Work of George Edmund Street RA', *RIBA Journal*, 25 Nov. 1916, 17.

70. Millard [note 67], 100.

71. G.G. King (ed.), G.E. Street, *Some Account of Gothic Architecture in Spain*, 2, Dent, 1914, 20.

72. A.E. Street [note 5], 81.

73. Street, 'On Italian Pointed Architecture', *The Ecclesiologist*, 23, 1862, 16.

74. See Butterfield's vicarage at Great Woolstone, Buckinghamshire, 1851. Butterfield first went to Italy in 1854.

75. Street [note 52], 43.

76. For a discussion of constructional polychromy see N. Jackson, 'Clarity or Camouflage? The Development of Constructional Polychromy in the 1850s and Early 1860s', *Architectural History*, 47, 2004, 201-26.

77. Broletto, Brescia, details of archivolts, p. 67; S. Zenone, Verona, cloisters, p. 98; Italian brickwork, p. 104; Mantua, window in Ducal Palace, p. 184.

78. Street [note 4], xv.

79. 'New Churches', *The Ecclesiologist*, 20, 1859, 426.

80. J. Ruskin, *The Seven Lamps of Architecture*, Smith, Elder, 1849, paras. vi and vii.

81. Street [note 4], 263.

82. The tower at All Saints, Boyn Hill, proposed in 1858 but not built until 1865, was also detached from the church but became connected when A.E. Street extended the nave in 1907-11. Although banded and suggestive of Italian polychromy, the

tower, with its two-light belfry openings and tall broach spire with three tiers of lucarnes recalls that at the thirteenth to early fourteenth-century St Mary, Irchester, Northamptonshire, to which Street had referred in his paper on 'The True Principles of Architecture, and the Possibility of Development', [note 22], 225. See also G.E. Street, 'On Colour as applied to Architecture', *Associated Architectural Societies Reports and Papers,* 3:2, 1855, 351-2, and G.E. Street [note 4], 283.

83. In this design, which was placed seventh, the tower actually rises from the middle of the building and was intended for ventilation.

84. For an analysis of this church, see Jackson [note 17].

85. C.L. Eastlake, *A History of the Gothic Revival,* Longmans, 1872, 321.

86. G.E. Street, 'An Architect's Tour to Munster and Soest', *The Ecclesiologist,* 16, 1855, 364.

87. The best remaining examples at Genoa are S. Giovanni di Pre and S. Agostino. In a notebook kept during his Italian tour of Aug./Sept. 1857, Street notes how the campanile at Siena Cathedral was 'capped with square spirelets at the angles, and a low octagon spire ' King [note 11] 73.

88. Hitchcock [note 13], 163, n.81.

89. In 1873 Street was to use the same spire in the Anglican church of the Holy Ghost, Genoa. Here, A.E. Street writes, 'local peculiarities have been happily made to serve as a basis without being slavishly borrowed', A.E. Street [note 5], 105.

90. G.E. Street, 'On Italian Pointed Architecture', *The Ecclesiologist,* 23, 1862, 5.

91. Street [note 4], 160.

92. Ibid., 154, illus. facing 153.

93. Here Street clearly regretted the 'hideous classic edifice' which Alberti had 'tacked' on to the earlier campanile. See Street [note 4], 186. In the second edition of the book he calls it a 'hideous Renaissance edifice', see G.E. Street, *Brick and Marble in the Middle Ages, Notes of a Tour in the North of Italy,* John Murray, 1874, 258.

94. Street [note 4], 186-7.

95. In 1858 Street visited Fécamp, Rouen, Nantes, Beauvais, Soissons, Reims, Laon, Châlons-sur-Marne, Metz, Trèves, Cologne and Liège.

96. G.E. Street, 'Architectural Notes in France, 1,' *The Ecclesiologist,* 19, 1858, 362.

97. RIBA Drawings Collection, SKB 334/4, 79.

98. RIBA Drawings Collection, SKB 334/4, 41. At St James the Less, similar paired columns support the aisle arcade where it meets the chancel arch. These also have a stiff-leaf where the rounded torus of the base meets the square plinth, as in Street's sketch.

99. RIBA Drawings Collection, SKB 334/4, 28. The location of these capitals in the chapter house is assumed since the chapter house plan is shown on the facing page (p. 27v.). The pagination, which is handwritten, is at this point inconsistent.

100. King [note 11], 138.

101. RIBA Drawings Collection, SKB 334/4, 100. The plan (which is unidentified), showing the two bays of quadripartite vaulting and the radial vaulting which comprise the apse, is on 99.

102. King [note 11], 159

103. Street, 'Colour' [note 82], 355.

104. See Street [note 4], 162. A similar illustration, showing a capital at Burgos Cathedral,

appears in *Gothic Architecture in Spain*, 36. Although this would have been too late to influence the work at St James the Less, the discovery of the carving of the foliage, which he thought was 'good and very plentiful', must have given him reassurance.

105. 'There is a principal of truth in all good architecture, careful obedience to which is the only and the universal test of success ... This principle is to be found more in true construction than in anything else.' Street [note 22], p. 261. The title of this paper recalls that Pugin's, *The True Principles* (1841), which says, in its second sentence, 'that there should be no features about a building which are not necessary for convenience, construction, or propriety'.

106. 'New Churches', *The Ecclesiologist*, 20, 1859, 426.

107. Street [note 4], 98.

108. Ibid., and plate facing 98.

109. See RIBA Drawings Collection, SKB 335/4: San Pablo, 63; Gerona, with dimensions, 103; Montmajour, 180 with note on 179.

110. 'Church of St James-the-Less, Garden-Street, Westminster', *The Builder*, 17, 1859, 410-11.

111. See RIBA Drawings Collection, SKB 334/4, 69. See also 78 for another drawing of a cresting and part of an iron screen with a large quatrefoil decoration, with dimensions.

112. King [note 71], 66-68.

113. Ibid., 68.

114. 'The admirable iron screen, copied from that round the tomb of one of the Scaligers at Verona', 'Shottesbrook and Boyn Hill,' *The Ecclesiologist*, 19, 1858, 317.

115. Ibid., 19, 1858, 379.

116. Street [note 4], ix.

117. Ibid., vii.

118. The tour was led by the firm's continental agent, probably John Ripley. I am grateful to Paul Smith, archivist at Thomas Cook UK and Ireland, for information about this tour.

119. Both these critiques are included in an advertisement which Murray inserted on the *verso* of the sub-title page of the 1874 edition of *Brick and Marble in the Middle Ages*.

120. Anon, 'Mr Street's Italian Tour', *The Ecclesiologist*, 16, 1855, 299.

121. King [note 71], 2.

122. The first edition of Murray's *Northern Italy* was heavily criticised by Ruskin and when the second edition was published, it carried a note disassociating itself from Palgrave.

123. Street [note 4], xvi.

124. For Murray's *Handbooks*, see, W.C.B. Lister, *Murray's Handbooks for Travellers*, University Publications of America, 1993.

125. King [note 71], xviii.

126. This was written by the founding Cambridge Camdenian and Ecclesiologist, and friend of Benjamin Webb, John Mason Neale.

127. The German Karl Baedeker had been publishing guides since 1835.

128. King, [note 71], xi.

129. RIBA Drawings Collection, SKB 334/4, 172.

130. Ibid., 146.

131. RIBA Drawings Collection, SKB 335/2, 238. Street actually gives the date, incorrectly, as 1860. See also King [note 71] 349, para. 1.

132. RIBA Drawings Collection, SKB 335/2, 210.

133. RIBA Drawings Collection, SKB 335/4, 155. See also King [note 71], 65.

134. King [note 71], 65.

135. RIBA Council, 20 Aug. 1874, *Proceedings of the Royal Institute of British Architects*, 1st ser., 1873-4, 111 (preliminaries, hand-numbered).

136. See 'Report of the Council to the Annual Meeting', 4 May 1874, 6, *Proceedings of the RIBA*, 1st ser., 1873-4, 64 (preliminaries, hand-numbered).

137. A.E. Street [note 5], 227.

138. The presentation was made, probably at the RIBA premises on Conduit Street, Hanover Square, London, on 2 Nov.; Mariquita had died on 16 Oct. I am grateful to Elizabeth Walder for her advice on the 1874 Royal Gold Medal.

139. I. Nairn and N. Pevsner, *Buildings of England: Surrey*, Penguin, 1971, 315.

140. Goodhart-Rendel [note 8], 142.

141. J. Sherwood and N. Pevsner, *Buildings of England: Oxfordshire*, Penguin, 1974, 298.

142. Goodhart-Rendel [note 8], 146.

143. R. Blomfield, *Richard Norman Shaw RA*, Batsford, 1940, 16, quoted in A. Saint, *Richard Norman Shaw*, Yale U.P., 1976, 17.

144. A. E. Street [note 5], 21, 81. The quote on 21 actually reads '*Very Italian*, and that is not so good as *very English*': note the italics and the conjunction/relative pronoun.

145. Ibid., 81.

146. See E. Blau, *Ruskinian Gothic: The Architecture of Deane and Woodward, 1845-1861*, Princeton U.P., 1982.

147. Quoted in 'The Late Mr G.E. Street RA', *The Architect,* 24 Dec. 1881, 413.

148. Goodhart-Rendel [note 8], 142.

149. 'The Late G.E. Street RA', *The Builder*, 39, 1881, 778.

150. Street [note 93], 381.

151. Ibid.

152. Millard says that Street 'prepared some 3,000 drawings with his own hand' [note 69], 24.

153. The first bricks were laid rather unceremoniously, first by the contractor Henry W. Bull and then by his wife, and then his son, on 1 May 1874. See Brownlee [note 1], 297.

154. Gladstone was a friend and supporter of Street. They had first met in 1858 and in 1866 Gladstone had been one of the judges for the Law Courts competition. In 1865 Street dedicated *Gothic Architecture in Spain* to him 'as a testimony of the author's respect and admiration.' At Street's funeral, William Henry Gladstone MP, representing his father who was then once again Prime Minister, was one of the pallbearers.

155. The election was held from 31 Jan. to 17 Feb. and Disraeli, who had won the greater number of seats (for not all were contested), took office on 18 Feb. 1874.

156. See A.E. Musson, 'The Great Depression in Britain, 1873-1896: A Reappraisal', *Journal of Economic History*, 19:2, 1959, 199-228.

6

'A man at once strong in the present and reverent of the past' – John Thomas Micklethwaite (1843-1906)

Peter Howell

John Thomas Micklethwaite (**6.1**) was born on 3 May 1843 at Rishworth House, Wakefield.[1] His father James was a worsted spinner and colliery owner. He spent much of his childhood at Hopton Hall, Mirfield, a sixteenth-century house where the Micklethwaites had lived for over 150 years.[2] He was educated at private schools, before entering King's College, London, as a student in the engineering and applied science department. Because of problems with his eyesight, it was thought that it might be best for him to take holy orders rather than train as an architect. However, in 1862 he entered the office of George Gilbert Scott, in Spring Gardens, London. The best account of that office is the one given by Thomas Graham Jackson in his *Recollections*: he had entered it in October 1858. Although it was a 'very large' one, and little was seen of Scott himself, the presence of heads of rooms who were 'capable men with a good knowledge of construction', and the 'sharp fire of criticism' which pupils endured, ensured that they were well trained.[3] Jackson's apprenticeship had ended in 1861.

Micklethwaite formed a friendship with his fellow pupil Somers Clarke (1841-1926), cousin of the highly individual architect George Somers Clarke. He remained in Scott's office as an assistant until he set up his own practice in 1869, though he continued to work for Scott afterwards (as did Jackson). In February 1866 he was a founder member of the Spring

6.1: J.T. Micklethwaite. (Building News, *58, 1890, 256.*)

Gardens Sketching Club, a group of men in the office whose sketches of architectural specimens were published as lithographs. Micklethwaite's eight contributions included two of screens, one of a chasuble, and one of Ashburnham House, Westminster, built *c.*1662, which showed his interest in post-medieval architecture. The obituary by William Niven (a fellow pupil of Scott, best known for the church of St Alban, Teddington) points out that Micklethwaite did not choose to be an architect because he could draw, describing him as 'no draughtsman': 'he held that, though useful, good draughtsmanship was hardly more necessary to an architect than writing in a good hand to its author'.[4]

Publications

Niven also stated that 'it may be safely said that never did archaeology, or more strictly ecclesiology, enter so largely into the professional practice of an architect as in Micklethwaite's career'. This interest was obviously encouraged by his work for Scott. In 1870 he read to the Society of Antiquaries a paper on the Chapel of St Erasmus at Westminster Abbey, as a result of which he was elected a Fellow. He recorded Scott's help in his investigation.[5] His first paper to the Royal Archaeological Institute, given in September 1872, was on the shrine of St Alban at St Alban's Abbey, the fragments of which were discovered in February of that year. As Scott's wife died in that month, Micklethwaite stood in for him at St Alban's.[6]

He went on to write a further twenty articles for the *Archaeological Journal* (and became a vice-president of the RAI), as well as six for *Archaeologia* and two for the *Yorkshire Archaeological Journal*. Among his special interests was Cistercian architecture, which he knew from the order's Yorkshire houses. Although he does not seem to have published on the subject, he was said to have had such an expert knowledge of the Carthusians that the prior of Parkminster, their house in Sussex, called upon his help for his history of the order. In his later years he devoted much of his time to Saxon architecture. We are told that he almost never missed one of the annual 'country meetings' of the RAI, and for a retiring bachelor they must have provided welcome companionship. He rarely missed a meeting of the Society of Antiquaries, and became a vice-president of that body also. He spent a good deal of his time answering antiquarian queries by correspondence.

Micklethwaite's antiquarian interests led to two significant friendships. The first was with James Thomas Irvine (1826-1900), a former apprentice of Scott who became one of Scott's most trusted clerks of works, and who had a passion for archaeology. From about 1892 until 1896 he acted as clerk of works for Micklethwaite's restoration of Kirkstall Abbey, Leeds. This was a commission which Micklethwaite received after a report had been produced in 1890 by W.H. St John Hope. Hope was assistant secretary of the Society of Antiquaries from 1885 until 1910, and a founder of the Alcuin Club. Micklethwaite often took him to meetings of the Art Workers' Guild, and they were closely associated in various protests and projects.

In 1870 Micklethwaite was asked by the editor of *The Sacristy: A Quarterly*

Review of Ecclesiastical Art and Literature to contribute a series of articles, which were published in 1874 as *Modern Parish Churches: Their Plan, Design, and Furniture.* The book is full of common sense and learning, presented in a dogmatic and sometimes humorous manner. Micklethwaite attacks the idea of 'correctness', the dead letter of an often imperfectly understood medievalism. (Niven reports that, when asked what was the 'correct' place for the font, he replied 'I really don't know. Possibly the "correct" place is the centre of the chancel, but if I were you I'd put it near the door most used by the congregation.') On the other hand, tradition should always be respected.

He begins by discussing the general plan. He claims that most chancels are too short: they should be 'little, if at all, narrower than the nave, and little more than half its length' (p. 14). It is not necessary for the altar to be visible from everywhere: that would require the use of the modern theatre as a model. The 'remarkable logic' of this passage particularly struck the German Protestant Hermann Muthesius in his book of 1901 about recent church-building in England: he saw it as evidence of a backward-looking movement which blindly clung to a previous ideal, and wanted nothing to do with the means of its own time.[7] This criticism would not have pleased Micklethwaite, who was far from holding any such opinion, though his

6.2: St Hilda, Cross Green, Leeds, from the north-west in 1900 (J.T. Micklethwaite, 1876-82). (*Stephen Savage.*)

insistence that sermons must be heard will have been more acceptable. He even thought that galleries, denounced by the Ecclesiologists, might be useful.

Micklethwaite is most insistent on the importance of screens, which should be among the first furnishings put into a church. They should always be of wood, they should be tall, and they should be kept locked. Lofts could be used for the epistle and gospel, and on special occasions for orchestras. Pulpits should also be of wood. Stone altars are becoming fashionable, but wood has the advantage that it was the material of the Cross (a rare reference to symbolism, which Micklethwaite thought much exaggerated). Fixed pews are preferable to chairs, as they facilitate kneeling (he seems to have changed his mind about this later). Despite his preference for wood, he claims that, despite the good work done for Pugin and Carpenter, there is now no one in England fit to carve a reredos (later, however, he found J.E. Knox – see below).

So far as style was concerned, Micklethwaite, like Bodley, claimed that, like the use of language, it was of little importance. Michael Hall sees this as essentially 'an argument against innovation or originality for the sake of it'.[8] Micklethwaite argued that Perpendicular was best, partly because he held that the best models for church furnishings dated from the fifteenth century. Hall thinks that 'one could argue that it is only slightly exaggerated to say that Micklethwaite was at heart a designer of furnishings rather than a designer of buildings. His argument that Perpendicular should be the point of departure for modern Gothic was echoed by Sedding, and as with Sedding I think it was based in part on a desire to bring back all the ornament permitted by the Prayer Book rubric, which Micklethwaite – tendentiously – claimed amounted to virtually everything in late-medieval worship'. Hall also points out that Micklethwaite's way of arguing that what he is proposing is the sensible way of doing things 'makes it easy to forget that [the book] came out in the same year as the Public Worship Regulation Act and a great number of his recommendations would have been wildly controversial if actually carried out' (for example, the use of rood-lofts). He denounces both 'cockney "Gothic"' and 'Manchester "Gothic"', and also the 'go' so popular in High Victorian times. Again like Bodley, and others, he thought that there should be fewer but larger churches. His final command is 'BE NATURAL'.

The anonymous reviewer in *The Builder* greatly disliked the book.[9] He was obviously biased by his Protestantism and describes the book as 'in many respects antiquated and superstitious, but enlightened by gleams of practical common sense'. He liked the chapter on the organ, which was provided by Somers Clarke, but he deplored Micklethwaite's 'lamentable amount of overstrong language and abuse of everything that has been done by other architects'. *The Architect* published a much longer review by Edmund B. Ferrey.[10] Although much more sympathetic, Ferrey also criticised Micklethwaite for his 'too strong expressions', and 'too much dogmatism, almost bigotry, especially in his condemnation of modern work'. He concludes, however: 'If, as I hope, Mr Micklethwaite is but a type (and a good type) of that school who reverence medieval work, while earnestly endeavouring to think and act for themselves according to their lights, then the coming era of ecclesiastical architecture may prove no barren field.' In fairness to Micklethwaite, it has to be remembered that he wrote the book as a young man, with little experience of actual church-building. And his Yorkshire bluntness is commented on by his obituarists.

In 1891 he contributed a trenchant essay on 'Architecture and construction' to *Architecture a Profession or an Art: Thirteen Short Essays on the Qualification and Training of Architects*, edited by R. Norman Shaw and T.G. Jackson. This was a protest against the proposal by the RIBA to make architecture a 'closed' profession, and Micklethwaite was in congenial company, the other contributors including G.F. Bodley, W.R. Lethaby and W.B. Richmond. His ecclesiological interests led to his being one of the founders of the Alcuin Club (whose first publication, in 1897, was his *The Ornaments of the Rubric)* the Henry Bradshaw Society, and the St Paul's Ecclesiological Society.

Between 1899 and 1905 he published a series of fifteen articles in *The Church Builder*. They were republished as a pamphlet, 'at the request of many friends', in 1908, with the title *Occasional Notes on Church Furniture and Arrangement*. Some of his ideas had matured since he wrote his book, but the tone of common sense seasoned with humour remains. He prefers a mixture of pews and chairs. 'He who tries to keep a seat for his hat as well as one for himself is properly served if his neighbour sits on it.' Chancels should not have too many steps. Wooden ceilings are useful, if thick enough, but vaults of stone, brick or concrete, or even plaster, are best. He praises the best Georgian churches, such as 'Mr Hammond Roberson's at Liversedge' (the Gothic Christ Church, 1812-16, by Thomas Taylor, see Chapter 3). He disapproves of the basilican plan, which had been used several times in recent years. He continues to insist on the importance of screens, which give scale (St Peter's in Rome looks a quarter of its real size). The worst kind are of thin metalwork: to be transparent, screens must be visible.

Architectural practice

In his practice as an architect, Micklethwaite's work is somewhat elusive.

6.3: St Hilda, Cross Green, interior. (*Building News, 10 November 1882, Stephen Savage.*)

This is for a variety of reasons. From 1876, he and Somers Clarke worked in partnership, and it is not easy to distinguish their contributions. The partnership officially came to an end when Clarke 'retired from active work in 1892', handing over all current work, but the practice continued to be called 'J.T. Micklethwaite and Somers Clarke, architects'. It comes as a surprise that in the sequence of letters concerning the Liddon Chapel at Keble College, Oxford, which are all, after 1891, from Micklethwaite, there is one, of July 1894, from Somers Clarke: despite the dissolution of the partnership, Clarke by no means gave up architectural work, serving as Surveyor to St Paul's Cathedral from 1897 until 1906, and as Surveyor of Chichester Cathedral from 1900 until 1922. Micklethwaite's churches were built for High Church parishes at a time when lavish funds were not so readily available as they had been earlier in the century, and all too often the

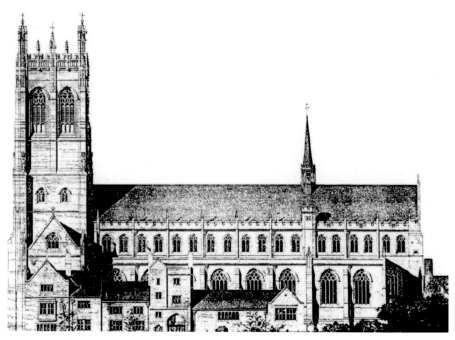

6.4: St John the Divine, Gainsborough, Lincolnshire, proposed south elevation (Micklethwaite and Somers Clarke, begun 1881-2).

buildings remained unfinished. As a church restorer, he was so self-effacing that it is often difficult to discover what he actually did.

The names of some of those who worked in the office are known. A.G. Wallace, son of the vicar who completed the Church of the Ascension, Lavender Hill, to the design of Micklethwaite and Clarke, in 1893-8, was a pupil and remained in the office for twenty years (see below). J.W. Bloe was there almost as long, and designed some screens. George Gilbert Irvine (son of J.T. Irvine) served his articles there, from 1890 to 1893. William Weir, formerly assistant to Philip Webb, assisted in the office in 1897-8.

New churches

Micklethwaite's first church seems to have been St Anne, Wrenthorpe, a small brick building of 1873-4 in a Yorkshire mining village near Wakefield. The disproportionately large east window has Geometrical tracery. This is probably the church referred to in *Modern Parish Churches* as now building, 'which, I think, will not cost more than £4 per sitting'.[11] His first significant work was St Hilda, Cross Green, Leeds (1876-82), founded as a daughter-church of Pusey's St Saviour (**6.2, 6.3**). Although begun in the first year of his partnership with Somers Clarke (who had already built the magnificent

St Martin, Brighton, in 1872-5), it is said to have been his own design, and it was shown under his name alone at the Royal Academy in 1881. He recalled that he had met the vicar of St Saviour, the Revd Richard Collins, 'by chance in 1872', and Collins asked him for designs. The exterior is plain, in brick, but tall and impressive – very much a 'town church' on the lines proposed by Street. The windows have Geometrical tracery, and the clerestory has lancets. There is no structural division between nave and chancel, a standard feature of Micklethwaite's work. The arcades are elegant, and the roof panelled. Items of furniture due to Micklethwaite include the returned stalls, the font of Frosterley marble, the pulpit (1882), and the rood (1904). The church was seated with chairs. He intended that there should be a screen, but one was installed only in 1922-3, by W.H. Wood, who modified Micklethwaite's design. The reredos and font-cover are also later, but thoroughly in keeping, and the stained glass (1891-1905) is by Burlison and Grylls. The clergy house (1894) is also by Micklethwaite. The church's effect is described in the *Buildings of England* volume as 'power through austerity', and it continues to provide a superb setting for High Church worship.[12]

A joint work in which the chief share was claimed by Clarke was St John

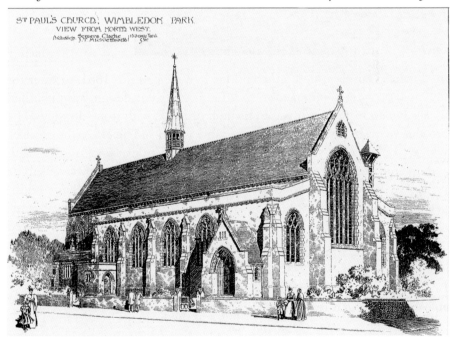

6.5: St Paul, Wimbledon Park, London, from the north-west: engraving dated 1895. The chancel, built in 1888-9, was mainly the responsibility of Clarke, but the nave was built in 1896 under Micklethwaite's supervision. (*St Paul's PCC*.)

6.6: St Paul, Wimbledon Park, from the north-east: undated engraving. (*St Paul's PCC.*)

the Divine, Gainsborough, Lincolnshire. It was begun in 1881, to cater for the rapid growth in population, and the magnificent design was published in *The Builder* in 1884.[13] It was to be built of brick, with stone dressings. The broad nave of six bays was to be of the same width and height as the chancel, which would have a screen and returned stalls, a side-chapel on the south and organ chamber on the north. The grand pinnacled west tower was to be flanked by tall transepts. South of the church the three-storey clergy house, parsonage and school would stand around a courtyard (**6.4**). To begin with, in 1881–2, the chancel and three bays of the nave were built, but roofed below clerestory level, with a wall set outside the arcade piers, pierced by groups of lancets. The chancel has the altar set above five steps, and fine sedilia. The nave was lengthened by five further bays, without aisles, in 1902, but the church was never completed, and is now used by a performing arts club. The small school dates from 1883, and the former vicarage from 1887.

Another joint work was St Paul, Wimbledon Park (**6.5, 6.6**). The chancel of 1888–9 was mainly the responsibility of Clarke, but the nave was built in 1896 under the supervision of Micklethwaite. As usual, the exterior is of brick, with nave and chancel under one roof, the junction marked by a flèche. The Lady Chapel is north of the chancel, and the vestry on the south. The window tracery, arcades and other details are of great elegance. The furnishings came later. The rood-screen, installed in about 1896, is attributed to C.E. Kempe, but actually follows the design in the engraving produced in connection with the appeal for funds (apart from the rood) (**6.7**). The pulpit (1898) and reredos (1907) are also by Kempe. The font is not characteristic of Micklethwaite. Kempe also did the glass. The church was described by Canon B.F.L. Clarke as 'the late Victorian suburban church at its best'.[14]

The next church of the partnership was at Morton, near Gainsborough. The benefactor was Sir Hickman Bacon, premier baronet of England:

6.7: St Paul, Wimbledon Park, proposed interior: engraving dated 1895. (*St Paul's PCC.*)

6.8: St Paul, Morton, exterior, rebuilt (apart from the tower of 1845) by Micklethwaite and Somers Clarke, 1891. (The Builder, *60, 1891, 261-2.*)

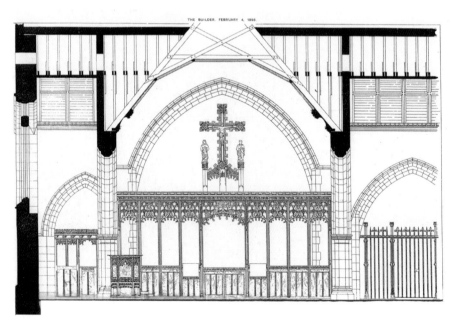

6.9: St Paul, Morton, Lincolnshire, section showing the rood-screen. (The Builder, *64, 1893, 91-2.*)

Micklethwaite also worked at his nearby house, Thonock Hall.[15] The church of St Paul had been built in 1845 by Thomas Johnson, of Lichfield, and only the west tower of this was kept. The new building, of 1891, has a wide nave and narrow aisles. The south transept is flanked by wide projecting bays. It is all kept low, and picturesquely varied (**6.8**). The church is particularly remarkable for its complete decoration and fittings, all done under the architects' direction. The oak furniture, carved by James Erskine Knox of Kennington (who had done the remarkable woodwork at St Martin, Brighton, and who regularly worked for J.F. Bentley), included the rood-screen and pulpit (**6.9**). The fine organ-case is painted and gilded. There is a wrought-iron screen to the side-chapel. The large font, again of Frosterley marble, is by Farmer and Brindley, and has a tall oak cover. The original light fittings survive. The ceilings are painted.[16] The glass is by Morris and Co., the earliest in the chancel and side-chapel. In view of his critical remarks about their glass in *Modern Parish Churches* (p. 292), Micklethwaite must have preferred the windows showing the stoning of St Stephen and St Paul

6.10: All Saints, South Wimbledon, London, proposed exterior, by Micklethwaite and Somers Clarke. The south aisle remained unbuilt. (The Builder, *49, 1885, 786*.)

6.11: All Saints, South Wimbledon, proposed interior. (The Builder, *49, 1885, 786.*)

preaching (both of 1892) to the windows containing figures isolated against quarry backgrounds.[17]

In the same year, 1891, the church of All Saints, South Wimbledon, was begun, on a confined and inconspicuous site. The design proposed a wide nave, with aisles. The chancel, side-chapel, and vestry and organ-chamber would be the same width, and at the same height. The west end would have a bellcote. The church was consecrated in 1892, but the south aisle has never been built. The brick exterior is plain, but the interior is most effective, spacious and light, and enriched by the carved oak fittings which were put in over the next few years. These include the splendid rood-screen, the pulpit, and the two lecterns (**6.10, 6.11**). The font, given in memory of the publisher John Murray, is a superb great bowl of *verde antico* marble set on curved steps (**6.12**). The seating consists almost entirely of chairs. The altar curtains were from Morris and Co.'s local Merton factory, but have disappeared. The glass is by Kempe.[18]

The rebuilding of All Saints, Lower Brixham, Devon, was long drawn-out. The original church was built *c.*1819-24 by Thomas Lidstone, on a steeply sloping site. It had a north-west tower, and a flat ceiling. A small chancel and galleried transepts had come later. In 1883 a south aisle was added by Micklethwaite and Somers Clarke. The roof was of iron joists and concrete, covered with asphalt – a perhaps surprising use of modern materials. Beneath the concrete was a boarded ceiling. In 1892 a new north aisle was built, and the west wall of the nave was given a seven-light Decorated window. In 1898 the nave got a new open roof. Finally, in 1900-06, Micklethwaite provided the Lady Chapel, as an additional north aisle, and rebuilt the tower (the earlier work having been mainly attributed to Clarke). The rood-screen, and the other screens, shown in *The Builder* perspective were never installed.[19]

The masterpiece of Micklethwaite and Somers Clarke was the church of St Mary at Stretton, Staffordshire, now a suburb of Burton-on-Trent (**6.13, 6.14**). A church had been built in 1837-8. The new one, built in 1895-7, was given by John Gretton (1836-99), a local man who had become rich as a partner in the brewery of Bass, Ratcliffe and Gretton, and who wanted 'nothing but the best'. The cost was £30,000. Niven claimed that Micklethwaite 'thought it one of his best'. However, after Micklethwaite's death in 1906, Somers Clarke wrote to Mervyn Macartney, who was

6.12: All Saints, South Wimbledon, font. (*Author, 2010.*)

6.13: St Mary, Stretton, Staffordshire, from the south-east (Micklethwaite and Somers Clarke, 1895-7). (*Edward Diestelkamp, 2010.*)

proposing to publish photographs of the church in *Architectural Review* 'as a design of my old friend Micklethwaite', insisting that it was his design. '[I] esteemed him so much that I set no particular store by his usual method of absorbing things into his own personality ... Even to me he used to make me laugh inwardly at the way he absorbed the whole affair.' The design then dated from before 1892. Micklethwaite designed the furniture, except for the organ-case: 'I was always organ case hand in our office, being as I am much interested in the internal economy of that instrument.'[20] For once, the church is of stone (Derbyshire sandstone outside, Runcorn inside). As usual, the aisled and clerestoried nave and chancel are of the same height. Over the choir, as recommended in *Modern Parish Churches* (p. 16), rises a noble buttressed tower, with pyramidal roof. South of the chancel is a chapel, and on the north a vestry, closed off by a stone screen, with organ-chamber above. The interior is light and dignified. The roofs are prettily painted. Excellent woodwork (again carved by Knox) includes pews, pulpit, rood-screen, organ-case, and the tall cover to the shapely Frosterley marble font. The chancel floor is of black and white marble. There are five powerful and richly coloured stained-glass windows (the east and side windows of the chancel, and two in the side-chapel), made by Powell's to designs by Sir William Blake Richmond. The east window dates from 1897, the chancel side windows from 1898, and the side-chapel windows from 1903. Presumably the commission came about as a result of Richmond's work at St Paul's Cathedral (where his glass in the apse was destroyed in the Second World War).[21] Micklethwaite's up-to-date tastes in stained glass are shown by his commissioning in 1897 of an east window from Christopher Whall for St Mary, Haversham, Buckinghamshire, which he repaired. There are also two windows by Whall (1901 and 1903) at St Saviour, Folkestone, a church designed by Somers Clarke, but supervised by Micklethwaite.

Stretton must have been a great encouragement to Micklethwaite, but his next two churches were less fortunate. St Peter, Bocking, Essex, was begun in 1896-7, but only the nave and chancel were executed. The aisles and tower at the south-east were never achieved. What there is is described in the *Buildings of England* as 'competent and sensitive'.[22] St Saviour, Luton, Bedfordshire, was begun in 1897-8, with the north aisle and Lady Chapel.

6.14: St Mary, Stretton, tower from south (*Edward Diestelkamp, 2010.*)

6.15: St John, Wakefield, from the south-east: built 1791-5, easternmost bay of nave and chancel added by Micklethwaite, designed 1884, built 1904-5. (*Stephen Simpson, 2011.*)

In 1904-5 the nave and chancel were added, but the south aisle was never built. In brick and stone, the north elevation to the street has the windows set between buttresses (as at Southsea).[23]

St Matthew, Southsea, was designed in 1898, and built between 1902 and 1924 (when it was completed by Sir Charles Nicholson). The aisles were almost as tall as the nave, and the ten bays had a continuous roof. Buttresses rose from a battered plinth, between the windows.[24] Micklethwaite is said to have wanted to try the effect of black-painted walls in the nave, with the roof white and the piers gilded, and reduced his fees to secure the vicar's agreement. The effect must have been remarkable. The church was gutted in 1941, and rebuilt by Stephen Dykes Bower with the dedication to the Holy Spirit.[25]

Micklethwaite's final church was even less fortunate. St Bartholomew, East Ham, was a brick church in Early English style, built in 1901-10. It was gutted in 1941, restored in 1949-52, but demolished to make way for a new church of 1979-83. Only the font, typically octagonal and of Frosterley marble, seems to have survived.[26]

Church restorations

Two substantial additions to post-medieval churches may be mentioned first. St Peter, the parish church of Brighton, had been built in 1824-8 by the young Charles Barry. It had a very shallow canted apse at the east end, with the vestry behind a straight plaster screen. This unsatisfactory arrangement led to proposals for works, including a new chancel, put forward in 1874 by Somers Clarke's father, as clerk to the vestry. His son was to be the architect. The younger Clarke had to wait until 1889 for his chance to build, along with Micklethwaite, a new south-east chapel. This was finished in 1898, but their new chancel was not completed until 1906. These additions have been criticised for their failure to match the nave, either in material (sandstone

6.16: St John, Wakefield, new chancel interior. (*Church Builder* 1905, 62-8.)

instead of Portland) or in style, but they are spacious and handsome. H.S.Goodhart-Rendel conceded that they were discordant, but described them as 'noble' and 'sumptuous'.[27] In 1885 Clarke had added 'a picturesque Gothic façade' to the 1817 church of the Holy Trinity, Brighton.[28]

It was Micklethwaite who was responsible for the addition of a new chancel to a church in his home town of Wakefield (**6.15, 6.16**). St John was built in 1791-5 by William Lindley and Charles Watson, a handsome Classical building set in a matching square. In 1881 Micklethwaite was called in.[29] Some thought the church was ugly, and should be replaced, but he advised that it should be kept, but improved. A faculty was obtained in 1883. The old pews were replaced with chairs, new porches were added, and in 1889 the galleries were removed. A new pulpit, marble font, and choir-stalls were given. The tower was taken down and rebuilt in 1895-6.[30] In 1905 he built the new chancel, which is tunnel-vaulted, and has a 'big reredos à la Wren and Gibbons' (Pevsner).[31] On the exterior is a statue of St John, in memory of the architect. Micklethwaite's work is thoroughly sympathetic. Already in *Modern Parish Churches* he had shown respect for eighteenth-century Classical churches, and deplored their Gothicisation.[32]

In the same book he had written powerfully about the treatment of older churches: 'hundreds of our old churches have been destroyed by the process which, with an irony trebly bitter by its unconsciousness, is called restoration'.[33] It is a tribute to his own care and restraint that, in looking up accounts of the churches where he worked (for example, in the *Buildings of England*, it is often extremely difficult to find any evidence of his activity. In his obituary, W.R. Lethaby wrote (referring to Westminster Abbey): 'he did that best and most difficult thing for an architect who has charge of a noble monument – very little'.[34] For example, at the great medieval church of St Margaret of Antioch, Cley-next-the-Sea, Norfolk, it must have been he who renewed the rainwater goods, which bear the date 1901, but hardly anything else is apparent, though he repaired the fifteenth-century roofs of the aisles in 1901-3, and he seems to have put back gargoyles which had been found in 1893.[35] Similarly, his repair work at the splendid church of St Thomas, Winchelsea, East Sussex, goes unnoticed.[36]

An excellent specimen of his approach is St Michael and All Angels, Lydbury North, Shropshire. Very little had been done to this attractive medieval building in the nineteenth century, and by the time Micklethwaite was called in by the Earl of Powis in 1900 it was in a parlous state. His report recommended repairs to the foundations, walls and tower. So far as the fittings were concerned, he wrote that 'the west gallery and the more recent pews are poor and may be taken away without loss', but the church should be fitted up with the old pews. 'The screen must be kept'. The nave was restored in 1901-2, and the chancel in 1908. The tower had to wait until 1950. The early seventeenth-century pews were restored and added to: Micklethwaite wrote that 'the like of [them] is seldom to be seen in a country church'. The late medieval screen retains the painted Commandment boards above, dating from 1615. The medieval porch was carefully repaired. The south transept, whose upper part had been used as a schoolroom until 1843, was given a new arch to the nave, and new windows and pews. Newman rightly calls the restoration 'sensitive'.[37]

St Helen, Ranworth, is celebrated for its fifteenth-century screen, the finest in Norfolk. Micklethwaite's restoration again goes unacknowledged, though, after inspecting the church for the Society of Antiquaries in 1898, he restored the whole building from 1901, the work being completed in 1910 after his death. He replaced the nave roof of 1811.[38] Another great East Anglian church where he worked is St Bartholomew, Orford, Suffolk. The chancel had been in ruins since the eighteenth century, and part of the tower collapsed in 1830. In 1892 it was found that the nave roof, dating from 1562, was in such a poor state that the nave had to be abandoned, and only the south aisle was used. The SPAB was asked whether the parish should get A.E. Street to carry out his father's proposal of 1881, which involved rebuilding both chancel and tower. The SPAB instead recommended Micklethwaite. Work began in 1895, with the new nave roof. Then a new east window was provided, high above a newly raised altar. Flying buttresses supported the east wall. The north side of the church was repaired; in the course of the work Norman stonework was discovered in the north-east corner. The west gallery was removed. No pews were put in. In 1899 a new pulpit was installed, and the south aisle was restored. A row blew up over the sale of the pews in this aisle, which had been given by a former rector, but Micklethwaite justified it on the grounds that they were both uncomfortable and poorly made. In 1900 the fifteenth-century porch was restored. Micklethwaite's work is described by Jane Allen as 'sensitive and sensible'. The wooden screens were designed in 1921 by Sidney Tugwell.[39]

Micklethwaite's most celebrated restoration was that of St John the Baptist, Inglesham, Wiltshire (**6.17**). An inscription states: 'This church was repaired in 1888-9 through the energy and with the help of William Morris, who loved it.' It is close to his home, Kelmscott Manor. Oswald Birchall, rector of Buscot and Inglesham, was a friend of his, and in 1885 the SPAB was asked to oversee the work of repair. The result is that this delightful church, mostly of the thirteenth century, shows almost no sign of nineteenth-century work.[40]

6.17: St John the Baptist, Inglesham, Wiltshire, interior after restoration in 1888-9 by Micklethwaite. (*Henry Taunt, 1902, National Monuments Record.*)

On one occasion Micklethwaite's High Church beliefs got him into difficulties. At the church of St Mary Magdalen, Madingley, near Cambridge, he was called in in 1897 by the vicar, T.A. Lacey, to do repairs, and to install a stone altar. Micklethwaite advised that no faculty was needed, as did the Ecclesiastical Commissioners, who were the rectors. He also recommended that a chancel screen should be erected, with a cross bearing paintings of Our Saviour, the Blessed Virgin Mary, and St John, and also incorporating six sixteenth-century paintings of Apostles, already in the church. The lord of the manor, H.W. Hurrell, objected, and at a Consistory Court in 1899 the chancellor of the Diocese of Ely, G.J. Talbot, ordered that the altar be removed, while admitting that it was legal, and permitting the vicar to apply for a faculty, but refused the petition for the screen, despite the fact that he thought it would be an improvement, in the interest of parish peace.[41]

Westminster Abbey

Micklethwaite's paper on the Chapel of St Erasmus, read in 1870, has already been mentioned. Gilbert Scott was succeeded as Surveyor in 1879 by John Loughborough Pearson. Scott had begun the restoration of the north transept, and this was continued by Pearson. Both earned the scorn of the SPAB. Micklethwaite thought the work mistaken, but wrote to explain that he felt no personal animosity towards Pearson. He had already allied himself with the SPAB in opposing Pearson's work at Peterborough Cathedral, and had joined Somers Clarke, J.J. Stevenson and William Morris in criticising his proposals for Westminster Hall. When examined in 1885 before the Select Parliamentary Committee on the restoration, Micklethwaite (described by Chris Miele as 'the best informed of Pearson's critics'), when asked whether he thought the new work should harmonise with the old, replied: 'architecturally it should, but not pseudo-archaeologically'. Asked what style he would choose, he replied: 'I should aim at no style at all. I never do in my own repair work.' Although obviously not entirely true, this was an interesting response.[42]

On Pearson's death in 1897, Micklethwaite was appointed to succeed him at the Abbey. It is impossible to understand why Donald Buttress should describe him as 'not the obvious choice'.[43] Niven said that he was 'undoubtedly ... the wisest choice that could have been made',[44] while Lethaby thought that the position was one 'for which his long study of the Abbey church and buildings pre-eminently fitted him'.[45] Lethaby also quoted the words of the dean; 'he studied the Abbey during the main part of his life, and gave his whole heart to it'. Lethaby praised him for doing 'very little'. 'Large works of renewal' on the west front and south transept were carried out in his time, but Lethaby writes that 'he was not concerned with them'. They were supervised by W.D. Caröe, in his capacity as Pearson's former assistant. Not long before he died he and Caröe jointly produced a scheme for the repair of the exterior, chiefly on the north side.[46] His own work included the decoration on the west side of the shrine of St Edward the Confessor, which he designed at the time of the coronation of Edward VII. He also designed, for that occasion, an altar, a gilded wooden crucifix (currently in use on the nave altar), the copes, a high altar frontal, and a pall for the Confessor's shrine, all made by Watts and Co.[47]

In 1895 his paper on the Abbey buildings was republished in E.T. Bradley's *Annals of Westminster Abbey*, and it was included again in 1899, 'with some alterations', in a lavish book by H.J. Feasey.[48] Lethaby, who himself succeeded Micklethwaite on his death, noted that 'one of his fresh departures' was to experiment with the preservative effect of limewash on decaying stonework. Lethaby continued this work.

St Paul's Cathedral

In 1871 the first number of *The Sacristy* opened with an article on 'The completion of St Paul's'. Micklethwaite was named as the author, but the plan showing how the cathedral should be arranged bears a note (in Latin) stating that it was worked out by him and Somers Clarke *inter se disputando* (in discussion).[49] In 1874 this was followed by a longer pamphlet, in the names of both, with the title *What shall be done with St Paul's? Remarks and suggestions as to the alterations made and proposed to be made.* It was dedicated 'to the shade of Sir Christopher Wren, the greatest English architect from the time of William of Wyckham [*sic*] to that of Sir Charles Barry'. It was a response to the exhibition of the 'long-promised models' at the Royal Academy, which showed the proposals made by William Burges for the decoration of the interior with marble veneer, bronze ornaments, painting and gilding, *opus sectile*, *opus vermiculatum*, and so on.

They agreed with G.E. Street, who had published a pamphlet in 1871, and 'had asked more than once why the work of a great architect who lived in the seventeenth century and worked in the classic style should be less respected than if he had lived earlier and worked in Gothic'. They expressed their surprise that the only voices in defence of Wren were 'those of some half dozen architects all of the school traditionally supposed to despise him'. They thought that Burges would produce 'a very gorgeous interior, which we should be glad to see executed, but not at St Paul's'.

Burges's scheme did not affect the plan, except that the altar would be put back at the extreme east end, and the stalls would be moved 30 feet west.

6.18: Stapleford Park, Leicestershire, from the south-west: built *c.*1680, the central section added by Micklethwaite, 1894. (*Edward Diestelkamp, 2010.*)

Micklethwaite and Clarke agreed with Street and others that the choir-screen, taken down in 1860 under the direction of F.C. Penrose, and its parts put in various places, should be replaced, with the organ above it, and a new altar should be set up under the eastern arch of the dome, with a raised choir in front enclosed by marble walls. This should be done before any decorative schemes were considered.

In 1897 Somers Clarke was appointed Surveyor to St Paul's, in succession to Penrose. This might seem surprising, as his own successor, Mervyn Macartney, claimed that he 'never missed an opportunity of making critical allusions to Classic design and construction'. Macartney admitted, however, that Clarke 'took an enormous interest in the Cathedral', and 'did some very useful work there', directing attention away from decorative schemes to structural matters. Despite the dissolution of their formal partnership five years before, Micklethwaite was associated with the work, not least because Clarke's poor health meant that he spent half the year in Egypt. Macartney noted that 'Micklethwaite was a very efficient partner, but difficult.' This led to trouble over the electric lighting, the Chapel of St Michael and St George, and the completion of the decorative scheme.[50] These problems contributed to Clarke's decision in 1906, the year of Micklethwaite's death, to resign, and, soon after, to retire permanently to Egypt.

Secular buildings

It is hardly surprising that an architect so closely associated with ecclesiastical building should have received fewer secular commissions. Only three, remarkably different in character, need be mentioned. The earliest, and least expected, was his remodelling of Stapleford Park, Leicestershire, which was bought in 1894 by John Gretton, the brewer for whom Micklethwaite was building St Mary's, Stretton, at the same time. The work was largely complete by the time of Gretton's death in 1899.[51] The house is celebrated for the wing dated 1500, but rebuilt in 1633, with its twelve statues in niches and well-preserved reliefs. The rest of the house was rebuilt around 1680, and a century later further remodelling took place. In the words of Giles Worsley, 'Micklethwaite completely remodelled Stapleford to make it as luxurious as possible.' His principal external work was to fill in the space between the projecting wings on the south side with a taller range (**6.18**). For this he used a Jacobean style, modelled on the older part of the house, with tall mullioned windows and a projecting bay in the centre, surmounted by a curved gable. Christopher Hussey called it 'honest and restrained'. On the ground floor is the drawing room, with the fireplace in a columned recess (**6.19**). Above was a long gallery, no doubt intended for hunt balls, but

6.19: Stapleford Park, drawing room (Micklethwaite, 1894). (*Edward Diestelkamp, 2010.*)

this was never completed and is now subdivided. Micklethwaite also created two large top-lit halls, one containing a heavy mahogany staircase, rising from a floor of onyx, and the other a magnificent marble chimneypiece. These impressive spaces give the house a patrician central focus. For the dining room Micklethwaite used a seventeenth-century overmantel and overdoors, and an eighteenth-century chimneypiece.[52] In the year of his death, Gretton built a magnificent new stableyard, appropriate for his estate's position in England's best hunting country. This, however, was not designed by Micklethwaite, but by Peter Dollar, of London, who was perhaps a specialist.[53]

In 1892 Micklethwaite and Somers Clarke made a contribution to the City of London street scene, with nos 47 and 48 Chancery Lane (**6.20**). Here the style, again in brick and stone, was a more conventional Jacobean, with large mullioned windows and recessed gables above. No. 49 was added later by another architect, to match, but has gone. The Micklethwaite buildings are now nos 46-47, and are called Oldebourne House. The gables on top have disappeared.[54]

The Wimbledon Technical Institute, in Gladstone Road, was built for Surrey County Council in 1903. It was a brick building of three storeys, rising to a fourth in the central gable, in a rather plain style, more or less Jacobean, but with large windows. The 'original scheme' was completed (at the back) in 1910. The Institute was demolished in 1989.[55]

One unexecuted project deserves mention. Micklethwaite and Clarke were among the six practices asked to submit designs for Church House in Dean's Yard, Westminster (which is where their office was). It was intended

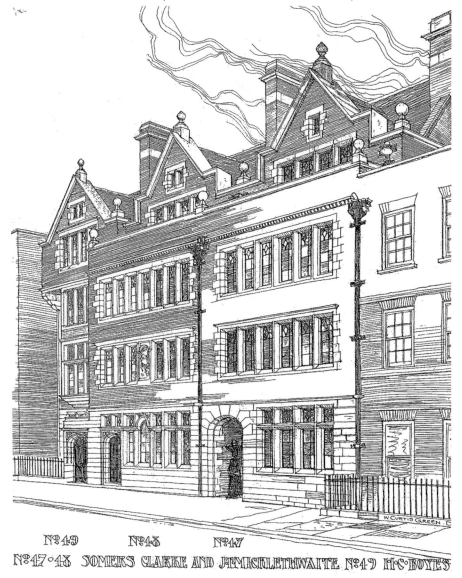

6.20: 47-48 Chancery Lane, London (Micklethwaite, 1892). (*The Builder, 77, 1899, 607.*)

as the Church of England's commemoration of Queen Victoria's Jubilee, and to be its 'central legislative and business house'. Their design was shown at the Royal Academy in 1890, and published in *The Builder*.[56] It proposed a very large late Gothic building, with a pinnacled tower between a tall six-bay chapel, whose undercroft would serve as a library, and a four-storey block arranged around a courtyard. The design of Sir Arthur Blomfield was chosen, and part of it was built, removed later to make way for Sir Herbert Baker's building of 1937-40.[57]

Epilogue

Micklethwaite died, unmarried, in 1906, 'after some years of failing health', at his home, 27 St George's Square, SW1. He was buried in the west cloister of Westminster Abbey. He left the large sum of £12,000.[58] Somers Clarke, as his executor, hoped to place the uncompleted jobs with A.G. Wallace, a pupil of Micklethwaite who had been in the office for twenty years.[59] His archaeological and ecclesiological affiliations have already been mentioned. In 1893 he was Master of the Art Workers' Guild, and his bronze relief portrait by Roscoe Mullins (who had carried out sculpture for him at St Saviour, Folkestone, and at the Liddon Chapel at Keble College, Oxford) adorns its hall. His architectural appointments included those of architect for St George's Chapel, Windsor (in 1900), and as an honorary consulting architect for the Incorporated Church Building Society. Although William Morris asked him in 1881 to join the SPAB, and become a member of its committee ('you would be hearty in the cause against the destroying Philistine'), he never did so, though he did join in some of its protests.[60] The reason may be provided by his assurance to the Parliamentary Committee on the restoration of Westminster Hall, opposition to which was principally organised by the SPAB, that he was not a member.[61]

Those who knew Micklethwaite agreed that he could be blunt, as befitted a true Yorkshireman, and that he particularly disliked 'humbug', but he was a kind, lovable and loyal friend, with a keen sense of humour. His scholarship, with which he was freely generous, was highly praised by Lethaby, who saw him as' the successor of Professor Willis'. He described him as 'a ready speaker, a powerful presence, and an able controversialist', and also as 'an honest and devoted Churchman'. Somers Clarke was much upset by the death of 'poor old Tom', after '43 years of the most intimate friendship and cooperation'. He admitted that Micklethwaite was 'of boastful temperament and saw himself very large but never, in intentions, hurt a fly. A more true or steadfast friend never was.'[62]

Lethaby said of Micklethwaite's architectural work: 'a strain of bald common sense well made up for the lack of more exquisite aesthetic gifts'. This seems rather unfair. According to Niven, 'William Morris used to say to him that without effort he naturally produced fourteenth-century architecture', but 'his principle really was to move with the times and make use of modern inventions so far as they could rightly be brought into service' (his use of iron and concrete at Brixham has already been mentioned). On the other hand, Niven also expressed the opinion that he would be chiefly remembered as an ecclesiologist. In fact, it is probably true to say that he is best known now for his book.[63] Nevertheless, his architectural work is well worth seeking out. Although less individual than that of (say) Sedding, it is always handsome and well-detailed, and (in the case of his new churches) appropriate to its High Church origins. He deserves to be honoured for his treatment of older churches, not least because of its scholarly restraint.

Notes

1. The principal sources for Micklethwaite's life and career are the article in the *Oxford Dictionary of National Biography* (by Paul Waterhouse, revised by Donald Findlay); *Building News*, 58, 1890, 256; and the obituaries: *The Builder*, 91, 1906, 516; W. Niven, *Architectural Review*, 20, 1906, 317; W.R. Lethaby, *The Athenaeum*, 10 Nov. 1906, 589-90; Lord Avebury, *Proceedings of the Society of Antiquaries*, 2nd ser., 21, 1907, 435-6; W. Niven, *Archaeological Journal*, 64, 1907, 58-62. The quotation in the title is from the end of Lethaby's obituary. The assistance of Nicholas Antram, Peter Cormack, Edward Diestelkamp, Michael Hall, Kenneth Powell, Andrew Saint, Elizabeth Simon, Paul Velluet, and the editor is gratefully acknowledged.
2. For eighteenth-century weaving in Hyde Hall hamlet, see D. Linstrum, *West Yorkshire Architects and Architecture*, Lund Humphries, 1978, 125.
3. T.G. Jackson, *Recollections*, new edition edited by Sir Nicholas Jackson, Unicorn Press, 2003, 54-72; W. Whyte, *Oxford Jackson*, Oxford U.P., 2006, 12-13.
4. *Architectural Review*, 20, 1906, 317.
5. The paper was published in *Archaeologia*, 44, 1873, 92-9.
6. *Archaeological Journal*, 29, 1872, 201-11; see also G.G. Scott, *Personal and Professional Recollections*, Sampson Low *et al.*, 1879, 325.
7. H. Muthesius, *Die neuere kirchliche Baukunst in England*, Wilhelm Ernst & Sohn, 1901, 83-4.
8. I am deeply indebted to Michael Hall for his most helpful comments.
9. *The Builder*, 32, 1874, 364.
10. *The Architect*, 11, 1874, 195-7, 210-12.
11. *Modern Parish Churches*, Henry S. King, 1874, 341, n. 1.
12. P. Leach and N. Pevsner, *The Buildings of England: Yorkshire: West Riding, Leeds, Bradford and the North*, Yale U.P., 2009, 53. See Revd J.S. Willimott, *The Story of St Hilda's, Leeds, 1845-1932*, Leeds, 1932, which quotes the Micklethwaite letter.
13. *The Builder*, 46, 1884, 939. A view of the proposed south elevation can be found at http://www.flickr.com/photos/tatraskoda/4930451796/ (accessed Mar. 2011).
14. E. Simon, *Guide to St Paul's Church, Wimbledon Park*, 1996; B.F.L. Clarke, *Parish Churches of London*, Batsford, 1966, 277.

15. The house has been demolished: H. Thorold, *Lincolnshire Houses*, Michael Russell, 1999, 98-9, 194.
16. *The Builder*, 61, 1891, 261-2; 64, 1893, 91-2, with plan of east end and illustrations of the screen and organ-case.
17. For the former, see A.C. Sewter, *The Stained Glass of William Morris and his Circle*, Yale U.P., 1974-5, figs. 610-11; for the latter, fig. 632.
18. *The Builder*, 49, 1885, 786.
19. *The Builder*, 59, 1890, 228-9.
20. W. Niven, *Architectural Review*, 20, 1906, 317; Somers Clarke to Mervyn Macartney, 15 Dec. 1906 (transcript by Andrew Saint of a letter in the St Paul's Cathedral Fabric Archives).
21. M. Harrison, *Victorian Stained Glass*, London, 1980, 67; S. Reynolds, *William Blake Richmond: An Artist's Life,* Norwich, 1995, 294. The dates were provided by Peter Cormack.
22. J. Bettley and N. Pevsner, *The Buildings of England: Essex*, Yale U.P., 2007, 147.
23. *Church Builder*, 1904, 116, 139; C. Pickford (ed.), *Bedfordshire Churches in the Nineteenth Century*, Part IV, Bedfordshire Historical Record Society, 2001, 933-4.
24. *Church Builder*, 1898, 39-45.
25. J. Offord, *Churches, Chapels and Places of Worship on Portsea Island*, John Harman, 1989, 55-8.
26. B. Cherry, C. O'Brien, N. Pevsner, *The Buildings of England: London 5: East*, Yale U.P., 2005, 267-8.
27. H.S. Goodhart-Rendel, *Architectural Review*, 44, 1918, 25-6.
28. Ibid., 25.
29. *Church Builder*, 1905, 62-8.
30. *Church Builder*, 1903, 83.
31. N. Pevsner, *The Buildings of England: Yorkshire, The West Riding*, Penguin, 1967, 530-1.
32. Micklethwaite [note 11], 298, n.1.
33. Micklethwaite [note 11], 239-40; see also *Archaeological Journal*, 38, 1881, 352-60.
34. *The Athenaeum*, 10 Nov. 1906, 590.
35. *Church Builder*, 1901, 76-7, 86-90; 1903, 80; M. Missen, *A History and Guide to the Parish Church of St Margaret of Antioch, Cley-next-the-Sea, Norfolk*, Cley Parochial Church Council, 2005, 15.
36. *Church Builder*, 1903, 76-7; 1904, 126-32; Church Plans Online (1904-11).
37. *Church Builder*, 1901, 72-3; E Rossington, *St Michael and All Angels, Lydbury North: A Visitor's Guide*, 1999; J. Newman and N. Pevsner, *The Buildings of England: Shropshire*, Yale U.P., 2006, 388-90.
38. Claudia Marx, 'The restoration of cathedrals and major churches in England during the nineteenth century and after', unpublished Ph.D. thesis, University of Cambridge, 2009, 186, n. 132; *Church Builder*, 1900, 41; 1903, 48. E.F. Strange, *The Rood-Screen of Ranworth Church*, Norwich, 1902, was published in support of the restoration.
39. *Church Builder*, 1898, 70; 1900, 50; J. Allen, *The Wallace Connection: The Story of the Restoration of Orford Church*, Orford Museum, 2008, 130.
40. Marx [note 38], 154-5; C. Miele, '"Their interest and habit": professionalism and the restoration of medieval churches, 1837-77', in C. Brooks and A. Saint (eds), *The Victorian Church: Architecture and Society*, Manchester U.P., 1995, 170-1.
41. *The Guardian*, 5 Apr. 1899, 471-2; *The Victoria County History of Cambridgeshire*, vol. 9, Oxford U.P., 1989, 175-6.
42. His evidence included the 'very pithy diagram' reproduced in *The Builder*, 51, 1886,

370-1. See C. Miele, 'The battle for Westminster Hall', *Architectural History*, 41, 1998, 236-7.

43. T. Cocke (ed.), *900 Years: The Restorations of Westminster Abbey*, Harvey Miller, 1995, 87.

44. *Archaeological Journal*, 64, 1907, 62.

45. *The Athenaeum*, 10 Nov. 1906, 590.

46. Buttress, quoted in Cocke [note 43], 87-90, ascribes the work on the west front to Micklethwaite.

47. The crucifix and copes are illustrated in Cocke [note 43], 148 and pls xviii-xix.

48. H.J. Feasey, *Westminster Abbey Historically Described*, G. Bell and Sons, 1899, 63-90.

49. *The Sacristy*, 1, 1871, 1-5.

50. M. Macartney, *RIBA Journal*, 3rd ser., 33, 1925-6, 617-18; see also D. Keene, A. Burns, A. Saint (eds), *St Paul's: The Cathedral Church of London 604-2004*, Yale U.P., 2004, 259, 298.

51. O. Barron, *Country Life*, 23, 1908, 270-5; C. Hussey, ibid., 56, 1924, 288-96; G. Worsley, ibid., 182, 1988, 160-3. The remodelling of Raveningham Hall, Norfolk, for Sir Hickman Bacon's brother, was similar in character, but is attributed to Somers Clarke.

52. The lavish plaster ceiling of this room dates from after 1924 (see fig. 18 in Hussey [note 51]).

53. G. Worsley, *The British Stable*, Yale U.P., 2004, 249, 268, 270-1.

54. *The Builder*, 77, 1899, 607.

55. Photographs and information in Merton Local Studies Centre.

56. *The Builder*, 58, 1890, 376.

57. H. Baker, *The Church House*, Publications Board of the Church Assembly, 1940.

58. *ODNB*.

59. Somers Clarke to M. Macartney, 17 Nov. 1906 [note 20].

60. *Archaeological Journal*, 64, 1907, 61.

61. Miele [note 42], 237.

62. Somers Clarke to M. Macartney, 17 Nov. and 15 Dec. 1907 [note 20].

63. For its impact, see A. Symondson in Brooks and Saint [note 40], 199-200.

Notes on the contributors

Dr John Elliott taught art and architectural history at the University of Reading and Royal Holloway University of London. He is now retired from teaching but still active as a director of Spire Books. He lives near Salisbury.

Dr Terry Friedman, retired Principal Keeper of Leeds City Art Gallery and the Henry Moore Centre for Studies in Sculpture, is an architectural historian based in Leeds. He is the author of *James Gibbs* and *The Eighteenth Century Church in Britain* (Yale University Press, 2011), and has written widely on Yorkshire's eighteenth-century buildings, most recently two chapters in *Building a Great Victorian City: Leeds Architects and Architecture 1790-1914*.

Peter Howell taught Classics at Bedford and Royal Holloway Colleges in the University of London for 35 years. He is a former chairman of the Victorian Society, and has written extensively on nineteenth-century architecture. His publications include *The Faber Guide to Victorian Churches* (co-edited with Ian Sutton).

Professor Neil Jackson is an architect and architectural historian, and holds the Charles Reilly Chair of Architecture at the University of Liverpool. He has published widely on British and American nineteenth and twentieth-century architecture and is currently researching the architectural dialogue between Japan and the West. His book on the California architect *Craig Ellwood* (2002) won the Sir Banister Fletcher Award.

Professor Michael Port is emeritus professor of Modern History, Queen Mary, University of London. His interest in Rickman was stimulated by working on his thesis on 'The Church Building Commission, 1818-56', which led to the publication of *Six Hundred New Churches* (SPCK, 1961), re-published by Spire Books in a greatly enlarged second edition in 2006. A co-founder of *The London Journal* in 1975, he has published extensively on metropolitan and architectural history.

Christopher Webster is an architectural historian who has published widely on the late-Georgian and early-Victorian periods. He has a particular interest in post-Waterloo stylistic debates, the development of the provincial architectural profession in this period and the early work of the Cambridge Camden Society. His *R.D. Chantrell (1793-1872) and the architecture of a lost generation* was published in 2010, and in 2011 he edited *Building a Great Victorian City: Leeds Architects and Architecture 1790-1914.*

Picture editor

Ruth Baumberg read mathematics at Somerville College, Oxford and spent her working life in the computer industry. She has an interest in late-Victorian Art Pottery and has published articles on Burmantofts pottery. She is a member of the Victorian Society, enjoys looking at buildings and has always had an interest in photography.

Index

★ denotes architects
Bold denotes pages with illustrations

235